In Search of the F

Michael Asher was born in Stamfor̶d̶ ̶ ̶ ̶ ̶ ̶ ̶ ̶. ̶A̶f̶t̶e̶r̶
leaving school he served in the Para̶c̶h̶u̶t̶e̶ R̶egiment in Malaysia,
northern Europe and Northern Ireland. He later served in the
Special Air Service Regiment. He attended the University of Leeds
from 1974 to 1977 and took a degree in English. From there he
went on to train as a teacher at Carnegie College, Leeds, where he
specialized in physical education with a particular interest in outdoor pursuits.

From 1979 to 1982 he worked as a teacher in the Sudan, and during
this time became interested in the life of the nomads living on the
fringe of the Libyan Desert. In his spare time and vacations he
travelled thousands of miles by camel with these peoples, learning
their customs and language. These experiences form the basis of *In
Search of the Forty Days Road*. When the book was completed, he
gave up teaching and went to live with one of these tribes, the
Kababish. With them he saw the devastating effects of the drought
on their way of life. In 1985 he wrote his second book, *A Desert
Dies*, which concerns his three years with this tribe and in the same
year he led the first UNICEF camel expedition into the Red Sea
Hills to bring aid to nomads cut off in remote regions.

IN SEARCH OF THE

Michael Asher

FORTY DAYS ROAD

Penguin Books

Penguin Books Ltd, Harmondsworth, Middlesex, England
Viking Penguin Inc., 40 West 23rd Street, New York, New York 10010, U.S.A.
Penguin Books Australia Ltd, Ringwood, Victoria, Australia
Penguin Books Canada Limited, 2801 John Street, Markham, Ontario, Canada L3R 1B4
Penguin Books (N.Z.) Ltd, 182–190 Wairau Road, Auckland 10, New Zealand

First published by Longman 1984
Published in Penguin Books 1986

Made and printed in Great Britain by
Richard Clay (The Chaucer Press) Ltd,
Bungay, Suffolk
Filmset in Monophoto Plantin Light

To Katie Mitchell,
Wherever Time May Find You,
Allah Yabaarik Fiiki

CONTENTS

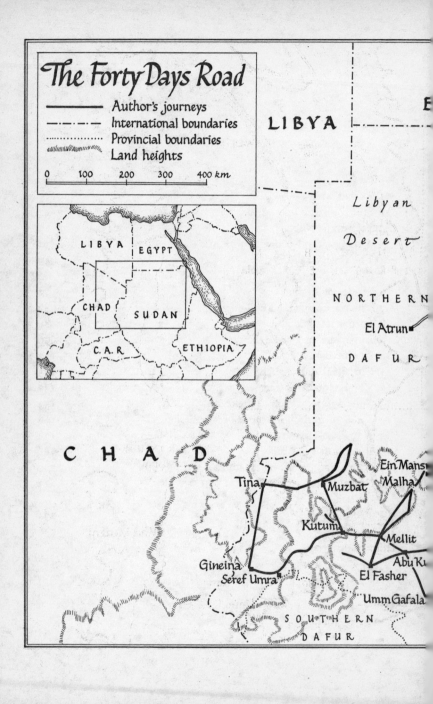

The Forty Days Road

- ——— Author's journeys
- —·—·— International boundaries
- ·········· Provincial boundaries
- ⸿⸿⸿⸿⸿ Land heights

0   100   200   300   400 km

LIBYA   EGYPT

CHAD   SUDAN

C.A.R.   ETHIOPIA

LIBYA

E

Libyan

Desert

NORTHERN

El Atrun

DAFUR

C H A D

Tina

Muzbat

Ein Mansi

Malha

Kutum

Mellit

Abu Ku

Gineina
Seref Umra

El Fasher

Umm Gafala

SOUTHERN

DAFUR

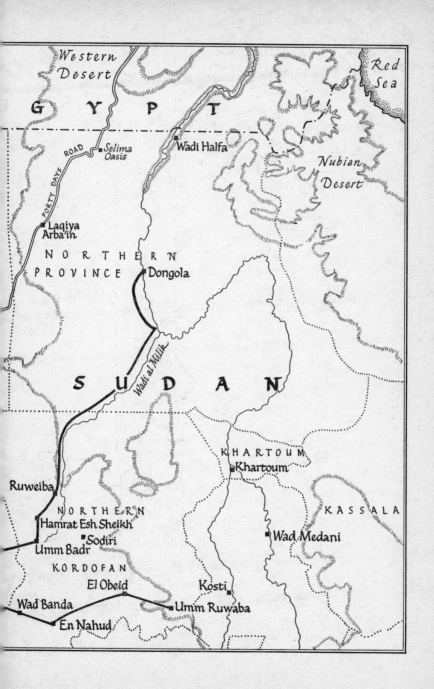

LIST OF ILLUSTRATIONS

PREFACE

This book is the result of a love affair. Like many Englishmen, I was captivated by the desert from the moment I first saw it, and even now my image of its grandeur and beauty is undiminished. But perfect as it is, the desert is no more than sun, sand and stars, and perhaps man should not bestow his affections so easily on something inert. My romance, therefore, was not with the Libyan desert, but with its peoples: the Arabs and other tribes which inhabit the desert and its fringes, without whom my journeys would have been meaningless. This work is a tribute to them.

During my years in the Sudan, I received help and interest from many quarters. Amongst my colleagues, fellow volunteer teachers, I owe a great debt to Kathleen Mitchell, who both inspired and encouraged my interest in the desert and its peoples, and to my other friends in Dongola, Maria Laudenbach and Marc Weedon-Newstead. My thanks are also due to Donald Friend, who showed me how well an Englishman could adopt the customs and language of a foreign people. I am also indebted to John Armstrong, who acted as 'midwife' for many of my ideas. Nothing could surpass my indebtedness to my parents whose support has been unshakeable.

David Granville, English Teaching recruitment officer at the Sudanese Cultural Centre in Knightsbridge, also deserves my thanks for allowing me to pursue my researches in the library there.

The Sudanese teachers, administrators and others who gave me assistance and hospitality during this time are too numerous to mention, but I am especially obliged to Awad Abu Zayd and his family who were true friends in Dongola, to Mohammed Hissein Mukhtar of the Zayadiyya, who acted as guide on my journey amongst the Mahamid Arabs in Dar Mesalit, and to Awad Abdal Kariim of the North Darfur Veterinary Department, who was instrumental in organizing my expedition across the Libyan Desert with the Rizayqat. I must also thank Farah Yusif Suleiman of the Forestry Commission for his patience in teaching me about the problems of desert encroachment. I am indebted to my friends in Gineina, especially Mohammed Zakariyya who was always ready to help in the organization of my schemes, and to the neighbour who came before the house, Ahmad Abdal Faraaj Ahmad, now a member of the People's National Council of the Sudan.

My greatest debt, however, I owe to the nomadic peoples of the Sudan, to the Rizayqat, Kababish, Hamar, Bedayatt, Zaghawa, Zayadiyya, Awlad Rashid and others with whom and amongst whom I travelled. These men will never see their names in print, nor appreciate the concept of this book, yet they taught me some of the most profound lessons of my life. I salute, therefore, the tribesmen who for three years were my companions along the way.

M.J.A.
Gineina, North Darfur,
The Democratic Republic of the Sudan
January 1982

AUTHOR'S NOTE

In transliterating Arabic sounds I have followed convention in rendering *qaaf* as 'q', though the reader should note that this is pronounced 'g' in the Sudan. Thus the name of one of the principal tribes, the Rizayqat, is pronounced *Rizaygat*. The Arabic sound *'ayn* is represented by the apostrophe '. The sound is difficult for most English speakers, and is pronounced by a slight retching effect in the back of the throat; it is a consonant not a vowel. The diphthong *ei* is represented generally by 'ay', although where it occurs in proper names of an accepted English spelling it has been left.

I have taken the liberty of giving some Arabic words anglicized plurals, as the plural system is complicated in Arabic. Thus the plural of *qayd*, a hobbling rope for a camel, is written *qayds* although it is actually *qiyuud*. The exception to this is in tribal names where I have preserved the singular and plural forms. The singular of Rizayqat is *Rizayqi*, Kababish *Kabbashi*, Bedayatt *Bedayi*, and so on.

The reader should note that some of the dialogue has been translated literally, not idiomatically, in an attempt to preserve the texture of the original. All translations are my own.

Finally, the names of a few of the prominent characters have been changed in the interests of their privacy and security.

M.J.A.

1

SURVIVORS OF A LOST WORLD

Ask of the neighbour before the house
And of the companion before the way.

Arab saying

The tents of the Mahamid lay on the banks of a wadi. The rainy season had been over for a month, and the nomads were making their way back south to where the old and weak members of their families lay in the *damra*, their semi-permanent camp. The watercourse, only weeks ago flooded with fast-moving water, was dry: a bed of flat, yellow sand, decorated with blue boulders, worn smooth by the annual passage of the rainwater over centuries.

It was night and the weather sharp. In the camp amongst the acacia trees, the fires were no more than glowing spills, their lingering smoke draping the thorn trees like gossamer. Most of the men slept in the square tents, which were gathered in family groups, but the unmarried and the hardy lay in the hearth area, the *dara*, on rugs and mats. Not far away from them, the camels were drawn up in a great crescent, drowsing in the depths of the moonless night. A couple of stallions were tethered to posts which had been driven into the ground, and a clutch of sleek hunting-dogs were curled up under the eaves of the tents. All was silent and peaceful on the wadi-banks. The tribesmen, exhausted after a day's watering, slept deep in the knowledge that the next day they must move to richer pastures further south.

Unknown to the sleeping men, other figures lay beyond the perimeter of the camp, cowled against the night but far from sleep. They had come amongst the trees like assassins, moving downwind of the dogs, leaving a nest of riding-camels not a stone's throw away. The camels under guard could not cry out, for their jaws were bound tightly with cloth.

Now the figures began to move towards the Arab encampment,

leopard-crawling like trained saboteurs, camouflaged by the shadows, until they were amongst the herd. A dagger was thrust forwards in the darkness, and the hobbling rope of one of the female camels was severed, then another and another. Finally, the stealthy figures moved back into the bushes whence they had come.

Some moments passed; one of the camels stood up quietly. She remembered some tasty thorn leaves, just a few yards away, and began to move towards them. One of her sisters, finding herself free, followed out of curiosity, then another. When the five females whose ropes had been cut were feeding busily in the shrubbery, out of sight of the camp, one of the cowled figures appeared and began to hustle them towards the couched pack of camels. So skilfully did he coax them on that there was not a hint of a cry or groan. Only when the raiders were mounted and beginning to move away did one of the females let out a roar of objection. A dog barked in response, and the Arabs in the camp were awake and leaping to their feet; rifles were seized as the Arabs raced through the bushes in pursuit of the raiders. But they were too late; the Bedayatt had come and gone with the expert precision born of years of practice, and even the most experienced of the Arab's trackers could not follow them quickly in this darkness. The Arabs could do nothing but wait till the first embers of dawn lit up the desert, to pick out the trail of the raiders. They would follow them on their little stallions, and perhaps, they thought, they would recapture their camels. Perhaps there would be fighting, and tribesmen would be killed. Most likely, they would not see the camels again: they would be dispersed, their brands changed, to be sold in the small markets all over the region.

I heard this story one night in an Arab camp. Sitting by a flickering fire, with the stars out like tiny jewels laid on the black velvet screen of the night sky, my host Hassan Abdal Kariim, a young man in his early twenties, told me the tale with all the oratory and rhetoric of a master storyteller. It could have been a heroic story from the legends of the tribe: an epic from the deep past, of Hassan's ancestors in Arabia. But it was not. Hassan had been one of the victims of the raid, which had occurred in the winter of 1980. The place was the Province of Darfur, an area in the west of the Republic of the Sudan.

When I first went to the Sudan, I never dreamed that I should find there the survivors of a lost world. I thought I knew the Arabs: that word lay in the sump of my memory, where it had been since as a child I had read the simplified *Arabian Nights*, as a youth I had seen *Lawrence of Arabia*, and as a young man I had read the poetry of James Elroy Flecker. I did not know, however, that the images which these romantic works conveyed were composites, created through the rose-tinted glasses of my own culture. They had little connection with the real figures which loomed up dimly behind the celluloid strip and the romantic phrases.

The Arabs had once been the nomadic tribes of the Arabian Peninsula, and that name was given to them by the townsmen with whom they interacted. They called themselves *Bedu*, the people of the desert, and indeed their environment was amongst the worst of all imaginable worlds. It was a vast shelf of rock and sand, where monotony and sterility were broken by the occasional clump of trees or patch of grass around a well.

Many different Arab tribes came to the Sudan between the ninth and fifteenth centuries, and eventually established dominance over the area. Many tribes settled along the river, but bedouin such as these, who were ancestors of the Mahamid, never gave up their wandering lives, and even now, generations later, they continued in the same pattern of nomadic existence.

The *Bedu* lived a life which was strictly regulated by rules of honour and chivalry. The various tribes were constantly in competition for grazing and water, and this led to raids on enemy tribes, battles and blood-feuds. But this competition was also a factor which preserved the vigour and vitality of bedouin life, provided an opportunity for the equalization of wealth, and promoted many of the Arabs' qualities of chivalry, courage and tribal solidarity.

The Prophet Mohammed, born in Mecca in the seventh century AD, was the first man to impose an uneasy unity on the tribes. They rallied under the banner of Allah, the One God, and instead of fighting each other, poured their considerable energies into conquering half their known world, a venture which they achieved within a few generations. The faith of Islam perhaps came from the city, but it was the character of the *Bedu* which stamped it most powerfully.

In due course, the tide of empire ebbed, and the nomads returned to the life they loved. Some were by now far from the Arabian Peninsula, but always they gravitated to the desolate places they knew and understood.

After thousands of years of eking out a precarious living in their harsh environment all over the Arab world, it was discovered that for all that time the *Bedu* had been sitting on a material which was beyond

price: oil. Discovery of oil in the Gulf, Saudi Arabia and North
Africa brought to an end the way of life which the bedouin had preserved for so long. They became the labourers in the first oil-fields,
and for the first time in their history, affluence came to the desert
people. As their stock of western material goods increased, so their
mobility decreased. In the past, material goods had been an embarrassment to the nomads, who had to carry everything on a few
camels. Jobs and the new possessions meant settlement, and led to the
death of their animals. All over the Middle East and North Africa,
the bedouin drifted into towns in search of the new comforts to be
found there, but their values were not those of the townsmen, and
the new wealth slipped through their fingers and often left them
stranded at society's lowest levels, bereft of the dignity which even
as poor desert dwellers they had known. The spirit which spawned
their greatness was diminished, leaving in places a flotsam on the
desert's edges, a hollow imitation neither of the east nor of the west,
but combining some of the worst facets of both.

The disappearance of the *Bedu* from the deserts was speeded by the
new central governments which were growing up in the first half of the
twentieth century in the Arab world. It was not in the interest of such
governments to have powerful forces, whose allegiance was not to
them, wandering within their borders. *Bedu* raiding of peasants and of
each other was a threat to the stability of the state, and had to be
prevented.

Libya, until recently a country largely populated by bedouin tribes,
tried to settle her nomads overnight into luxurious flat complexes with
all modern conveniences, but without any instruction as to how they
should be used. The bedouin ripped out wash-basins to use as
watering-troughs for their goats, unravelled electric cable for tethering-
rope and carried their livestock up and down in the electric lifts. They
grazed their flocks on the ornamental lawns and often slept outside
below the stars with their animals, disdaining the tight confines of
their new homes.

The new technology transformed the lives of many bedouin even if
they refused to settle or be settled. Motor transport meant that for the
first time water could be taken in large quantities to the herds, creating
a situation where the herds no longer had to be moved, and making the
traditional lines of migration unnecessary. This in turn led to over-
grazing, and as a result the production of camels, the traditional
occupation of the bedouin, declined. The skills of the desert were lost,

and eventually, in some places, the culture which had stamped the Arab coin in its own image became all but unrecognizable.

In *Arabian Sands*, the explorer Wilfred Thesiger wrote:

> Life in the desert ceased to be possible when the few but entirely essential commodities that the Bedu had hitherto been able to buy in exchange for the products of the desert became too expensive for them to afford, and when no one any longer required the things which they produced.

In the Sudan, however, there has been no breakdown in the economy of the nomads. The bedouin culture has survived in countries where the oil boom has yet to take place, where perhaps the state lacks the resources or the inclination to settle its nomads, or where the wages and material goods are simply not available. The Sudan is such a country. The nomadic Arabs there are the survivors of a heroic age which was once the property of the entire Arab world. These are the principal characters of this book.

These people do not know the word *Bedu*, though they are proud to call themselves *Al Arab*, and despite some admixture of African blood, it is they who preserve so nearly the culture and values of their ancestors. They are as proud of their lineage as any of the so-called noble tribes. The latter are no longer able to produce camels in the same numbers, but the Arabs of the Sudan are producing more than any people has ever produced, and even exporting them to other countries. Whereas other bedouin tribes may have become Syrians, Libyans, Saudis, Algerians, Jordanians and Yemenites, the Arab of the Sudan has remained an Arab, with allegiance only to his tribe and its interests. Whereas technology may have transformed their lives and culture, his culture remains almost unchanged, and his economy intact.

Camels are still required by cultivating tribes such as the Fur and Mesalit for use as beasts of burden, for ploughing and carrying. Similarly, the townsfolk are still keen to obtain the animal products which the Arabs provide: buttermilk, skins, leatherwork, goats, sheep and horses. From the sale of these items, the nomads are able to buy the commodities which they themselves cannot produce, such as grain, sugar, tea, vegetable oil, salt, cloth, swords, daggers and rifles. Some of the Arabs have settled near towns and become charcoal-burners and woodcutters, but the majority still prefer the tribal society of the desert and semi-desert, which has been their home for centuries.

Not all my companions in the Sudan were Arabs, neither were they all nomads. The Zaghawa and Bedayatt, for example, are black Saharan nomads and semi-nomads, whose relationship with the Arabs has traditionally been one of mistrust. These people, who claim Arab ancestry but do not speak Arabic as their mother-tongue, nor resemble the Arabs racially, have no less a claim than the bedouin to be the ancient stock of a great desert. I also travelled with tribes such as the Hamar, whose transition from nomadism to sedentarism was brought about by impoverishment rather than policy. Their views provided an important counterpoint for me against the attitudes of the pure nomad. I myself made no distinctions of quality between the various tribes and cultures, and the opinions I recorded were those of others. Nevertheless, because I speak their language, it was to the Arabs that I felt most strongly attracted.

Many of the tribesmen whom I met knew nothing of my own culture. They knew only of those British administrators who had ruled their lands until 1956. Two of the most famous of these in the west were Guy Moore and Wilfred Thesiger. Moore had been inspector in Kutum, a small town in Darfur Province, from 1936 to 1948. Tales of 'Mr Moore' were passed down from generation to generation and people delighted in recounting them. Thesiger, who had been Moore's assistant in Kutum, was remembered as a skilled hunter. Years later he became world-famous as the explorer of Arabia's notorious Empty Quarter. I admired these men in many ways, and was proud to be associated with them in as much as they were remembered as men of good character. Nevertheless, their political power had placed them in quite a different class from me. Often I felt glad that my relationship to those with whom I travelled was one of equality, not of dominance. I knew, though, that these men, particularly Moore, had struggled with some of the same paradoxes involved in living in another culture which I had encountered.

Like me, Moore delighted in Sudanese culture. He and Thesiger travelled light, without the retinue of servants and cooks which usually accompanied an official party. Moore could speak Arabic fluently and often amazed Muslims with his knowledge of the Koran. He would eat squatting on his haunches from the communal bowl like the local people, a thing unheard of for British officials, and he observed local feast-days and customs. He was renowned for his generosity, but equally for his harsh treatment of offenders. He maintained a large prison in Kutum, held public floggings and kept firm control of the movement of people in and out of the district. He respected the simplicity of Sudanese life, and considered that innovation and advance were a dangerous threat to it. Because of this he opposed the advent of motor transport and forbade people to wear European clothes or wrist watches. Unfortunately, in a country which was already struggling with the idea of independence, such conservatism was bound to be taken amiss. A prominent Sudanese journalist was sent by a national periodical to investigate the rumours about Moore's 'private kingdom' in Kutum. Moore refused him permission to enter the town, and the journalist, infuriated by such high-handed treatment, wrote a series of inflammatory articles about what he referred to as 'rule by inspectors'. The articles created a great stir and perturbed the colonial government, which was already preparing for a peaceful handover of autonomy to the Sudanese. Moore was obliged to resign, and left the Sudan under a cloud. From what I had heard of Moore, I felt sure that he had acted with the best of intentions, yet the story remained a salutary example to me of the dangers of toying with another culture, no matter how much value one may see in it.

Yet the nomads whom I met during my years in the country seemed very resistant to change. During December 1981, for example, when I was spending some time with the Awlad Januub in Wadi Habiila, an incident occurred which has always remained in my memory. The tribe were in their winter camp and their tents were slate-coloured canvas, stretched over wooden frames, almost hidden in the thick bush which had broken out into yellow flower. At sunset I sat with my host, Mohammed Belal, in a straw shelter which had been erected in my honour. Above us the sky was candy-floss pink lit by veins of gold which threw the sharp heads of the bushes into silhouette. Mohammed sat across the fire from me with his four small sons, huddled close. He was a raw, big-boned man with a massive head and an aggressive expression. His sons were slim boys with berry-red faces and shaven heads on which small coxcombs of hair had been left, in the Arab custom. Mohammed picked up the smallest child, a baby of less than a year old, and began to dandle him. The baby babbled in delight and the man gibbered back, echoing his baby-talk. Finally he sat the child on one of his knees, and peered across at me with an intense expression. 'Have you got any sons?' he asked.

'No,' I replied.

'Then you should have some. You could dandle them like this. It does your heart good.'

'But what about the future?' I asked. 'Don't you want to send your boys to school?'

'School?' he exclaimed. 'Why? What good is school?' He lifted his small son up once again. 'Shall I send this one away from me? To live in a house in a town?' He lowered his voice, 'Look around you, *khawaja*.' He gestured towards the bush, where his herd of camels shifted and belched in the shadows. 'Green bushes. Tall grass. Water. Fat camels which eat well. What more do we need? We don't have houses like you. We can move our tents where we like, by God! We don't need lorries. Our camels carry everything. What would my son do in the town, away from the herd and away from his family? No, he doesn't need school. His school is here in the ranges and the wadis.'

I had intended to try to explain the advantages of education, the need for engineering and technology in the advancement of the country. But I knew that I could never argue with the honest logic of this simple man.

It may be, though, that the nomadic tribes of the Sudan may not stay as they are for much longer. Already the government has plans to settle them, and those amongst them who are educated or 'enlightened' are beginning to claim the right of education and other services. The government has refused to provide these unless the nomads agree to settle. Alternatively, the oil which is already beginning to trickle from Sudanese fields may provide the nomads with technology which will transform their culture.

For the three years in which I made my convoluted arabesque of journeys across and around the Libyan Desert, these peoples were my friends, companions and sometimes my enemies. Although I started out with the illusion that the Libyan Desert was somehow to be conquered', as a man may climb a mountain, I soon came to realize that it was in being able to call these men companions that I was truly privileged.

2

SOJOURN IN NUBIA

In these deserts the river was life itself.

A. Moorehead, *The White Nile*

I first saw the Libyan Desert from the porthole of a Fokker Friendship, cruising down through serene and cloudless skies over the small town of Dongola in the Northern Sudan, the place to which I had been posted as a teacher for the next nine months.

Framed by the small window, I saw in microscopic display the elements which were to play such a large role in my life. I saw the thin green ribbon of the Nile, meandering like a serpent on its way north, between thick yellow wedges of desert. The entire area seemed devoid of vegetation, though as the plane dropped nearer I noticed some islands in the stream which were verdant and leaf-shaped. A little closer the nail-parings of green along the river banks, Dongola's famous palm groves, became visible, but from this height any greenery was swallowed up by the enormity of the desert and rendered as insignificant as scum along the edges of its vast emptiness.

My view of the scene was both obscured and distracted by the face of a pretty English girl, who was rapt in contemplation of the same landscape. Her name was Katie, and we were to be colleagues together in Dongola. I did not guess at that time that I would come to love all that I saw before me at that moment: the river Nile and its palette of colours, its inestimable poetry, the desert with its power and its unfathomable mystery, and Katie, who had a poetry and a mystery which were all her own.

When I was a child my father spoke to me of the lure of the desert. His words had no meaning to me, however, until the moment I stepped on to the tiny airstrip outside Dongola. When the pilot cut the aircraft's engines, and the dust had settled, I immediately became aware of the appalling aridity of my new environment. It was 'The Desert': a vast roll of paper, dried and corrugated, laid out to a dazzling horizon. It seemed a virgin stage, and almost at once I sensed that I should take some role upon it. Its only props were rocks and lonely bushes, its backdrop distant mountains hanging like grey ghosts beyond the sky-line, its lighting the stinging sun which seemed all enemy and without mercy.

I felt drawn to this wasteland, in no way that I could yet articulate, but through a growing sense of excitement within. For the moment I stood there, green from England, a neatly pressed shirt on my back, my hair combed and in place. I had never eaten with my fingers from a communal bowl, or sat in a Sudanese squat, and I knew no Arabic.

It was pure chance that brought me to Dongola. Only a few weeks before I arrived in the Sudan, in August 1979, I was kicking my heels around Belfast city centre with a Walther PP pistol snugly lodged under the waistband of my jeans. By chance I bought a copy of the *Guardian*, a paper which appeared rarely on the news-stands there. Scanning the Situations Vacant columns, I came across the following advertisement:

Teachers wanted for the Sudan. The Sudan is a developing country and cannot afford to pay expatriate salaries. Enthusiasm more important than experience. Climate harsh but people friendly.

For some time I had been looking for a way out of the prison that life had become – the bars imposed by the permanently cocked pistol in its waistband holster, and by the dangers of speaking in my English accent which had caused me to become silent and unresponsive.

The twenty-six years of my life in Britain seemed to have been a maze of blind alleys, of doorways leading nowhere, always in pursuit of that elusive quality – adventure.

I had searched for it in the ranks of the Parachute Regiment and later in the reserve of the Special Air Service Regiment. Finally the quest had led me to the bleak streets of Ulster as an officer engaged in anti-terrorist activities.

As a security officer in Northern Ireland, I had become disillusioned and cynical, and my alienation was beginning to show. When in 1979 I heard a rumour that the Special Branch were about to put a trace on me, I decided it was time to go.

I applied for the job, and was successful, and on one Saturday in July, I found myself handing back my weapon to a superior, laying out my thirty bronze-nosed slugs in a neat row on his desk, and watching as he placed the Walther carefully away in a drawer. It seemed to me at that moment that I had cast away with the weapon the chains of a life of controlled aggression which had begun when, as a youth of eighteen, I had first worn the maroon-red beret of the Parachute Regiment.

I had seen action in Northern Ireland at the height of the troubles, when gun-battles and bombings had been commonplace. I had worked in a small airborne intelligence section in the jungles of Malaysia, responsible for mapping out routes in the almost impenetrable rain forest. I had operated in small boats in the Baltic and dropped by parachute into the forests of Germany. Later, while an undergraduate at the University of Leeds, I had continued my military connection, serving with a reserve 'Sabre' squadron of the Special Air Service Regiment, in which I received specialist training in clandestine warfare, and learned to carry my world in a rucksack over vast distances in adverse conditions. Later still, I had turned this military necessity into a pleasurable pastime, training as a teacher of physical education at Carnegie College in Leeds, where my main interests were in outdoor pursuits.

Eventually, however, I rejected the dull routine which teaching in Britain seemed to offer, and was lured once again to Northern Ireland, this time as a civilian, by that same obscure desire for adventure.

I learned many things during my protracted training, however, which would prove of use later. I learned to live and work alone and in tiny groups for extended periods and in harsh and sometimes dangerous conditions. I learned to navigate accurately in all weathers, to hunt and trap food, to cross rivers and climb mountains. Above all I had had an opportunity to assess my strengths and weaknesses, to observe my physical and mental abilities in situations of stress and challenge. However, on that Saturday in 1979, when I put away my pistol for the last time, I was determined that I should never again seek such challenge in a situation likely to be detrimental to any but myself.

Now I was beginning a new chapter in the quest for adventure. Standing there, neat and British, on the Dongola airstrip, I felt the powerful thrill of Africa.

Dongola is the heart of the ancient African land of Nubia. It was old when the Arabs came here in the fifteenth century, and its people had lived for millennia along its gravel river terraces. At least once during its history a Nubian king had extended his power into the very core of

Egypt, and the fortitude of Nubian soldiers delayed the Arab invasion of the Sudan for many centuries.

I soon grew attached to Dongola, this town of strange curves and angles, with its matrix of mud walls, every shade of brown. It is a stark town, with little shelter from the hunting sun. Its walls are cracked and scarred by years of resisting the sandblazing wind from the north, the savage *haboob* which blows almost constantly in Dongola. Because of this the Dongolese look to the Nile for comfort – the cool shade of its palm groves, the cooler embrace of its waters. The Nile is mother to the Nubians, and like a woman her beauty changes its subtle tones with her times. The river seems to have moulded these people from her very clay, for they reflect her nobility, her beauty and her grace.

It was from Katie that I first learned to shed some of the prejudices of my European upbringing, and to see in a new perspective a society which had little in common with my own. I found the hospitality and generosity of the Sudanese astonishing. It was by no means uncommon to be invited to supper by a stranger whom one had met in the street, or to find on leaving a coffee-house that some unknown person had paid one's bill and left.

More difficult to assimilate was the communal nature of everything the Sudanese did. Here the family was still of the utmost importance, and each individual, weak or strong, was assured of a place within its structure. It was a society without alienation, where even outcasts belonged. The family was a powerful entity, both supporting and depending on its members. We had been reared to believe that, as individuals, our desires and ambitions were of paramount importance. Now we found ourselves in a society whose separate parts were of less significance than the sum of those parts.

Memories of those nine months in Dongola come flooding back in vivid intensity; they are among the happiest of my life. Memories of the flux of colours in the river at sunset; of feasts in the narrow streets of Nubian villages; of riding amongst a cavalcade of white donkeys with youths of the Mahas tribe as they sang an ancient melody in their native tongue; of the beat of drums, bounding across the sand-hills from the straw huts of a Bishari village; of a line of Mahas women wading through the river shallows with lengths of cloth, trawling for fish.

I can see again the spectacle of scores of Nubian women dancing at a wedding, dressed in splendid rainbow colours, swaying erotically to the hypnotic beat, flinging their braided, butter-smeared hair from side to side and rattling their gold bracelets, while groups of men danced up to them hand in hand, each one vying for the honour of being touched by the swinging hair of the women.

I remember the excitement of the date harvest in September, the brown limbs of the young boys as they scaled the knotted trunks of the date palms, holding curved blades in their teeth, the flash of gold as the cut bunches of dates slithered through the fronds, the singing of the teams of women below, their hands stained with henna and faces tattooed with kohl, as they shredded the fallen branches.

I remember too the great fishing barges putting out into midstream while the sunlight made patterns through the butterfly wings of their sails, of the Danaqla fishermen hauling in the majestic vessels before sunset, laying out their baskets of still squirming bream and perch along the muddy quay.

For the Nubian river tribesmen of Dongola, the great river forms the hub of their existence. They turn their backs on that very different world which lies to the west.

This shadowless wasteland is the Libyan Desert: a misleading term, perhaps, for much of it lies within the borders of the Sudan. From the Nile it reaches away west till it merges with the great Sahara, rising to the baked chimneystacks of Tibesti, in Chad, and the sunburnt peaks of the Hoggar, in Algeria. It finally comes to rest on the shores of the rolling Atlantic, over three thousand miles away in Mauretania.

This is a scavenging, dust-choked place, a place of old bones and spiked bushes, where the scarecrows of cairns mark a man's unlooked-for grave. It is a land like a parched throat, a land like dried cardboard, and this tiny bastion, Dongola, lies under its eaves, part of it, yet no part.

As I settled down in Dongola, I saw this world from my door every day. It seemed a place of mystery, fearsome, infinite, as alien to men as the surface of the moon. Yet I knew that men lived there, for I had seen camel herds, great mobs of loose-limbed beasts crawling over the flat sands like giant insects. In their wake came fierce-looking men who rode masterfully on enormous bull camels, cracking rawhide whips and chanting odd songs: the breath of an alien domain. The lives of these camel-men were quite different from those of the river tribesmen amongst whom I lived. They did not shun the desert, for their lives were centred on the well and the camel, lives of constant movement over the vast plains of their homelands.

When I learnt that these camel-men were 'Arabs', the word immediately triggered off a complex series of associations in my mind. There were memories, recently formed, of hordes of white-robed figures sweeping, not over the desert, but along the streets of London in summer, wearing spotless white headcloths, and followed by trains of women in vampire-like masks. These images were coupled with vague pictures of oil derricks, concrete palaces and squadrons of gauche American cars. But these memories had submerged a far older stratum of associations – the vivid childhood characters of the *Arabian Nights*, mysterious, hawkish men in furled turbans with viciously curved daggers, camel-riders, their faces swathed in white cloth, carrying ancient and ungainly flintlocks, black tents in the desert, dim figures moving beneath the palms at an oasis – ghosts which still lurked in the darker recesses of my memory. These ghosts, I thought, belonged to a world created by childish fantasy, a world which, if it had ever existed at all, had long since faded.

I knew that the other, latter-day world did exist in the Sudan. There were rich merchants who flew regularly to Paris and London, just as there were diesel lorries, TV, telephones and discotheques in the country. I soon realized, however, that these things were as alien to some sections of the population as cornflakes and pork pie, and with delight and amazement I discovered that these desert camel-men of the Sudan seemed to correspond much more nearly to the earlier stratum of my imagination.

Occasionally the Arabs would come into the marketplace in Dongola, looking raggedly regal as they led their camels across the dust-bowl square, the beasts towering above the donkeys and horses of the local people. Their presence added a new element to the bustle of the market, amongst the Nubian tribespeople of the Mahas and Danaqla tribes. The lines of uneven tables which formed the stalls were piled high with fruit, vegetables, spices, sweetmeats and bric-à-brac. Young girls sold bushels of groundnuts and melon seeds, and in the shadow of the teetering, mud-cake walls, old women nursed baskets of eggs and bread and hoary old roosters for sale. The odour of dung, spices, tea, coffee, tobacco, sweat and urine hung in the air like a vapour amongst the merchants and the farmers, the buyers and the sellers.

Only the Arabs seemed to stand aloof from all this. They rarely bought fruit or allowed themselves the luxury of fresh bread. For them, the purchase of non-essentials was an encumbrance, an extra item with which to burden their camels in the heat of the desert. Their faces, paler, lean and predatory, set them apart from the dark, broad-faced

Nubians. They spoke to no one without good reason, and in vain did I try to engage them in conversation. I longed to discover their destinations and origins, yet the terse, monosyllabic answers which I received only served to increase for me their aura of mystery and fascination.

Exotic and fascinating as I found the Nubian culture of Dongola, it was always to the desert that my imagination returned. Its delights were of a subtler, more delicate nature: the flame of a camp fire seen far off, just after sundown; the discovery of three charred stones, surrounded by camel droppings, which told their own story of an overnight camp. Such simple experiences filled me with excitement.

It was Katie who had first told me of the nomadic peoples of the Sudan, and who first articulated for me the idea of a desert journey by camel. Katie was five years my senior and had spent half her life travelling in remote and obscure corners of the world. A natural curiosity, a penchant for the exotic and a considerable personal charm had enabled her to penetrate deep under the surface of other societies. She encouraged and understood my interest in the desert and its peoples. She convinced me that although some westerners were already lamenting the passing of the nomadic way of life, here in the Sudan nomadic Arabs, still possessed of the skills and traditions of desert travel, continue in a pattern of existence which has been essentially unchanged for centuries.

Yet this microcosm of an ancient world is hidden, shielded from the senses of those who follow the new dictates of motor and air travel. By its very essence the domain of these camel-men moves at its own speed, occupying a very different time span. The time of this world is measured by the pace of the camel and the eternal cycle of the seasons, unmodified by the artificial environment of the motor vehicle. These two worlds exist side by side in the Sudan, sharing much of the same ground, but rarely mixing: two separate dimensions in time. It was this second, hidden dimension which, in the fullness of time, it was my ambition to find.

3

A THOUSAND MILES
BEGINS WITH ONE STEP

What's the name of them wild beasts with humps,
Old Chap?

Charles Dickens, *Great Expectations*

It was in Dongola that I first heard of the ancient caravan route known as the 'Forty Days Road'. It began in the far west of the Sudan, in the region known as Darfur, traversing the Libyan Desert by way of a chain of oases, meeting the Nile in northern Egypt. It was an historic route which had played a major role in trade between Africa and the Mediterranean for centuries, and I was assured that it was still used by Arabs who took their camels that way for sale in Egypt.

I was fascinated by the idea of travelling on this ancient route, for it seemed an ideal way to discover the inner world of the desert which I sought. I formed a plan to travel to the west by conventional means, and there to contact Arabs who were taking their stock north along the Forty Days Road. With this plan still raw in my mind I left Dongola in March 1980, bound for Khartoum. As chance would have it, however, my first camel journey was not to be in the Libyan Desert proper at all, but a five-hundred-mile trek across the semi-desert scrubland of Kordofan and Darfur.

From Khartoum, I crossed the river to the city of Omdurman, and obtained a seat on the back of a merchant's lorry, travelling to El Fasher in the west.

There were about ten other passengers on the truck, all of us perched precariously upon sacks of cotton and cartons of soap, completely at the mercy of the driver as the truck lurched and grated out of the tortuous streets of Omdurman. We pulled out of the sprawling city just after sunset, and as the garish neon tubes of green and orange which decorated the mosques and shops faded slowly in the darkness, we found ourselves in an eerie no man's land where shrouds of dust hung on the night like cobwebs and herds of ghostly cattle stamped and snorted on the periphery of our vision. The passengers huddled together, holding on with a kind of desperate grit as the vehicle banked and staggered.

For two days we travelled like 'his, passing small settlements of mud and straw buildings, snatching a few hours' sleep at night under the eaves of a lean-to shelter or on the open range. I felt completely cut off from my surroundings and their inhabitants, hardly noticing the beauty of the landscape or the sights along the way. I became increasingly irritated, and wondered not only why my fellow passengers had abandoned their animals for this uncomfortable and humiliating means of transport, but also why I myself had succumbed to its lure.

It was with this feeling that I awoke from an uneasy doze on the morning of the third day to find the truck limping into the town of Umm Ruwaba, nursing a blown-out tyre. As I climbed wearily down with the other passengers, I heard the driver telling someone that the repairs would probably take all day. Depressed by this extra blow, I followed the others to the centre of the marketplace, where we found a shelter of grass stalks near a well, and an old woman served us with coffee in the customary thimble-like cups.

As the sun rose higher, I took the opportunity to survey the town. It was quite different from the moulded mud settlements which had been a familiar sight in Nubia. The centre of the town was arranged along a system of wide, sand-filled boulevards, lined with shops of mud and timber, and around the perimeter of the town were rank upon rank of the conical, beehive-like huts known here as *ghautiyyas*. It was the first time I had seen one of these Kordofan towns, and the rows of huts and the rolling bushland beyond were unmistakably African. My feelings were confirmed when I watched a group of youths at the water troughs. They were heavy-set, powerful-looking men with very dark skin and negro features. I watched as they strained on the ropes together, hoisting bucket after bucket from the lip of the trough. I was told that they belonged to the local Jawa'ama tribe, an Arabic-speaking people whose ancestors had been amongst the first bedouin immigrants to the Sudan. Looking at them now, I could see that their ancestry belonged at least as much to those African races with whom the Arabs had mixed, and whose features were imprinted upon their faces.

As I sat there, rather disconsolately sipping coffee, my attention was drawn to a train of three camels that were being led by two men, who I guessed were father and son. Their appearance was quite distinct from that of the Jawa'ama lads at the water trough. They were small, slight men with fair skin, dressed in knee-length shirts which were ragged and filthy. They wore wooden prayer-beads around their necks, and their headcloths were knotted across their temples. Both were barefooted and wore daggers, and they moved with a consummate grace which belied the uncouthness of their clothing. Their narrow, aquiline features at once reminded me of the Arabs I had seen in Dongola.

The camels looked magnificent as they stalked in, tied head to tail. As they reached the well, the men began to tug on the headropes, making a *sha sha sha* sound, trying to couch them. The first two animals went down without protest, but the last one roared, belched and backed off, spitting and gurgling and spewing a slick of green cud on the man's clothing. Still he tugged, patiently and firmly, until finally the camel flopped down on its knees. It was then that my gaze fell on two cow-skins, bulging with water, which lay like bloated slugs in the mud at the well-head. I watched as the two men inspected them and realized that they intended to load them on to the camels. Suddenly, the younger man turned and walked directly to our shelter with a curiously delicate, mincing step. He stopped before us, and began speaking in a dialect that I found difficult to understand. As he spoke he moved his hands in languid gestures, almost as if he were reciting poetry, and indeed his words themselves seemed to have some of the qualities of verse.

Whatever it was that he said had little effect on the audience, who regarded him with silent indifference. I heard someone whisper, 'Arabs!' with distaste, and I realized that the young man had been asking for help in lifting the waterskins, which were obviously too heavy for himself and his father. Flushed with embarrassment, I impulsively stood up and followed him to the well-head. We lifted the skins so that they rested on the wooden frame of the camel's wooden pack-saddle, while the older man tied them securely to the saddle horns.

When it was finished, neither of the men expressed any thanks, but the younger one looked at me appraisingly and nodded. I nodded back, then on another sudden impulse, said, 'Which are your people?'

'Our people? We're Baza'a. We're camel-men, Arab.'

'You sell camels?'

'Sometimes – but if you want to buy a camel go to the camel *suq*.' He gestured to another part of the market. 'That's the market. Ask for Shaykh Mohammed 'Esa, he will help you.'

With that he turned and went about adjusting the camel's headrope. I walked off, feeling with a flush of excitement that this was the nearest I had yet been to that parallel dimension. Already I had the urge to forget the lorry and its dubious glory: I would go and have a look at the camel-market, if only to examine the animals for sale.

I found a small square filled with sand and shaded by a few *nim* trees, surrounded by tightly packed mud-brick shops. In the soft sand were couched about twenty camels, and small groups of men stood around talking or merely sitting in the shade. Most of these, by their appearance, were Jawa'ama, but I noticed a few of the more roughly dressed Baza'a amongst them. There seemed to be very little business in progress, and my arrival caused a stir of excitement, something I had got used to in a country where a European *khawaja* was a rare sight.

Shaykh Mohammed 'Esa was a withered old stick of a man, with a narrow head and bird-like features, but there was no mistaking his Arab origins, nor the watchful, evaluating nature of his stare. He listened to my questions without apparent surprise, but almost immediately a group of men and youngsters gathered around to listen to the conversation, and I heard some familiar remarks passed:

'Is he a Palestinian?'

'No, he's Egyptian!'

'He's a merchant from Omdurman, come to buy our camels!'

'He's from the government!'

Mohammed 'Esa took all this in his stride, leading me by the hand on a tour of inspection of the animals for sale and showing off their qualities. 'This is a fast one, but it won't be good over long distances,' or 'This one is strong, and well behaved, it will be good for you.'

I felt a little disarmed by his frank manner. In Dongola I had asked repeatedly about the qualities of a good camel. 'Look for strong legs without excess fat,' I had been told. 'Make sure it has shiny eyes and pointed ears. Its neck should be arched, its chest broad, and its hump directly above its belly.'

Now, with twenty camels to choose from, I realized how pathetically inadequate such information was. To appreciate the quality of any animal, whether horse, dog, donkey or camel, one requires a rich store of experience. Those such as Mohammed 'Esa had camels in their blood: they had been gathering such experience since they first learned to walk.

Eventually, however, my eye alighted on a camel which seemed to incorporate some of these characteristics: it was a male of medium size, which the shaykh told me was a seven-year-old.

'Do you want to try it?' he asked.

Thinking that I had little to lose, I answered that I would. Several men stood on the animal's front legs, while I struggled awkwardly into the saddle. I took the headrope and held on tightly to the saddle horn as the camel's back tilted violently backwards, then forwards, then backwards again. Then I was up, and the beast was walking at a steady pace around the square. Mohammed shouted to me to guide the creature's head with the rope, so that it walked round in a circle. There were guffaws from the crowd, but I ignored them. This was my first camel ride: I felt a new surge of excitement as the animal obeyed my commands to move left and right. It was something primitive welling up inside me – man's mastery over the beast. I was almost disappointed when Mohammed took the headrope and couched the animal. He looked at me inquiringly. I stood deep in thought, trying to master my emotions. There was no doubt that I was already hooked: the lorry had gone completely from my mind.

'How much?' I said.

There followed a great deal of shifting and discussion, in which I was urged unsuccessfully to suggest a good price.

Finally the shaykh said, '£500.'

I returned his hard stare. I did not know camels, but one thing I had inquired about carefully was current prices. I had been told that a good camel should be between £300 and £400, depending on size and quality, and as far as I could tell, this one did not seem exceptional in either. I offered £250, and the crowd almost booed with disapproval. Various people poked and prodded the camel and more remarks were passed:

'Look how well behaved he is!'

'By God, he's a good camel!'

Once again I was up against the Sudanese group effort: it seemed that the entire community was involved in the task of selling me this camel. The bargaining went on, following an intricate ritual of offer and rejection, which I was to see enacted many times in the Sudan. Eventually, however, the shaykh and I reached stalemate at £400 and £350 respectively. I mumbled regrets and stalked off back towards the well-head. There seemed no alternative now to another long and unproductive period on the truck, being tossed about like flotsam, isolated from this magnificent landscape. I was hovering on the brink of two worlds, unable to settle in either.

Suddenly a small boy touched my sleeve, and as I turned towards him I heard a shout, and saw not far away a group of Baza'a who had been closely engaged in the bargaining. They beckoned me over to them.

'Have you got the money with you now?' one of them asked. The question alerted my suspicions for a moment: it seemed dangerous to admit that I was carrying a large amount of cash.

'That camel is ours,' said another. 'If you have the money, we'll take £350, but we must go quickly to the house of the clerk, to register!'

At once I felt ashamed of my suspicions: throughout the sale I had been worried that these people would try to cheat or rob me. This was not entirely the paranoia of a stranger in a foreign land, but also the result of tales I had heard in various places about the rapaciousness of the Arabs. In retrospect I can say that these Baza'a and Jawa'ama treated me with scrupulous honesty, for I had come to Umm Ruwaba totally ignorant of camels, and could easily have been sold a bad one. In fact my first camel brought a profit when I eventually sold it.

The official clerk, 'Ali Ahmed Gad Allah, lived in a house composed of grass huts and incorporating a cool yard where we sat on rugs and were served tea by a small boy, waiting for the actual owner of the camel to be found. Meanwhile 'Ali Ahmed, a rotund and cheery Jawa'ami, harangued me on the lunacy of my trip west.

'You can't sleep in the open without a rifle or pistol to protect you,' he said. 'Especially on the other side of El Obeid. The tribes there, like the Hamar and the Kababish, don't respect life. They are heavily armed, by God! They'll kill you and take your camel as easily as eating their food!'

I found myself listening to this talk with a certain disbelief. I had already heard tales of Arabs roaming about toting automatic rifles and sub-machine-guns. To me, it seemed unlikely, a memory of the past. I put it down to the natural distrust between townsmen and nomads. I was not aware how soon I would discover the truth of such stories.

Meanwhile the old Baza'a who owned the camel arrived with a group of ragged kinsmen, some of whom I recognized from the market. They looked wild and proud as they sat amongst us. The owner, Yusuf Hassan, was a bowed old man with a face like polished *babanoss*: he seemed miserable to be losing his camel. Nevertheless, the deal was concluded, and I counted out the thirty-five pinkish £10 notes into the hand of 'Ali Ahmed. He counted them again into the hand of Yusuf Hassan, who counted them himself, just to make sure. He looked at me almost reproachfully, as if I had stolen a daughter, but the others smiled and there was profuse hand-shaking. 'Ali presented me with a yellow slip, which was my certificate of ownership. There were persistent offers of hospitality, but I explained that I was anxious to set off as soon as possible, and walked outside to find my camel couched amongst several others. I noticed the Arabs hanging back, with smirks on their faces, and I realized that they were waiting to see if I would recognize my own animal. Luckily I remembered the complicated brand-mark on his flank, which I had been told belonged to the Jellaba Howara, a tribe renowned as travelling merchants.

I had bought an old saddle with the camel, and an old waterskin. The Arabs showed me how to fit the saddle, mounting the two double wedges of wood on the leather pads which protected the animal's back, buckling the girths which held the timber in place. Someone brought my waterskin, half-filled, and I hung it from the saddle horns on one side, having suspended my rucksack from the other. A small crowd had gathered to see me off, and I walked around shaking hands with everyone. Things had happened so quickly, and so sudden had been my change of plan that I hardly knew what my intentions were. All I knew was that I wanted to get away as quickly as possible to the quiet of the bush.

The Arabs held the camel as I mounted, and I heard 'Ali Ahmed saying, 'Watch out for those Hamar!' Then I was magically up and pacing out towards the marketplace, riding my first camel. I felt king of all I surveyed, deaf to the cheers and cat-calls which rippled amongst the pedestrians in the street. I rode deliberately past the stranded lorry and waved wildly at the passengers, whose faces dropped in amazement. I imagined that I was cocking a snook at the monster of motor transport in all its infamy.

The various stages of the buying process had taken nearly the whole day, and it was almost sunset by the time I had cleared the town. The camel seemed easy to handle, though he travelled at his own pace, which seemed to be 'slow'. Someone had given me a switch, but I was reluctant to use it, not knowing what result it would produce, and I began to suspect quite quickly that there was more to riding than just sitting in the saddle.

The sun was a golden sovereign lodged on the edge of the world, lighting the sky with bars of gold which gave a strange, mystical luminosity to the whispering bush. As darkness came, the moon blinked out like a bleary eye, enveloped by a bank of alto-cumuli. The silence of the day was replaced by the chorus of the night: a million crickets rasping in the grasses, a hundred thousand lizards scampering in the dusk. The dim lights of Umm Ruwaba flickered up behind me, and I felt serene and content, to be at last here with the wide open spaces of Africa before me.

The shell of serenity was crushed suddenly by the roar of an engine, and I saw to the north the merciless beam of a lorry as it headed west. I wondered idly if it were the same truck on which I had entered the town that morning, that lifetime away. My mind formed a fleeting image of the passengers, huddled together on its back, rattling across this vast plain, oblivious to and unconnected with its harsh beauty, carrying their false world like a bubble around them, travelling blind in an indifferent universe. It seemed to me then that already, almost imperceptibly, I had passed into the other dimension.

This sense of perfect peace, however, was destined not to last. Some way out of the town, I decided that I had had enough for the first day, and that I would make camp. This was when my problems started. I tugged on the headrope, but the camel did not respond. I tugged harder, and he merely shifted about, nibbling at tufts of grass and shrubs, as if nonchalantly unconcerned about my presence on his back. After swearing profusely, still without result, I jumped from his back, and found myself suddenly covered in viciously sharp thistles, which embedded themselves in my arms, legs and face. The faster I tried to extract them, the more they stuck: they worked themselves inside my trousers, up the sleeves of my shirt and even into my lips and ears. It was my first experience of *heskaniit* grass, the desert traveller's nightmare.

Meanwhile the camel, whose rope I was still holding, began to wander off, following tasty trails of thornbush and *mukhayyit*. I pulled against him, but he pulled harder, dragging me for yards through a grove of acacia bushes, whose needle-like armaments were even more deadly than the *heskaniit*. It was all I could do to retain my hold on the animal: my shirt was torn, my limbs deeply scratched. For more than an hour I fought a battle of strength with him, cursing and swearing at my ineptitude. Suddenly, however, he sat down of his own volition, without any warning. As quick as a flash, I secured his front leg with a loop of rope, as I had been shown, to prevent him from rising again. I dared not remove the saddle, for fear I should not be able to replace it in the morning.

I laid out my meagre possessions, a sleeping-bag and some clothes, and found to my dismay that they were immediately covered in *heskaniit* thorns. The moon suddenly went down and I was alone in the pitch darkness of the bush. With the aid of a torch I tried to light a fire, but there was no dry wood, and every step I took in search of some took me further into the *heskaniit*. I broke up some *mukhayyit* twigs, but they were too green to burn, so after a while I gave up the attempt and rolled out my sleeping-bag, only to find that the zip had broken. Everything possible seemed to be going wrong. Certainly this was not how I had imagined my first night travelling by camel. Trying somehow to get into the sleeping-bag and to ignore the *heskaniit* all over me, I settled down to the most miserable night I ever spent in the wilds of the Sudan. Somewhere out across the wide bush, a dog or some other unhappy animal set up a haunting wail, as if lamenting the fallen moon.

The first thing I saw as I awoke was a camel-rider bearing down upon me. He couched his camel and came over to where I was lying in the *heskaniit*.

'What on earth are you doing here in the thorns?' he asked incredulously. 'Why didn't you go to the village?' He pointed west and shook his head, 'It's dangerous to sleep in the open. The country's full of bandits. They'll take your camel and kill you!'

Later, I realized how incredible it must have seemed to him to find a *khawaja* sleeping in such uncomfortable conditions, when there was hospitality to be found at any village. But at this time I had not yet understood that the Arab concept of hospitality was nearer to being a right than a privilege: something which could be freely asked for, and was freely offered.

The sudden appearance of the rider and his talk of bandits had alarmed me slightly, and I rolled out of my sleeping-bag and picked up the dagger which I had been carrying. The tribesman, who I guessed was a Jawa'ami, took the hint, and I watched him as he mounted and rode off. Only then did I remember that I had not yet mastered the couching of my camel.

Luckily, a few minutes later, I spotted two Jawa'ama lads passing near by on donkeys. I called them over, and explained shamefacedly that I could not couch the animal. They grinned from ear to ear and gave each other knowing looks, as if to say: 'Damned *khawajas*, playing with camels!' They demonstrated how to tug the headrope downwards rather than backwards, as I had been doing, and to mouth the *sha sha sha* sound, which I had forgotten.

'Don't be afraid of him!' said one of them. 'The camel will know if you're afraid!'

I nodded, and practised the movement several times, much to the camel's annoyance. Then I packed up my things and rode away in the wake of the Jawa'ama, trying desperately to hold on with hands which were red and swollen from the *heskaniit*. The boys pointed out to me the pitched roofs of a village not far away, and I urged the camel towards it.

As I approached, a magnificent sight met my eyes. Outside the village was a well, and, even at this early hour, almost every inhabitant of the village must have been there. The well was surrounded by cattle, sheep and goats, pressing and pawing at each other so that a cloud of fine dust layered the air above them. Together with a few camels and a contingent of donkeys they set up a tremendous cacophony of noise: they seemed to be moving in continuous circles, always chased by ragged little children armed with sticks.

Moving nearer, I saw lines of adults, men and women, straining on the leather ropes which hoisted the ribbed, rawhide buckets to the surface, where the water was poured into wooden troughs made from hollowed-out tree trunks. Many of the workers were teenage girls wearing loincloths or wraps of coarse cotton, their hair tightly braided and decorated with chains of gold trinkets. The men, their heads shiny with sweat, grunted rhythmically as they heaved on the ropes, continually shouting and exhorting each other.

Though I have seen hundreds of wells in the Sudan, I have never forgotten this sight, on my first morning travelling by camel. It brought home to me with sudden intensity the realities of the place which I had chosen to travel in. Everywhere man's life depends on water, but in our tap-supplied, pipe-infested houses we are far less conscious of its immediate importance. It is something taken for granted. In parched Kordofan it is a treasure, the extraction of which occupies a large part of the day.

I couched my camel, and greeted the villagers. Some of them answered my greeting, but all continued in their task.

Eventually a toothless old man came up and asked if I was from the *Ingleez*. When I answered that I was, a broad smile of nostalgia spread across his face. 'I remember the *Ingleez*,' he said. 'Those were good times. When a chicken cost only five piastres in the market. Now everything is so expensive!'

I had not the heart to tell him that Britain was not quite the country it had been in those days, or that rising prices were due partly to a trend of world inflation. He instructed a couple of young girls to fill my waterskin and to give my camel water. The girls giggled as they lugged the heavy leather buckets from the well-head, occasionally casting huge doe-like eyes in my direction. For them, at least, the *Ingleez* had no explaining to do.

The memories of those first three days have become little more than a blur in my mind. I do remember, though, the vivid beauty of the semi-desert plain I was crossing, in places nothing but red sand or cracked grey soil, in others thick with vegetation: the golden *heskaniit* grass underfoot, deep groves of acacia overhead. I passed through stretches of woodland where the giant baobab trees stood close together, tangled with thorns and creepers, through the vast bowls of valleys, where nothing grew above calf-height, through narrow ravines beneath the volcanic plugs of mountains. I rode into many villages and always found an enthusiastic welcome, especially from the children, who crowded around to see the strange white face of the man on the camel. Without the warmth and friendliness of the Jawa'ama and Jellaaba peoples whom I met in those first days, I would probably have made little progress, for I was still having trouble from the camel. Although I had now mastered the art of couching, I had trouble mounting. Often the animal seemed to wait until I had swung my leg over the saddle, an instant before the fulcrum of my weight was actually resting on it, then skip to his feet, sending me stumbling into the sand or the evil *heskaniit*. It was almost certain to happen if I was mounting before a group of village children, who naturally found the sight of a *khawaja* falling off a camel much to their taste, for they howled with laughter to display their approval. The saddle also gave me problems: it regularly slipped while I was riding, and once came off completely, just over a particularly rich patch of *heskaniit*.

No matter how amusing they thought the whole idea, the villagers were always ready to give assistance and advice. I soon realized how totally ignorant I was. I had imagined that keeping a camel would be somehow like maintaining a motorcycle. I now had to get used to the idea that my transport was a thing of flesh and blood with desires of its own: it needed to eat, drink and rest. I learned from the Jawa'ama how to feed it on grain, and found that it responded well, moving at a comfortable trot which placed less strain on the back. Travelling in this way, I arrived in the city of El Obeid, capital of the North Kordofan, within four days. I stopped only briefly in the town, for it was difficult to control the camel amongst the hooting of trucks and the growl of their engines. Instead, I camped outside under a great baobab tree. The next day I headed west towards En Nahud. The weather had turned unexpectedly damp, the sun dim and sickly pale behind a bank of grey cloud, and a cool wind blew in gusts across the red plain. These changes were the harbingers of a day which almost proved to be my last on a camel in the Sudan.

It was afternoon, and I had stopped in the shade of an acacia tree for a much-needed rest. For the first two days, my muscles had ached continuously from the unaccustomed strain of riding, and although this had largely disappeared, I was still feeling tired. I decided, however, that it was time for another effort, and began to load my luggage on the camel. As I began to mount, the animal suddenly sprang up with a jerk and I felt the headrope slipping through my fingers like a fishing-line on a reel. Then it was out of my grasp, trailing in front of me, and as I stooped to regain it, the camel kicked backwards, then bounded away into the bush in the direction from which we had come. Within seconds it was a hundred yards away. I gave chase hotly and desperately, visions passing through my mind of myself crawling on hands and knees into El Obeid, the laughing-stock of the town, without even my passport, money or my precious return ticket to London. There were bubbles of self-criticism too: the plan to travel by camel seemed to have been laid bare in all its naïve arrogance. Then I noticed that the beast had stopped running and was browsing on a rich patch of vegetation, on the crest of a ridge. I began to hope. I approached at a cautious walk and miraculously got within striking distance of the headrope. I made a lightning grab, but too slow for the camel's reflexes, for he bounced off at a gallop kicking up dust and dropping cushions and cloths from the saddle. My heart sank: the horrific idea struck me that the fugitive was playing this cat-and-mouse game with deliberate and calculated spite. I remembered hearing that camels could be both vicious and vindictive.

For many minutes the unpleasant game continued, the camel stopping to graze, making off again as soon as I drew near. The fourth time, however, it seemed that I was going to get away with it. Perhaps he had tired of this amusement, I thought, as I inched my way cautiously inside his guard and felt my fingers close on the plaited strand. Immediately the camel kicked and spat, leaping away. I held the rope tightly, but to my utter dismay, his jerky movement had undone the securing knot at his neck, and now the useless halter came away in my hand, as the animal skipped off. Now I was doubly desperate as I pursued him, for I could not imagine how I should capture him without a rope to grasp, and I realized with a shudder how late the afternoon was. Already the fiery nucleus of the sun was beginning to mellow: unless I got him by sunset, all hope would be gone.

As I followed breathlessly, I lost sight of him for a while. There was no doubt in my mind that he was heading for home, as he was running due east, as if following some inbuilt homing compass. I reached the brow of a second ridge and stopped for breath, getting the miscreant back in my sights as I did so. Almost simultaneously, about a quarter of a mile away to the south in a bowl of dead ground, I spotted the figures of two camel-riders, heading west. I jumped up and down, frantically, shouting, 'Hai, the camel! The camel!' gesturing with my hands to where he stood, calmly chewing leaves. For a few moments the riders seemed not to have heard. Then the second of the two figures wheeled around lazily, like a battleship, setting off at a slow trot towards my animal. His companion turned even more slowly and shambled off after him.

I watched, feeling helpless as the two riders circled the grazing animal carefully. Then the first man dropped from his saddle and walked towards him. As he approached, the beast turned sharply as if to apply his old tactics. Then, to my surprise, the man seized the camel's tail, tugging it hard and swinging himself round so that he was able to catch the animal's front leg in the crook of his elbow. Somehow, he transferred his grip to the camel's throat, grasping it almost like a wrestler holding a headlock. I felt like cheering.

I hurried towards the group, clutching the headrope, noticing as I did so how the second rider couched and dismounted from his camel, while holding the headrope of his companion's mount. As I drew near, I saw that my camel's captor was no more than a youth of perhaps seventeen or eighteen years: a tall, well-built figure, dressed in a full-length Arab shirt or *jellabiyya*, with a dirty lace skullcap tilted over one eye. His face was a smooth, nut-brown oval capped by a brush of curly hair, his nose and lips a little flattened like those of the Jawa'ama boys I had met. The second lad was perhaps a year or two younger, but his face, though thinner and smoother than the other's, told me at once that they were brothers. For a moment we stared at one another. They regarded me with a cool, disapproving silence, as if they were the adults and I a mere youth. The stare began to shake my confidence, creating an awkward pause, which I felt the need to puncture.

'Thank God you got him!' I said.

'Yes,' said the older of the two, slowly. 'And if we hadn't got him, you never would. It'll soon be dark.'

'I know,' I replied, 'and I'm grateful.'

'He's hungry,' said the younger one suddenly, without smiling. 'Don't you feed him?'

'Yes,' I said defensively. 'I fed him yesterday!'

'Yesterday!' cut in the elder. 'By the life of the Prophet, yesterday is too long ago! Don't you know a camel should eat every day, if he's to stay strong?'

I felt not angry, but somehow mildly cheated. Had people not told me that a camel would last for months without food? I was at this time, of course, too naïve to realize that though this remarkable animal can go for many days without food, it does not mean that the process is actually pleasant or desirable to him!

'Give me the headrope,' said the boy, and proceeded to thread it expertly around the camel's head. The animal was cowed and meek now, in the hands of a man of experience.

'What's your name?' asked the younger lad.

'Makil,' I said, clipping the diphthong, which was difficult in Arabic.

'I'm 'Ali,' said the boy, 'and this is my brother Osman.'

'Where are you going?' asked Osman.

I explained that my immediate destination was En Nahud. Osman smiled for the first time. 'That's where we're going,' he said. 'We shall go together?'

He seemed to take this for granted, but somehow I felt reluctant. There was something mildly sinister about the brooding youths, and the stories I had heard about bandits had put me on my guard. On the other hand these boys had rescued me from a very awkward situation, and anyhow, to travel with company would be far more interesting than going alone.

'What's your tribe?' I asked.

'We're Arab – Hamar.'

I hoped that the flush I felt spreading over my face was not too visible. Here were the very people I had been warned about repeatedly – I could have fallen into a trap, like a fly into a web. Yet it was too late to refuse their offer, for I had already told them that I was going to En

Nahud, and to change my mind now would be to insult their hospitality. I had no choice but to go along with them and hope the stories were fallacious.

We drank water from 'Ali's waterskin, sucking the tarry liquid from the mouth of the vessel. Then the Hamar stood on my camel's legs as I mounted. We rode together towards the melting sun which was already fading into the pale soup-mixture of the evening sky. My camel seemed to perk up, padding faster with the two larger bulls ridden by Osman and 'Ali. As we rode the camels formed and broke in endless patterns, sometimes in file, sometimes abreast. The Hamar lads rode lightly and easily, though I noticed that they both used the hard-framed pack-saddle, known as the *hawiyya*, piled with blankets, sheepskins, and canvas sheets. They rode at a steady pace rather than the skipping trot which I had found comfortable, and allowed the camels to munch grasses as they went, mouthing strange clicking and sucking noises and swinging their whips from side to side harmlessly.

At intervals they chatted, asking me about my country and my work in the Sudan. They digested the answers slowly, as if they could not believe that a *khawaja* would ride a camel. But their talk and manner was so courteous and friendly that my suspicions began to evaporate.

'We'll stay at Umm Gauda tonight,' said Osman. 'We'll arrive there after sunset. It's a village of the Bederiyya – a people not to be trusted, but it's better to sleep in the village than outside. No one would steal our things while we were under their protection.'

The light had faded almost completely when we reached Umm Gauda, but I was still able to make out the shape of a broken grass compound within which there were a few grass huts with pointed roofs. I followed Osman and 'Ali up to the gate and couched my camel by theirs.

'Peace be on you!' Osman called. 'O people of the house, peace be on you!'

Suddenly a gaggle of curly-headed children appeared at the doorway, laughing and pointing. Then a man came forward, a small, trim figure in a plain cotton robe, his face in the darkness like wrinkled rubber, and his hair chopped down to the bone.

'Welcome, welcome!' he said and shook hands with each of us in turn. 'By the will of God you are well?'

'Thanks to God we are well.'

He called to the children, and some older boys, who immediately began to unload the camels and carry the equipment into the compound. Then the camels were led away into a dark corner of the yard, while the Bederiyya brought sheaves of hay or *qeshsh* and laid it before them. We were ushered to an almost moribund fire outside one of the grass huts, where we squatted on straw mats, and our host began to warm a pot of coffee in the hearth. As he poured us each a cup in turn, he said that he was Juma' Salih of the Bederiyya, shaykh of this village, which consisted of few but his own family.

Juma' was curious to know about me and my origins, and when I explained that I was English, he said, 'Ah yes, I remember the *Ingleez*. But that was twenty-five years ago. You're the first one I've seen since then. Are the *Ingleez* coming back?'

I could not help chuckling a little at his obvious sincerity, and I assured him that the *Ingleez* were not coming back. He seemed disappointed.

As we talked, other men – sons, cousins and brothers of Juma', I imagined – came over to listen to the conversation, greeting us and taking their positions by the fire. Small boys would sidle up and sit quietly in the shadows, staring with wide eyes at the adults. As I fell more into the background of the talk, I began to perceive that, far from being imposed upon by our visit, Juma' seemed honoured and stimulated, as if our coming had for tonight shone the lamp of favour on his doorstep.

A little later, a boy brought a huge dish of *'asida*, a kind of stodgy pudding made from sorghum flour. This was my first experience of the staple diet of the western Sudan. It resembled half a football lying in a pool of sticky gravy, and after the boy had poured water over my hands I crouched around the bowl with the others and copied them, dipping my right hand into the soggy mass. To my dismay, I found that it was piping hot: it stuck to the fingertips and burned them unmercifully. I hid my discomfort as well as I could, however, and covertly watched my companions, trying to emulate their trick of covering the morsel with gravy before inserting it quickly in the mouth.

After the meal, the boy poured more water over our hands, and we settled down around the fire to drink tea. I will always remember this first night in a village in Kordofan: the camels shifting and chomping in the shadows, the pointed roofs of the huts looming up in the darkness, the flicker of the fire in the open grate, the smell of wood smoke and the tidal rise and fall of the talk around the fire. The Hamar boys and the Bederiyya were deep in conversation, which seemed to revolve around prices: the price of a camel in El Obeid, a cow or a goat in En Nahud, the current price of sugar, millet, sorghum and groundnuts. The men seemed to be juggling constantly with the figures, repeating them and reciting others from previous times. Later they broke up for their evening prayer, each man facing east and praying separately, making his own individual submission to God. It seemed to me that these individuals, not only in this tiny place, but in millions of such places all over the Islamic world were united to the core by this moment, this submission to a single idea. I felt humbled and envied them.

As the talk continued afterwards, I found it increasingly difficult to understand or take part. I found my attention wandering above the soft murmur of voices, drifting into the deep mystery of the night. It had been a day of strange reversals, but now I felt content, and above me the stars were out, in celebration of my euphoria, in their most royal gold. It was a privilege to be here.

4

THE BUSH ARABS

The distance between El Obeid and the wells of Abu Ku' in North Darfur is about four hundred miles. The way cuts through thousands of acres of rolling range-land, referred to in the geography books as marginal steppe or acacia scrub. The Arabs simply call this area *qoz*, meaning sand-dunes, a word reflecting the true essence of the country, which is in fact a sea of undulating red sand, the deep shades of which are given relief by the golden yellow of the coarse grasses which cover it like a carpet. These grasses are valuable beyond calculation, for the wealth of the Arabs, their cows, sheep and camels, depends on their abundance.

The ranges are also enhanced by rich veins of green bush, many species of acacia, *mukhayyit*, *ushur* and others. The *ushur* or Sodom's Apple grows like a fungus on the land, producing a tempting green fruit filled with a poisonous white pus. The acacia thornbush, however, is a vital source of food for camels, and one variety produces gum arabic, the soft amber resin which is an important export of this region. The scrub is dwarfed in places by the grotesquely magnificent figures of the giant baobab trees which occasionally raise their stark fingers over the landscape.

The *qoz* is dotted with villages: compounds of grass with straw-roofed huts which blend in with the colour and texture of their surroundings. These works of man are pinpricks against the background of the enormous dimensions of the range-lands, for this is a place where humankind has wrought little of permanence on the landscape, where nature, by sheer size and power, has resisted any encroachment on its autonomy.

As I travelled, I felt myself becoming totally immersed in my environment. This was not the desert I had seen from my house in Dongola, yet these desert marches still represented part of the world I had sought. It was a world existing within its own time span, and all but oblivious to the outside. I never regretted my decision to cross it by camel.

I travelled with the Hamar boys for four days, as far as the town of
En Nahud, and very quickly I perceived that the tales I had been told
of the Hamar were groundless. The boys were courteous and considerate, and treated me like an honoured guest. They would hold my camel
as I mounted, help me adjust my saddle, and perform all the small
tasks of caring for the animals without my help. After a while, in fact, I
found this rather irritating, for I saw it as a barrier between us. I
desperately wanted the Arabs to accept me as one of themselves, and in
a sense resented this special attention, as a result of which I learned
less about the handling of camels than I should otherwise have
done.

We followed the rise and fall of the land, and I became accustomed
to the deliberate yet unforced way in which the Arabs made the pace.
Their camels moved easily, with sweeping strides, and often I found
myself admiring the superb patience, grace and power of these animals.
My own bull was shorter and had a jerky stride, yet I tried to emulate
the light and easy manner of the Hamar, encouraging the camel with
clucking and sucking noises, tapping his shoulders with my heels and
his rear flank with my stick. Slowly, I overcame the difficulties I had
experienced in my first days of riding. I learned to fit the saddle
correctly and to master that most difficult of operations: mounting.
The trick, I discovered, was to stand at the animal's left shoulder
holding the headrope and the stick or whip in the left hand. One then
grasped the rear saddle horn with the right hand and cocked the right
knee carefully over the front horn, like a hook. The movement had to
be extremely careful, for most camels would rise as soon as they felt
pressure, and the hooking of the knee gave one a secure position as the
camel jumped up, whereupon the rider crossed his legs over the
animal's neck. This position, slightly forward of the hump, was quite
comfortable, despite the fact that the motion of the camel put a strain
on one's back and legs. Once up, the camel was controlled by the
headrope, held in the left hand, and by the stick or whip held in the
right.

As we rode, the Arabs filled the hours with endless talk, and I was
able to question them about their lives. I soon discovered that they
were not from a nomadic background, but villagers from near En
Nahud, the centre of the Hamar *dar*, or homeland. Their father, they
said, lived near En Nahud, and owned a few camels. They were on
their way back from El Obeid, where they had sold some camels in the
market. Since the Hamar was largely a sedentary tribe, practising

cultivation as well as pastoralism, I was interested to know how they reared their camels, for I understood that these animals required an annual cycle of movement.

'Once the Hamar were all nomads,' Osman told me. 'That was in the time of our great-grandfather, the time of the Khalifa Abdallahi. Now most of our people live in villages. Still, when the rains come, the young men take the camels and cattle north, as far as the *dar* of the Kababish. Then they move south again, after the rains, back to the villages. But, in truth, we have few camels now, not like the old times.'

'Once the Hamar were the most powerful tribe in Kordofan,' cut in 'Ali. 'By the life of my eyes, we had more than the Kababish – they only had goats! Then the watering-places dried up, and the Kababish stole many Hamar camels.'

'Is there still trouble between the Kababish and the Hamar?' I asked.

'The Kababish are savage men, and they have many weapons. They respect no one,' Osman said. 'And sometimes they take Hamar ani-mals.'

'The Kawahla are the same,' continued his brother. 'They come into our country to steal cows and camels, then they take them off into their own country. Only a month ago, one of our kinsmen lost five cows.'

'What about the police? Don't they help?'

Osman laughed. 'What can they do? These tribes are more numerous and better armed than the police. They know the country better, and know where to hide.'

I was still a little sceptical about this talk, though I could not help being fascinated by such stories. I had heard many tales of this kind, not least about the Hamar themselves, but I often suspected that they were engendered by spite against other tribes.

Occasionally, I felt disinclined to talk, and as I rode gazed around enjoying the overpowering beauty of the landscape. Here there was life in plenty: the scrub was full of birds and I saw orange-beaked hornbills, bee-catchers of bright yellow, indigo Abyssinian rollers, woodpeckers with scarlet plumage, dun-coloured plovers and crows of black and white. Often we disturbed colonies of giant vultures which regarded us with distaste, but did not fly off at our approach; sometimes I would catch sight of one of these birds perched high in the branches of a tall tree looking like the feathered monarch of some mythical domain. The grasses were alive with lizards, snakes and salamanders, and insect life was in great abundance. There were butterflies: swallow tails, admirals and whites, and sometimes the air hummed with the sound of locusts the size of young nestlings. 'Ali told me that the Hamar caught and ate these, considering them a great delicacy.

I once asked Osman why he preferred to stay in villages overnight rather than sleeping in the *qoz*. He looked at me blankly, then replied, 'Why sleep in the *qoz*, when everyone here will shelter us? It is the way of the Arabs: if we come to a village, they must give us hospitality. If not, how could they expect to receive it in our lands? Anyway, it would be shameful.'

'Who does not welcome guests in his house?' said 'Ali.

Indeed, in the Bederiyya villages at which we rested for the first three nights, we were always welcomed as readily as we had been at Umm Gauda. We were shown respect and treated with great politeness, almost as if we were ambassadors of our different tribes.

Each day we travelled until about noon, when the sun was a burnished hammer raining forty-degree blows upon our heads. We would halt for a rest at a hamlet or village, where the Bederiyya would help us to unsaddle our camels and carry the equipment into the shade. The Hamar would set the camels to graze in the bush, or feed them on sorghum grain bought from the villagers. Then we would be entertained under a shelter or in a hut where the shafts of sunlight penetrated the gloom like currents of warm water. We would eat *'asida* with the tribesmen, squatting in the sand or on straw mats, and afterwards drink tea and chat, or just rest until about three o'clock, when we would saddle up and set off again, travelling until after sunset.

Always our hosts were anxious to hear news from the outside world. Most of the villagers rarely ventured further than the nearest market and were fascinated to hear anything new. I was questioned in detail about my 'tribe'. The most common questions were personal ones: was I married? How many children had I? How many brothers? They were amazed to discover that I was not married, for amongst these people marriage came early, an arranged affair, often between first cousins. A man had to pay an agreed sum for a wife, or a number of cows or camels to the equivalent value. They took my bachelor status as a sign of poverty, and found it difficult to reconcile this with a belief that all *khawajas* were rich. When I explained that in my country it was the tradition for the woman's father to pay for the wedding, they were at first mystified, then assumed that men in

Britain were subservient to women, an assumption which, to their satisfaction, was borne out when I admitted that we were ruled by a queen and a woman prime minister.

Similarly, they were surprised at the small size of my family. The Arabs generally had large families, often with more than ten children, whom the parents relied on for support in their old age. A man who had many sons was respected and honoured. They wondered, too, at the fact that my family owned no livestock, for even amongst these largely settled Arabs, a man's status depended partly upon the number of camels or cows he owned. Other favourite questions concerned my people's agriculture: what crops did we grow? When did we harvest them? What type of soil did we grow them in? These were things which interested the tribesmen and with which they could identify. Most of them seemed to imagine the world as a great plain of sand and grass, populated by tribes of varying speech, colour and custom, but with basically the same lifestyle as their own. They rarely asked about the 'wonders' of modern technology, which they did not understand, and which had little bearing on their lives.

Osman and 'Ali, however, occasionally referred to relations who had gone off to work in the cities such as Khartoum or Wad Medani. They spoke of their imagined lives there almost with wistful yearning, which contrasted with the deep pride they had in their Arab traditions. They told me of their ancestor Abdalla Al Juhani, progenitor of the Juhayna families, one of the two great divisions of the Arabs of the Sudan, and the one to which many of the nomadic tribes belong. Their forefathers had left South Arabia in the seventh century, and had entered the Sudan in the fourteenth century by way of Egypt. It was strange to hear these youths referring to such events as if they had occurred only yesterday.

When they spoke of their tribe, I could see that they had a fierce sense of identity with it. It was a large family of which they felt themselves to be an integral and important part. The disadvantage of this strong sense of unity was that it led to mistrust of other tribes. The Hamar regarded the Bederiyya with something like disdain, because they were not Juhayna Arabs, and even their nearer kinsmen, such as the Kababish, a nomadic tribe from the desert fringes, were treated with suspicion.

But their awareness of another life outside their own, the life experienced by relatives in the large towns, had introduced a sense of uneasiness into the consciousness of these boys. A knowledge of schools, lorries, radio, aeroplanes and news of the outside world had begun to erode the confidence of their convictions, making them restless for things about which they could only dream. I felt that their way of life was far more satisfying than that of their contemporaries in places such as Khartoum, though I did not express this.

Like most tribesmen in Kordofan, 'Ali and Osman were strong Muslims. They prayed five times a day: at sunrise, noon, afternoon, sunset, and in the evening. If we were travelling, they would halt their camels and hobble them, then lay out prayer-mats of many colours on the sand. They had an old army water-bottle, which they would fill with water, and perform the ritual ablutions, washing the body's extremities in a certain sequence. Then they would face east, towards Mecca, and begin their prayers, murmuring verses from the Koran, bending forwards in submission, then kneeling and bowing so that their foreheads touched the ground. The number of ritual bows or *raka'* varied according to the time of day, but the boys generally only performed two, a special 'allowance' for travellers, for all except the sunset prayer, when three *raka'* were performed.

As I watched them, I could sense the power of their belief, the brotherhood of unity and equality which is at the core of Islam. It seemed in many ways a logical religion, requiring no great leaps of the imagination, but merely the acceptance that there is no God but God, and Mohammed is His Prophet. It was easy to surrender to the idea of God's omnipotence in this giant wilderness, and I realized that the submission to this all-embracing belief both reflected and arose from the desert genesis of the Arab people: it was a factor which had been of positive survival value to the Hamar's Juhayna ancestors, whose resilience had allowed them to cross one of the world's harshest environments. If anything could ensure the coherent survival of these peoples through the inevitable hazards of the twenty-first century, I felt that it would be Islam.

On the morning of the third day we passed the village of Khewei and out of the *dar* of the Bederiyya into *dar* Hamar. There seemed to be very little difference in the way the tribes lived, despite their different origins. The houses in which we rested were of similar construction, usually a compound of grass or cane which enclosed three other compounds, one for the men, another for the women, and a third for the animals. In the men's yard there would be two or three huts, and often a flat-roofed shelter or *rakuba*. One of the huts was the *khalwa dyuuf*, the 'guests' retreat', where we sometimes stayed, and another the *bayt kibiir* or 'big house', which was used by the head of the family. Most of the younger men slept outside under the *rakuba*, as the nights were still warm, and the smaller children slept in the women's quarters. The huts were very solid, built on eleven props of wood bound with strips of bark. The roof was supported by thirty-two smaller beams which were attached to a square frame of wood below the apex. Over-lapping layers of grass were then bound over the roof framework with thin strips of bark. The houses had to resist two long months of pounding rain in autumn, and they did so successfully. They were admirably adapted to their environment, and I felt sure that the Arabs had adopted them from the earlier indigenous inhabitants. Indeed, throughout this section of my journey, I had the constant impression that I was travelling on a demarcation line between two spheres. Here on the marches of the Libyan Desert was the place where Arab North Africa and the Negro interior met. This was the outer limit of Arabdom and these Bush Arabs, with their half-Arab, half-African way of life, were the border tribes of their domain.

As we moved west, the belts of baobab trees grew more common, and often we passed through spinneys of gum-producing acacia and flat fields of grey earth ripe with watermelons. Often, in the distance, we would see flocks of sheep and herds of cows being watched by wizened old women wearing nothing but loincloths of coarse blue cotton. I saw few camels, and no village seemed to have more than a dozen. Osman talked to me about his tribe's cultivation, telling me that they relied upon rainy-season crops such as sorghum, millet and groundnuts. Melons, he said, were an unreliable crop, since they were too sensitive to rainfall and difficult to transport; however, they were used for feeding animals. Certainly I noticed that the camels loved them, biting off great chunks and chewing them with obvious relish: it was only with great difficulty that one could wrest them from a melon-field once they had the taste for the succulent fruit. I was curious about the baobab trees, which the Hamar called *Hamari*, after their own tribe. The boys told me that the trees were an important means of water storage, and I was incredulous at first. One day, however, we halted under the spiky canopy of a giant specimen, and Osman pointed out to me the square opening high up amongst the boughs, where the water was poured inside.

'The water collects around the tree in the rainy season,' Osman explained. 'Then someone climbs up the trunk and hoists up the water in buckets. Of course, the inside of the tree is hollow: some can hold thousands of *jowloon* of water.'

'But there's been great dryness,' continued 'Ali. 'So now many of the people rely on *dawanki* for water.'

Dawanki, I learned, was the Arabicized plural of the word *donki*, which in the local dialect had come to mean an artesian well, so called after the European 'donkey-engines' which powered them. Lack of water had been a serious problem in this area for several years, as the rains had been slight. I had already noticed how careful people here were with water, as compared with the north. In houses it was stored in large porous jars, the evaporation from which kept it cool. In Dongola, when drinking from the jar, it had been the custom to give each drinker a fresh cup, throwing away the leftover amount; in Kordofan, however, the cup was passed around and not a drop wasted.

We spent the evening of the third day at the village of Mirkab. I noticed that the boys seemed much more at ease with their own kinsmen, who welcomed them like long-lost brothers. To me the Hamar seemed indistinguishable from the tribes I had encountered previously, but 'Ali and Osman assured me that they could tell a Hamari immediately from a Bederi or Jawa'ami, by his appearance, dress and accent. They looked down on these tribes, which were of the Ja'aliyyin family, the second great division of Arabs in the Sudan, whilst the Hamar considered themselves to be Ashraf, or noble Arabs, connected with the family of the Prophet Mohammed.

It was on the fourth day that the most memorable incident of the journey took place. It was late afternoon, and we had not been travelling for long when a cluster of camels broke light over a ridge to the south of us. They were moving very fast, and as they came nearer, I saw that there were two mounted men driving four unsaddled animals before them. The men were fair-skinned and dressed in tattered Arab shirts, and they trotted one on each side of the free camels, keeping them in a tight huddle. They moved north across our path, not more than two hundred yards distant. Suddenly, Osman and 'Ali halted their camels. A moment later, I noticed what they had already seen: both riders were carrying what appeared to be old service rifles, slung from their shoulders.

'Who are they?' 'Ali said.

'They look like Kawahla,' replied Osman. 'They're not Hamar.'

'But those are Hamar camels, by God!'

I had no idea how he was able to tell this, for although I knew that most camels had a brand-mark, this group was too far away for the marks to be distinguished.

Osman strained his eyes towards the rapidly moving figures. 'Yes, what are they doing with Hamar camels?'

'And carrying rifles like that in Hamar country! By God, they're bandits!'

'Now just a minute,' broke in Osman. 'Maybe they bought them.'

The boys began to speak very quickly, and I could not catch all the words. They seemed to be having a heated argument which lasted several minutes, by which time the camel-drivers had disappeared into *qoz*.

Finally Osman said: 'We must go on.'

'They're bandits!' muttered 'Ali as we set off.

Less than an hour later another group of men appeared on the sky-line, seven camel-riders sweeping over the *qoz* from the direction of En Nahud. They were a magnificent sight, riding at a fast trot, the necks of their mounts stretched out like those of flying swans. They made directly for us, and as they came near I got an impression of a mass of grizzled faces, expensive saddlery of wood and leather, the snapping of camels as they slowed down to meet us. I noticed with some consternation that these men too were carrying rifles and shot-guns slung from their saddle horns. The group greeted us with the usual *as salaam 'alaykum*, 'peace be upon you', and one of them, an oldish man with a fringe of white beard, spoke rapidly to Osman. Again I was not able to grasp all that was being said, but the riders seemed agitated and eyed me with unmasked suspicion.

'He's English – *khawaja*,' I heard Osman say. 'He's a teacher travel-ling to En Nahud . . . No, he's been with us for four days.'

I began to feel very selfconscious and wished I could understand what was happening, but again the man broke into a flood of rapid talk which I could not follow.

'We saw two men . . . back towards Mirkab . . . going the way of the wind . . . we couldn't tell . . . we come with you . . . maybe . . .' I picked out from Osman's words.

'No, go on! We'll find the sons of dogs!' The old man suddenly wheeled around and gestured to the others. 'Peace be on you!' he said.

'And on you,' we replied, and stood watching as the seven riders headed off to become dots on the vast plain.

Now it was my turn to ask: 'Who were they?'

'They were Hamar,' said Osman. 'Shaykh Hassan Mohammed from near En Nahud. They say that some raiders took six of their camels this morning. They blame the Kawahla. They've been following tracks all day, but lost them in the *qoz*.'

'And the men we saw, are they the ones?'

'Only God knows,' Osman shrugged. 'Perhaps, but it is a wide country – and those we saw had only four camels with them.'

'Perhaps there were two groups,' said 'Ali.

'Why were those men looking at me?' I asked.

'They said that you were a "red" man like the Kawahla. They were suspicious. I told them you were a teacher, a *khawaja*.'

'Will they catch the raiders?'

'It will be difficult. Sunset is not far away, and when the Kawahla get further north nothing can stop them. Anyway, it may be nothing to do with the men we saw.'

I was amazed by the sudden series of events. Quickly all my ideas about 'bandits' had come into sharp focus. This, at least, was reality, though it might be a far cry from some of the tall stories I had heard.

That night we spent with some Hamar near the village of Dawiana. News of the theft had spread quickly, and as we sat around the fire in the lee of the *khalwa*, we were asked repeatedly to tell of what we had seen. More and more Arabs came to join the conversation, which boiled over into a heated argument about weapons.

One lean-faced Hamari began to bang his stick on the sand, shouting, 'By the life of the Prophet, how long will this go on! They take our animals and we can do nothing!'

A young man's voice rose to meet the other's: 'We have no weapons to fight them, the government take some, the others we must hide in the ground!'

Everyone began to talk at once, and a babble of incoherent voices filled the night. It seemed that the Kababish and Kawahla, who lived on the borders of the Libyan Desert, found it easy to make incursions into Hamar country, making off with cows and camels into the desert where the less mobile Hamar could not follow. These two tribes were nomadic and because of their parched surroundings, very isolated. Here, beyond the effective jurisdiction of the government, they enjoyed an autonomy which compensated for the harshness of their environment. Although I sympathized with the Hamar, all I heard of these tribes fascinated me: they seemed to be as wild and free of outside influence as their ancestors had been, centuries ago. I was determined at some later time to find out more about them.

Suddenly a camel roared in the darkness beyond the grass walls, and a voice greeted the company. The discussion stopped abruptly, and we saw two dim figures framed in the doorway.

'Come closer, near to the fire,' called out one of the Hamar. As the men moved into the firelight and began to shake hands, I saw that they were dressed in the olive-green uniform of the *shorta*, the police Camel Corps, and carried automatic rifles. They sat down by the fire, a thickset man with a bulging black face and a slim youth who looked no older than Osman. There was silence, a brooding, resentful silence which hung in the air like a coming storm. The thickset man gazed about him, looking selfconscious, trying to find some way of breaking the deadlock. Then his eyes fixed upon me.

'Where's this person from?' he asked the assembled company. Osman began to explain that we had travelled together from near El Obeid. He looked at me with what was intended to be an intimidating stare. 'You have permission from security to be here?' I shook my head, and replied that I hadn't. 'No one is allowed in this area unless they have permission from security. You understand? You must come to En Nahud tomorrow and report to the secret police.'

I nodded, and he sat back, looking satisfied and self-important. Just then the lean-faced old Hamari said, 'Never mind *khawajas*, what about these Kawahla bandits, when will you stop them?'

'Yes,' someone broke in. 'When are you going to give us back our weapons?'

The babble of voices began again, reaching a new level of decibels. The *shorta* looked nervous, and began to shift, cradling their weapons protectively in their arms. A few moments later, they got up and left, having been made to swallow a rather large dose of public opinion.

The next day I entered En Nahud alone. I had already said goodbye to 'Ali and Osman, who were heading off to a village outside the town. I was genuinely sorry to see them go, for they had lightened my way and taught me a great deal. Under their tutelage I had begun to understand that alternative world that I had been seeking. Now, after only ten days of travelling I felt totally committed to this quest: it had already become the most interesting and fulfilling experience of my life.

5

CLOSE ENCOUNTERS

Alfred Mobile's office was equipped with an ancient fan which had probably stood motionless for decades, and shafts of heat throbbed in at the windows, lacing our brows with beads of sweat. The walls of the room were visibly crumbling, spotted with the red mud of old hornet nests and the streaky trails of termites. Alfred was a security man, tall and trim, with a rounded head scar which betrayed his origin amongst the Dinka, a tribe from the tropical lands of the Southern Sudan. He leaned over his desk and fixed me with the official stare.

'Who gave you permission to enter Kordofan by camel?' he asked.

I had to suppress a laugh: his near-perfect Oxford English seemed so incongruous.

'No one,' I answered. 'I just came.'

'Just came! You don't seem to understand the serious trouble you could have been in. Personally, I'm surprised the Hamar didn't attack you. Do you know how many reports we've had recently of camel thefts? With violence!'

I replied that I did not, but that I could guess.

'And now you intend to enter Darfur? They'll eat you! You must give up this idea at once. The way is lonely and dangerous. You can go by lorry.'

I explained that I wanted to meet the people in the remote villages and settlements, not merely to see the towns, which would not be possible if I travelled by lorry. I also told him of my idea of travelling north along the Forty Days Road. As I talked, I saw a glitter of interest in his eyes, and noticed that the official mask was slipping. When I had finished, he sat back, grinned and said, 'Are you a Protestant?'

'I was brought up as one, yes.'

'So am I. But they're all Muslims here. Nearly all of them. I have some friends – they are Syrians, Copts, we stick together, because we're Christians. You must come to dinner with us.'

'Thanks. But what about the journey into the desert?'

'Well, if you really insist on going, I'm not going to forbid you, but it's really up to the governor; you must speak to him.'

As we went out, Alfred chatted about his upbringing amongst the missionaries in the south. Like most southerners, he found the Muslim, Arabic-speaking northerners staid and clannish. He seemed delighted to have discovered another Christian in Kordofan, and welcomed the opportunity to speak English, which he had learned before Arabic.

Later we dined with his Coptic friends, who were wealthy merchants in the town, and afterwards I met a local government official, Mohammed Osman, a Shaygi from the Northern Province. He invited me to stay in the government rest-house and arranged for the Camel Corps to look after my camel in their barracks. He sent his two Hamar servants, Yusuf and Siraj, to bring me food and water.

The next two days were a busy round of visits and interviews. I was treated with unstinting hospitality, though almost everyone with whom I came into contact was from that educated class of Sudanese society which aspired to a western lifestyle. They felt a constant need to apologize for the poorness of everything, and I found this embarrassing since I was very much attracted by this town with its squares of mud-brick shops, its rows of leathersmiths and tailors, its clumps of wells and its tiny coffee-houses.

Most of these men were adminstrators from Khartoum or the Gezira, and considered that En Nahud was the very outpost of the known world. Almost all of them tried to persuade me to give up the idea of travelling by camel. I guessed that this was partly because the camel represented to them the economic backwardness of their country, something which they would rather have left behind in their movement towards 'civilization'. I found it difficult to explain that 'civilization', in my view, was not merely a matter of communications and high-rise blocks, but also a measure of man's treatment of his fellows. It seemed to me that many of the Sudanese I met, both simple tribesmen and more educated townsmen, were far more 'civilized' than many people I had met in Europe. I felt myself to be on a quest for an alternative to the materialistic civilization of my own culture, while these men were pursuing a vision of the very culture which I was rejecting. It was as if we were travellers meeting at a crossroads, the destination of each of us the starting-point of the other.

On the second day I was interviewed by the district governor. He was a thickly built, light-skinned man who sat behind a vast desk on a raised plinth, with the look of a benevolent autocrat giving audience.

He listened carefully to my plan to travel into Darfur by camel, then laughed, and declared in excellent English, 'I advise you strongly not to go by camel. By luck you've had no trouble so far. But beyond En Nahud the *qoz* is wild, and in Darfur the tribes are not like those in Kordofan. They are not to be trusted.'

I explained that I accepted the danger, and that I did not consider danger to be a serious excuse for abandoning anything worthwhile. At the same time I allowed myself a smug inward smile at his words about Darfur tribes, in view of what I knew about those in Kordofan.

'Very well,' he continued. 'I won't forbid you. You English are strange. But you should travel only by day, and spend your nights in villages. Only three months ago a Bederi left here by camel, alone, to visit relatives in Sherrif Kabashi. He camped in a wadi and lit a fire. He did not know that two thieves had followed him. When he was asleep they crept into his camp and loosed his camel. He woke up and drew his dagger but they beat him with clubs and finally stabbed him in the neck. Thanks to God he was a strong man and did not die. He was lucky.'

This spine-chilling story abruptly dispersed my secret sense of superiority. I could see from the way the governor had spoken that he was not exaggerating. 'I'll give you a letter to show to the shaykh of each village between here and the provincial border. They will give you shelter. After that I cannot guarantee your safety.'

I thanked him warmly, but as Alfred Mobil and I left the office, the Dinka turned to me and grinned cynically, 'That letter won't be much good. None of the shaykhs can read. And it won't be any protection against a high-powered rifle.'

Amongst the people I remember most clearly from the two days I spent in En Nahud were the two Hamar servants, Yusuf and Siraj. They were a Laurel-and-Hardy combination, Yusuf short and barrel-chested, while Siraj was tall, stringy and bird-like. The most pleasant intervals were when I walked with them in the market, touring the arched alleys, exploring the smells of fruit and spices, drinking in the rich scents of new leather, the laughter of the cobblers, the chatter of the spice women, watching camel trains laden with charcoal and gum arabic, and lines of women in colourful robes balancing water tins on their heads. We sat in the leather shops and coffee-houses, and the two Hamar helped to fit me out with new clothing, more suitable for riding camels than the nylon tracksuit I had been wearing. I ordered a Sudanese *araagi* – a shirt of coarse white cloth, which extended down to the knees – and its complementary *sirwel*, or baggy trousers, loose-fitting around the thighs but tight around the ankles, and so ideal for riding. I brought an *'imma*, the long strip of white cotton which makes up the Sudanese headcloth. At the advice of the Hamar, I increased my stock of saddlery. I bought a large rug of camelhair, a saddlebag of raw goatskin to replace the rucksack, and a new waterskin. The Arabs also advised me strongly to obtain a weapon of some kind. They talked about pistols and shotguns, but since these were officially illegal, I foresaw myself running into problems with any authorities I encountered. I had noticed, however, that some of the Hamar carried long swords, in addition to the traditional dagger, and I asked Siraj about these. At first he scoffed, saying, 'What use is a sword against an automatic rifle? They can attack you from far away. You'll never see them.' Then he thought for a moment, and became less scornful. 'The Hamar have always carried swords, we call them "white weapons". The old ones are the best – I've got one which was my father's. It's a good sword.'

I had always been fascinated by swords: at Stamford School I had been a keen fencer and had twice fenced in international tournaments. The Arabs took me to a shop where several weapons were hanging up. They were all of the same pattern, about three feet long with broad steel blades and cross-hilts bound in leather. I bought one for ten pounds, and asked the leathersmith to make me a scabbard which could be slung from a saddle horn. As we examined the weapon, a small crowd of boys gathered. Yusuf demonstrated the quality of the steel by bending the blade double, and I recalled testing foil blades in the same way. I had seen many tribesmen carrying such blades and I wondered how they would use one. One of the boys took the sword and demonstrated a crushing cut against the wooden prop of the leather shop, which brought a stream of abuse from the owner. Evidently, for the Sudanese the blade was mightier than the point!

My final task in En Nahud was to find, if possible, companions with whom I could travel to Darfur. Unfortunately, in Kordofan camel caravans were no longer used for long-distance trade as they were in Darfur: most of them carried gum and charcoal from local villages. I was introduced to some charcoal-burners who had a string of six camels, and were travelling to their encampment a few hours' journey outside the town. I spoke to the leader, a wild-looking man who wore neither shoes nor headcloth. He told me that people called him Ab' Gurun, 'father of horns', because his hair stuck out at odd angles from his broad head. He and three younger brothers had brought a load and intended to travel to their camp next day. They agreed to let me travel with them, though they pointed out that the journey would be a short one.

In the cool dawn of 2 April, I left En Nahud with the charcoal caravan. As we emerged from the thick gum groves which surrounded the town, I felt a new surge of exhilaration, the excitement of being once more unshackled from the chains of the town. The six camels were tied head to tail and each carried an old pack-saddle piled with jute sacks which the Arabs had obtained in the market. The animals moved over the soft *qoz* with a smooth, fluid stride, each seeming in perfect rhythm with the others, a superb, flowing pace which I had never witnessed amongst other creatures. Once again I marvelled at the graceful beauty of these strange animals, and wondered how anyone could find them ugly.

Ab' Gurun walked at the head of the column, a powerful, almost savage figure, black-skinned and barefooted, clad in yellowed breeches and a folded *tobe*, a blanket-like garment of soft wool, beneath which his rope-like muscles bulged, his wiry hair sprouting in all directions from his massive head. A dagger the size of a short-sword dangled from his left elbow, and a set of wooden prayer-beads curled around his throat. In his left hand he grasped the headrope of the leading camel, and in his right he carried the wood-hafted axe which was the badge of his calling. His younger brothers had placed themselves at intervals along the caravan. They were smaller versions of Ab' Gurun, hewn of the same rock, but with the rougher edges honed down to a finer finish. They too were barefoot, but their hair was neatly trimmed, and they wore knee-length shirts over their *sirwel*. The younger boys also carried axes, and as they walked made clicking noises to encourage the camels. Beside these barefoot Bush Arabs, I felt soft and inadequate, almost ashamed to be riding while they walked.

The country was breathtakingly beautiful on that morning. We descended into deep brakes of forest where acacias drooped over the track, where the air was scented with the perfume of flowers, purple, yellow and white. We passed over gentle hills of pastel pink sand, and down into valleys where the sunlight hung in golden threads from the thornbush, and the shadows of great baobabs cooled the hot earth.

Occasionally we met people coming in the opposite direction, going in to market: a boy in an immaculate white *jellabiyya* leading his pretty sister, who rode sidesaddle on a black donkey; a whole family of Hamar riding camels of various sizes, each appropriate to the size of its rider; pedestrians in ragged clothes, carrying staves and bundles of possessions, like Dick Whittington.

I would very much have liked to talk to the charcoal-burners, but though I tried each of them in turn, they seemed taciturn and unwilling to engage in conversation. By the end of the morning we had reached their camp east of the village of Dibrin. I was surprised to discover how spartan and comfortless the place was. A line of neatly stacked sacks of charcoal stood in front of the hut, and beside it, in the shade of a tree, lay an old oil-drum sideways on. Inside the shack were a mat and a few blankets. This was their world, and they seemed oblivious to its lack of comfort. As they couched their camels, a young boy appeared out of the bush. He was a youth of about fifteen, I guessed, probably another brother, dressed only in *sirwel* and carrying an axe and a dagger. He went through the usual profuse greeting with each of the brothers in turn, as if they had been away for months rather than days. Having greeted me last of all, he helped to hobble my camel, then led me into the shade of the shelter and offered me tea. The youth told me that his name was Ishaq, and at once I expected the usual interrogation: where was my country? where did I work? where was I going? how much did my camel cost? where did I buy him? I had grown so accustomed to receiving these questions from strangers that I could reel off the answers word-perfectly in Arabic. What surprised me was that Ishaq did not seem the least interested in who or what I was, but simply went about making a fire of wood chips upon which he set a blackened kettle. Meanwhile the camels growled and spat outside as the others unloaded them. Then Ab' Gurun and his brothers joined us, squatting on the sand floor, while the tea was served. The liquid was as black as the charcoal itself and a rainbow film of oil, I assumed from the oil-drum outside, floated on its surface. I drank it quickly, and asked for water, which I found to my disappointment to be similarly laced with a scum of oil.

The conversation settled down to a series of politenesses. Unlike the loquacious Osman and 'Ali, these charcoal-cutting Hamar seemed morose and silent, happy it seemed merely to be in each other's company, as if they had been so long together in lonely places that talk had long ago been exhausted. Getting them into conversation was like pushing a heavily laden wheelbarrow uphill. However, I eventually managed to get Ab' Gurun talking about his family. Once in gear, he was like a verbal bulldozer, and there was no stopping him.

'Is your father a charcoal-man?' I asked.

'Our father is dead,' he answered slowly. 'But he was a Hamar from near En Nahud. He had some camels and cows, then one day some thieves came and stole some of his camels. He and my uncle followed their tracks for days. Then they found a Kawahla camp, and the camels were there. My father asked for the return of the camels, but the Kawahla refused. Then he said he would return with a large party from his family and take them by force. As he walked away, one of them shot him in the leg. My uncle could do nothing, he had only white weapons. It was some time before the leg was treated. He could not ride properly after that. He lost all his animals in the end, and became a charcoal-cutter.'

This seemed an enormous speech for the silent Ab' Gurun, and when he had finished he took a swig of oily water and spat it out. Then he picked up his axe, threw off his *tobe* and stalked off into the bush. I wondered if the memory of his father's misfortune had angered him. The strange thing was that he had not expressed any hatred for the bandits, merely accepting what had happened as an act of fate.

I continued talking to the other boys, asking them if they lived here most of the time.

'No,' answered the eldest, Jibril. 'We cut the wood in one place but we don't take it all, just the biggest branches. That way there's always some left for next year.'

I ascertained that the charcoal was made from green wood, buried in a special mud-oven, and left for several days. 'When we have enough,' went on another of the brothers, 'we send it to En Nahud, then we move to another place where the wood is more plentiful.'

At that moment Ab' Gurun strode back into the camp. He was carrying a newly cut club and advanced on me with such a devilish look in his eyes that I stood up, thinking I was about to be attacked. All he did, however, was place the stick in my hand. 'Keep this close when you sleep,' he said. 'Watch out for thieves. It won't protect you from bullets, but it might be useful.' I was touched by this simple but thoughtful present, and wished that somehow I could repay the kindness of these tough, quiet men, who spent most of their lives in the wild bush of Kordofan.

Later, I rode off alone, and after a few hours came to the village of Dibrin, a Hamar settlement dominated by a vast pile of groundnuts which towered over the straw roofs of the village. I couched my camel in a small square between the grass walls, and was immediately surrounded by a crowd of curious Hamar boys, who brought me tea, this time without oil. As I sat under a *rakuba*, I noticed two camels couched in the shade on the opposite side of the square. One was a magnificent pure white bull bearing the circular brand of the Hamar on its rear leg. The other was a buff-coloured animal, a little smaller than the white. Both animals bore expensive riding saddles, surmounted by rich leather cushions, and I began to wonder idly who the owners were, when an old man came up to greet me. He began telling me a long tale about the last Englishman he had seen riding a camel, who, it seemed, was the British governor of En Nahud in the 1940s. I became interested and forgot the two camels.

Not long before sunset, I was continuing west across the open *qoz*, when I happened to glance behind me. To my surprise, about a quarter of a mile away was a pair of camel-riders, one of whom was mounted upon a brilliant white beast which I took to be the one I had seen in Dibrin. I hoped the men would catch up, thinking that it would be pleasant to spend the rest of the day with company. I was disappointed, however, when they came no nearer, even though I had slowed down slightly. I found it curious, for I had already learned that no Arab will fail to be excited at the prospect of new company. It suddenly struck me that the riders might be following me intentionally, and I recalled with a rush the governor's horrific story about the lone traveller. Perhaps these men were thieves, intent on stealing my camel! At once I condemned myself as infantile for this foolish fantasy, but still the idea persisted, lodged securely in my brain by the power of the storyteller.

I continued riding on the same trajectory almost till sunset, glancing around occasionally to assure myself that the riders were still following. Meanwhile the day neared its end, the sky filled with a veil of cloud and a fierce wind blew from the north, whipping across the wild claws of the desert scrub. The *qoz* looked grey, cold and uninviting, and as the light of the sun faded, the clouds welled up into strange spectral shapes. I had been hoping to come to a village at which I could rest for the night, but had passed none, nor in the gathering dusk could I make out the cosy, welcoming light of any such settlement in the distance. I had the choice of continuing on the offchance of finding a village or of camping down in the bush, with these two men coming up behind me.

I made a sudden impulsive decision. I turned sharply from the western route, and headed straight into a thicket of thornbush over a hundred yards away. I selected a place and couched my camel near a low tree. Then I stripped down to my *sirwel*, slung my broadsword over my shoulder, and went off to clear the area in the little light that remained, making sure that my camel was not visible and that there were no animal tracks passing close to my camp. I had hardly finished this task when I heard the soft murmur of men's voices in the veil of the darkness, which was now complete. Quickly I dropped to the ground at the base of a thornbush, hoping that my white face would not give me away. The voices came nearer, but the new thickness of the night, with no moon up, meant that I could not make out the figures of the riders until they were almost upon me. They were going quite slowly, and only about fifteen yards away, they stopped.

'I think he's gone off into the bush,' growled one of the men.

'No,' answered the other. 'He's gone on, that's for sure. He would have lit a fire by now.'

'Where's he gone to then?' cut in the first man. 'There's no village ahead.'

'He doesn't know that, he's a stranger.'

At that moment I felt certain that my hunch had been correct. I was no longer dealing with exaggerated stories, but with the real thing. They stood still, silently listening, for what seemed to me an endless period. I suddenly remembered lying camouflaged on a moor in Wales during an SAS evasion exercise, while two Gurkha trackers came within a few yards and miraculously missed me.

Finally, to my intense relief, one of the men said, 'Let's go.'

When I was sure that they had gone, I returned to my camp. On the way, I almost walked into some loose thorn branches that had been left by charcoal-cutters or wood collectors, armed with vicious two-inch spikes. I suddenly had an idea, and began to drag the cruel branches to my tree, arranging them in semicircular defence around myself and my camel. If anyone was going to sneak up on me in the night, I thought, they would find a surprise waiting for them. Then I sat on my rug and ate some sardines, with my sword laid ready near by. The ridiculous circumstances of my situation suddenly dawned on me. I was only a day's journey away from a town where there were diesel trucks and electric generators. Yet here I was, dressed like some medieval knight, with my trusty sword at hand, hiding from robbers under a thorn tree. My own place and time seemed suddenly a million light years away.

In the bleary, windswept light of day, however, the events of the previous night took on a different form in my mind, as nocturnal events often do. I wondered if, after all, those men had merely been

seeking company, since I had heard that it was the custom for travellers
to join together at night. Perhaps I had let the bloodthirsty warnings I
had had build up in my mind. The question, however, was never
resolved, for I never saw or heard of them again.

I found, anyway, that I had a more pressing problem. The little
water I had possessed had run out in the night. I was out of water, and
had no idea how far I was from a well or settlement. The sun came up
like a flaming halo above, the hours passed as I plodded on west. I
found not a single settlement. Even the thick semi-desert brush disappeared, and I found myself in a wasteland of plain sand, covered in
places with a light down of grass. By mid-morning, my throat was
already choked with dust; I smoked a cigarette, but this only made my
mouth drier and my throat sorer. I carried on, feeling drier and drier,
hoping desperately that I would meet someone from whom I could ask
directions. The *qoz* became increasingly desolate, and though I ran
into occasional patches of vegetation, I dared not stop to rest. All
through the burning afternoon the camel and I ploughed on, until I
was feeling faint from dehydration, mysterious pains shooting up my
spine. Then, when I had almost given up hope, a village appeared like
a mirage before me, a green orchard oasis in a sea of sand. It was the
Hamar town of Wad Banda, still so far away that it took me almost an
hour to reach the small marketplace.

I couched my camel, and asked the nearest person for water with
the last of my strength. A Camel Corps trooper came up and took
charge, urging me to sip the water gently rather than swill it down. He
then took me to the Police Post, tied up my camel, gave me tea and
coffee and invited me to stay for the night. I felt exhausted and weak
from the effects of dehydration and the sun, yet I knew the day's
experience had been a hard lesson: in this merciless land water is not a
thing to be taken lightly. I asked the police trooper how long a man
could last in this heat without water. 'Not more than two days,' he told
me. I thanked my lucky stars I had not been forced to spend another
night out in the *qoz*.

It took me another four days to reach the Darfur borders, and in
many ways they were the most difficult of my journey to the west. East
of En Nahud, I had come to rely on the Hamar's detailed knowledge of
the area. I now saw that it was this knowledge, rather than any fabulous
sixth sense, which was the Arabs' true strength: the same strength,
perhaps, which had allowed 'Ali to recognize Hamar camels without
seeing their markings. Our journey to En Nahud had gone smoothly

because 'Ali and Osman had known exactly how much ground to cover each day, but without such knowledge my progress was sporadic and inefficient.

An additional problem was the camel himself. I noticed quite early on that he would not travel so happily alone; camels, like humans, are social animals and are far more relaxed in a crowd. Quite often during those four days he refused to leave villages in which he had been well fed, or the cool shade of a tree in which we had rested, and I had to force him onwards with a stick. A particularly unpleasant trick of his was to wait until we were passing a thick acacia bush with low branches, then make a sudden dart into the shade. This could have been far nastier than it was, considering the size of the thorns; luckily I always escaped with small cuts or tears in my clothes.

Usually I stayed in a village, presenting my official letter to the shaykh. As Alfred Mobile had predicted, none of them could read, and I felt that even without the letter I would have been welcomed. Each Hamar village was different in character, and each retains a special memory for me. In Wad Banda, for instance, I remember the Kawahla girls who had come in from the *qoz* to water at the wells. I found them strikingly attractive with their creamy-brown skin and long black hair, their gold nose-rings, ivory bracelets and bare feet. Some Kawahla, I was told, had settled in the village, though most of these women escorted caravans of donkeys from their tiny camps in the open range, where their people raised the camels for which they were renowned.

I passed through Sulayl, and finally arrived in Ed Damm Jamud, the last sizeable settlement in Kordofan. It was dominated by three huge and ancient baobab trees which stood exactly in the centre of the place. I went to inspect the trees and found with a shock that they were covered in English graffiti: 'WTS', 'TC' and other initials carved into the massive trunk. At first I thought this must be a hoax, but I was told that the carvings were genuine. They had apparently been left by the soldiers of Wingate's force who had camped here on their way to Darfur in 1916.

They had marched to Darfur to defeat the Sultan Ali Dinar, autonomous prince of the Fur tribe from whom the region gets its name. After the fall of the Mahdi, in 1898, when Kitchener had destroyed Sudanese opposition at Omdurman, Darfur was the sole region of the Sudan which had retained its independence, protected by its remoteness. The trouble had begun, however, when the French advancing from the west had annexed part of the western border of

Darfur. The British were worried about French encroachment on their sphere of influence, and since the borders could not be settled while Darfur remained independent, the British had set out across Kordofan with two thousand soldiers and two aircraft. It was curious to think of British Tommies relaxing under these same great trees, all those decades before, and it seemed that the village had actually not changed at all since those days.

I stayed the night with some Hamar. It was perhaps the most beautiful evening I had experienced in the bush of Kordofan. As sunset came, I sat in the sand with the Arabs, whose voices played an endless fugue around each other in the silence of the day's end. The sun was an orange globe sinking over the sharp roofs of the huts, and before us the colossal trees seemed to preside over the orchestration of the sunset. Two large camels lumbered past, followed by a boy on a white stallion. Suddenly, the clear voice of a muezzin struck up, calling the faithful to prayer, the fine notes seeming to draw together the threads of magical African beauty I saw before me:

> 'God is greatest, God is greatest.
> I testify that there is no god but God.
> I testify that Mohammed is the Prophet of God.
> Come to the prayer,
> Come to the celebration,
> God is greatest,
> There is no god but God.'

6

SHADES OF ARABIA

Far are the shades of Arabia
Where the princes ride at noon.

Walter de la Mare, *Arabia*

In the cool hour after dawn, the Zayadiyya were already gathered at the wells of Abu Ku' to water their herds and flocks. A great mob of camels, reds, whites, blacks and buffs, were grazing on the sparse vegetation around the wells, and the long iron troughs were obscured by a press of donkeys, sheep, goats and camels vying for a place, bleating, roaring, spitting and bucking.

Women wearing brilliantly coloured dresses struggled and fought, hissing and chattering like excited birds over their waterskins, tossing their braided hair and their peach-brown shoulders. Ranks of the swollen skins lay amongst the mud and the animal filth, ready to be loaded on camels and donkeys, and men stood around in languid groups. They were fair-skinned and bearded, and clad in dust-coloured shirts, pantaloons and hand-stitched leather sandals, their headcloths fluttering exotically across their foreheads.

As I stood amongst them, dressed like them, it seemed to me that had entered another world, separate from the semi-desert land of Kordofan. Reflected in the faces around me, I could see the unmistakable shades of Arabia.

All around was an ocean of amber sand, and in the distance the craggy, broken red teeth of the hills erupted from the silent desert. The flocks and the camels, the pale Arab faces, the open sands: all these seemed at a far remove from the rich Kordofan bush in which I had been travelling.

As I watched, a young boy suddenly snatched an enamel bowl from an older girl. She snapped at him like an angry bitch, laying into him with tooth and claw, and seizing a heavy stick with which to lash out. It took four grown men to separate the children, and I was amazed at the strength and ferocity of this slip of a girl. Her volatile power gave me an unexpected insight into the nature of these Arabs.

I had arrrived at Abu Ku' that morning, about a week after crossing the borders of Darfur at the village of Sherrif Kabashi. As the days had passed, the landscape had become increasingly arid: the baobabs had disappeared and the green acacia scrub had been replaced by acres of petrified bush where the trees stood grey and bald as stones, their branches as brittle as glass. In places I crossed flats of open desert, relieved only by stunted grasses and low *mukhayyit*. I had passed through the broad basins of valleys and plateaux where mountains, prussian blue, slate grey and red ochre, lay like impenetrable barriers around the perimeter. Here for the first time in the west, I had encountered the withering *haboob*, the freak wind from the north which dragged the sands of the Libyan Desert south, obliterating the fertile lands of the Sudanic belt.

I had left the land of the Hamar far behind, and had rested in the settlements of a variety of tribes, amongst them the Jiledad, the Berti and the Bani Umm Ran. Their villages seemed bleak and severe after those of Kordofan, the African-style huts looked out of place in this more desiccated environment.

In Abu Ku', however, I had entered the *dar* of the Zayadiyya, a small Arab tribe inhabiting the southern skirts of the Libyan Desert. To my great excitement, I realized that for the first time I had come into contact with desert bedouin: the nomadic herdsmen whom I had journeyed so far to find.

In Abu Ku' I met two Zayadiyya who agreed to take me to Mellit, the gateway post between the Sudan and Libya, which was the centre of the land of the Zayadiyya. It was a journey of two days only, but a fairly difficult one, across trackless desert and through the belly of flinty hills. One of the Zayadiyya, called Taha, had fair skin and an eagle nose which displayed his unmistakable Semitic ancestry; the other, his cousin Ahmed, was a shade darker, but with the same finely formed features; both were small, lightly built men dressed in full-length *jellabiyyas* and layered headcloths.

Taha told me that they were travelling to Mellit to sell four camels in the market there, which was one of the largest in Darfur. He pointed out to me two fine seven-year-olds and two younger calves which were roped together in pairs, neck to neck. Finally, he studied my own camel appraisingly for a long time, his eyes missing nothing, working carefully over the saddle, the rug, the saddlebag and the waterskins. 'What's your work in Mellit?' he asked.

'I'm looking for some Arabs who are travelling up the Forty Days Road,' I said. 'I want to travel with them.' I realized at once how ridiculous my words must sound. Taha regarded me silently, without surprise. I understood later that this was partly because he had not the slightest idea what I was talking about, for later on he asked me the same question several times.

It was approaching mid-morning by the time the camels were watered and prepared for the journey, and we finally set out across the open waste. The Zayadiyya were riding lean bulls, and driving before them the four camels which they intended to sell. As we began Taha turned to me and said, 'Are you all right?' I looked around at the sweeping grandeur of the desert, the powerful dignity of the camels, the calm nobility of the Arabs, and answered, 'I'm complete!' Which indeed I was.

As we rode, the Zayadiyya questioned me, as usual, about my tribe and country. They were surprised to find the *Ingleez* had no camels, and seemed to think that I must be very clever to have learned to ride one here in the Sudan; I did not spoil the impression by telling them of the misfortunes I had suffered in Kordofan. They questioned me about my camel and about each item of equipment in turn. They identified my camel as a *Howari*, and told me that it had become weak.

'Anyway, it's not good for the desert,' Taha told me. 'Its stride is too short.' I noticed that though the camels which the Zayadiyya rode were no larger than mine, their stride was considerably longer. I was not displeased with my bull, however, for it had crossed four hundred miles of semi-desert and been subjected to the whims of an inexperienced handler.

Ahmed and Taha talked incessantly of camels, and it was obvious that their animals were the absorbing interest of their lives. Both were using riding-saddles of polished wood, far more expensive than my own, draped with precious furs and rugs, and a variety of saddlebags. They told me that the leatherwork and saddlery of the Zayadiyya were famous, and I learned later that the ornateness of a man's saddle amongst the Zayadiyya was a sign of status and a way of showing off to the girls.

As they rode, talking endlessly, their eyes never rested, but darted about, taking in everything. Once Taha pointed out a herd of camels at the base of a distant hill, looking no larger than ants, and often they drew each other's attention to the tracks and spoor of various animals in the dust, which alone I should never have noticed.

Taha told me that the Zayadiyya was a small tribe, of the same Juhayna family as the Hamar. 'But we have many camels, because our land is perfect for them,' he said. 'They prefer this dry land to the damp areas of the south; when the desert blooms, there is much grass and many trees.' He told me that the tribe had two important sections: the Awlad Jabir and the Awlad Jerbo'. While some of the Awlad Jabir were settled in Mellit, most of the Awlad Jerbo' were nomads and ranged their camels far into the Libyan Desert. Indeed, Taha did not exaggerate about the large numbers of camels owned by his tribe. Later that year, during my journey to Malemal Hosh in the Libyan Desert, I saw herds of up to two thousand camels owned by single families of the Zayadiyya.

At about midday we came across the dry bed of a wadi, along which some thornbush was growing, and the Zayadiyya decided to make camp for the afternoon. We couched and unsaddled the camels, and the Arabs showed me how to bind the forelegs of my *Howari* with a plaited leather thong, called a *qayd*, looped at one end and knotted at the other. The thong restricted the animal's movements while still allowing him to feed freely. The two men set up the camp methodically, erecting a canvas sheet between two thorn trees to allow us a few square feet of shade. Beneath it they laid out a similar sheet, on which they piled their rugs, sheepskins and blankets. They hung our water-skins carefully amongst the bushes, then poured out a bowlful of water. I watched as Taha added to this a little flour and sugar, mixing it in with a twig. The mixture, which was called *habsha*, was more refreshing than water, as the extra ingredients took away the taste of *gotran* or tar which continually tainted water carried in skins.

Ahmed made a fire from some bone-dry wood which he had collected, ignited by a fistful of straw. He laid out some cooking vessels, and began to make *'asida* from the yellow flour he carried. We ate crouching around the pot in the usual manner, and afterwards drank sweet tea.

After the meal, we settled down in the shade as the sun began to incinerate the amber sand around us. I asked Taha about his experience in the desert.

'I've been to Libya twice,' he told me. 'It's a journey of thirty days from Mellit, but by God it's a hard one. That desert is empty – no trees, no grass, nothing.'

I asked if it was a dangerous journey.

'Many have died out there,' he said. 'The Arabs go to Libya to sell camels, they take them to the oasis of Kufra. Then they are taken to Tripoli by lorry. Tripoli is a big market: camels come there from Algeria, Tunis and Niger, but camels from the Sudan are the best – the others are so small.'

'How do you find your way across the desert?' I asked.

'Every group has a *khabiir*, a pilot. He is a man who knows the desert routes. By day he follows the landmarks, the hills, the colour of the sands or even the direction of the wind. At night he follows the stars.'

'But since Libya became rich,' Ahmed joined in, 'many people have gone there just to get work. Some are Arabs, but many are townspeople, who know nothing of the desert.'

'Yes,' continued Taha, 'and many of them died. What about last year, you remember, brother, forty men were lost at once.'

'What happened?'

'Two men of the Meidob arrived in the oasis of Nukheila, the only well between El Atrun and the Libyan border. They were almost dead, and some say mad. Their story was that they had set out from Mellit with forty men, mostly townsmen. At first things went all right, but they had no pilot with them, so they followed lorry tracks! Lorry tracks by Almighty God! Of course, along came the *haboob*, and where were the tracks? The Meidob made their way to Nukheila, but no one but God knows what happened to the rest!'

'These people have no brain!' said Ahmed. 'They take with them bad skins which fall to pieces, then where is the water? They fight over what is left, or they drink too much at the beginning, and have none at the end. They are not real Arabs, these people, and they don't understand that the desert is a hard place.'

'Many of the Zayadiyya are pilots,' Taha told me, 'because they know the desert well. A good pilot can ride to Libya alone.'

'My cousin is a pilot,' Ahmed said. 'You know the story he told us? He was leading a large party, and one of them was a big, fat merchant from Nyala. After two days, he said he couldn't ride his camel any more. "My body hurts all over!" he said. My cousin said that if he didn't ride they'd leave him in the desert. "Leave me then!" he said. "But by God the Great, I'm not riding again! Never!" Do you know what they did? Tied him in a basket, and hung it from the saddle. That's how he made the journey! But, mind you, he was much thinner at the end!'

This talk was fascinating; like most Arabs, the Zayadiyya loved telling and listening to stories, and were skilled orators. I found that the constant practice of the previous month had improved my Arabic, and I was able to comprehend more of what they said. I felt sure these experienced Arabs could tell me about the Forty Days Road, which I still intended to find. I asked Taha about this but he looked at me with the same blank stare which had first accompanied my mention of the name.

'What does he mean?' he asked the other.

'You mean the Forties Way,' said Ahmed. 'But that's not in the desert, it goes to Omdurman!'

I tried to explain that this was not what I meant, but it became obvious that neither knew of the Forty Days Road. This was mystifying, for many people had talked about it, not only in Dongola, but also in Kordofan. How was it that these desert men who lived in Darfur itself did not know it?

As the blistering heat began to wane, Ahmed started to make more tea. While he lit the fire, Taha and I went to collect the seven camels, which had managed to wander a distance of about half a mile, despite the restricting qayds. We drove them back, swinging our sticks. Taha told me not to stand too close to their back legs.

'They kick,' he said. 'And if they do, that's the end!'

Everything was packed quickly and efficiently, and we mounted to begin the evening trek. As we travelled, the hills began to close in around us, unbroken chains of soft ochre rock, sculpted into towers and terraces by the forces of erosion. The hills passed, and gave way to legions of russet-brown knolls which rose unexpectedly out of the flat desert. By sunset these features were behind us, and we found ourselves in a rippling tableland, obscured at the edges by a blue mist which first washed the colours out of the sun, then drowned it completely.

Not long after dark, we came to an area of coarse grass, and the Arabs discussed making camp there. Ahmed decided to ride ahead a little, to see whether more abundant grazing was to be found, but he returned within half an hour, and told us that we had better make camp here. We set up the camp as before, laying out our equipment and turning the camels loose in the grass.

After supper of 'asida, we sat close together in the darkness, and Taha and Ahmed began to talk. I asked them a few questions, and realized that they actually knew very little about the world outside their own section of it. Their main interest in foreign countries seemed to be in the weapons they produced. I noticed that they themselves were not armed and asked if it was the custom not to carry firearms in this area.

'The Zayadiyya have many weapons,' Taha told me, 'and they know how to use them. Those who travel with herds are always armed. There are plenty of thieves out there.'

'Last year, in Wadi Howar,' began Ahmed. 'What about that, by God! The Bedayatt took six of our camels, may their fathers be cursed!'

'The Bedayatt?'

'They're a tribe from the Chad borders. They wear their headcloths like this . . .', and he swept his *'imma* across the lower part of his face. 'They don't know Allah, those men! They are notorious thieves. They took six of our camels, at night, by God!'

'What did you do?'

'We made a search-party and followed them. We knew where they'd be. The Tagabo hills. They always hide there because it's so rocky that tracks disappear. But we found them, by God, we found them in a wadi, with the camels eating. They saw us coming and opened fire. One of us was hit and fell down with his leg smashed, but there were eight of us and we all had rifles. I had a *Kalash* with me. My uncles said we should try to get around the other side of the wadi, so I and two others ran through the rocks and into the trees. Then we put our guns on tripods and fired and fired until the Bedayatt ran away, and left the camels. One of them was dead, though, because I saw them carrying him away.'

Ahmed shook his head, 'Those Bedayatt. They're animals! What happened two years ago in Mellit! Some Bedayatt came into the market with camels they'd stolen from the Zayadiyya. The owner was there and recognized his animals. He walked up to them. A brave man, by the life of the Prophet! But what happened? By God they drew their pistols and shot him dead! Then they jumped on their camels and rode off into the desert! Wild animals! Not people!'

I asked, as lightly as I could, whether the Zayadiyya also stole camels. Taha said, 'All tribes have their robbers. Even the Zayadiyya. Some families think that stealing is a test of manhood, and a man can't marry until he's stolen a few camels. The Arabs steal only a small number, not like the Bedayatt. They steal whole herds, and drive them off into Chad. Then their women make up poetry about the bravery of their men. Tsch!'

On my return to this area in 1982 I learned that Taha had been shot dead by some Kababish after a raid in which they suspected him of being involved. It transpired that he was notorious as a camel rustler.

As the conversation dwindled, the Arabs went off to collect the camels, and drove them into the camp, where they were knee-hobbled around the fire. It felt strange, yet oddly reassuring, to be surrounded by these reptile-like heads, bobbing and twitching. I lay down and drifted towards sleep.

Suddenly, I felt something, featherlight but distinct, crawling with a ticklish step over my hair. I awoke with a start and saw an enormous black spider shooting under Taha's blanket. I shouted a warning and seized my club: the Arabs were up instantly, battering away with their sticks until the assailant was dead. Then Taha laughed and told me it was a *karamba*, a harmless type of spider which inhabited this area. Feeling somewhat embarrassed I returned to my sleeping-bag and shortly fell into an undisturbed sleep.

The next day we entered Mellit at about eleven in the morning, and I waved farewell to the Zayadiyya, who were taking their camels off to the market. The town was set on a series of dunes which sloped down to a natural cleft in the rock, where rainwater gathered. There were hundreds of camels watering there when I arrived, but I rode past them and up to the police post. A rather mystified sergeant escorted me from the office of the police chief to that of the district governor, and showed me in. As I entered, I felt like a gatecrasher at an official reception. The governor sat behind the standard gargantuan desk and was in deep conversation with four portly, double-chinned gentlemen in tent-like but immaculate *jellabiyyas*. All faces turned to me, and reflected in the twitching of nostrils, I realized with mortification that I was still wearing the soiled *araagi* and bedraggled headcloth which had remained unwashed since I had left En Nahud.

The governor turned to me and said in English, 'What can I do for you?'

I related my story, and ended by saying that I had come with the intention of contacting Arabs who were travelling north along the Forty Days Road.

'Forty Days Road!' said the governor, incredulously, and there was a ripple of laughter from the portly gentlemen.

'Yes,' I added. 'The old caravan route to Egypt.'

'Oh, I know of it,' went on the officer. 'It's just that it hasn't been used for a hundred years! There's no water on that route now, and anyway there's no need to use it when the other ways are safe.'

There were more giggles from behind and I felt myself flushing. 'Do you mean that no camels are sent from here to Egypt?' I asked.

'Plenty, but they don't go by that way, and they don't go from Mellit itself and they don't go at this time of year, when the desert is difficult for even an Arab, but death for a European.'

I felt shattered. I had been planning this for a year, and had ridden almost five hundred miles just to get here.

'What you should do is sell your camel and . . .'

'Go by lorry? Yes, I know!'

Outside the office, I stood looking out across the stony square to where my camel was tethered beneath a *nim* tree. I began to understand what had happened, and why the Zayadiyya had known nothing of the road. Part of Sudanese hospitality was always to tell a guest what he most wanted to hear. Those I had spoken to in Dongola about the ancient route had been affected by my obvious enthusiasm, and their polite lies had built up in my mind into a vivid picture which was not close to reality.

As I stood there pondering this, a young man with a fresh, humorous face approached me, wearing the uniform of a local administrator. He introduced himself as Farah Yusuf, the local forestry officer. He had heard my story, he said, from the police chief, who shared his house, as did the governor, and he wondered if I would like to stay with them for a few days.

After a wash and a good meal, I felt better, and began to consider what I should do next. The journey which I had made had been interesting and eventful, but to me it had been no more than an apprenticeship, a chance to test myself against the harsh conditions of the Sudan in summer. Now I felt a tremendous sense of anticlimax, yet to go into the Libyan Desert alone would be madness.

I asked Farah why the Forty Days Road was no longer used. He told me: 'The caravans used to go that way because the routes further south were unstable, and liable to attack, as were those across to the river. The caravans only left once a year, and with huge numbers of camels. They might get attacked, but the desert is a big place, and they could stick together. Now of course it is no longer necessary to avoid southern routes.'

'Which route do they take?'

'That I cannot tell you, only the camel-men can do that.'

The smiling and energetic Farah was almost fanatically interested in forestry. He had been sent to Darfur to help prevent the deforestation which was taking place as a result of the southern movement of the desert. Each year, he told me, the desert moved up to ten kilometres south. At this horrifying rate, the whole of the fertile Sudanic belt would be desert within a few decades.

'The tribes have already been affected,' he said. 'Take the Zaghawa – thousands have run away to the cities, their herds and flocks dead, the same with some of the Berti and Zayadiyya. No one can actually live in the desert, you know, but the tribes were supported by the patches of vegetation and the water sources there. Now these are disappearing, and those which are left are very valuable. The tribes fight over them: there have been some serious battles between them.'

I was astounded to know that the traditional way of life of these tribes was being eroded, not by the adoption of western ideas, but by changes in the delicate balance of their own environment. Ironically, in technically advanced Libya, the problem was being tackled by using products of the oil industry, but the Sudan could not afford to preserve its ancient way of life by halting desert creep.

I spent the next day exploring the market, and examining the famous Zayadiyya leatherware and saddlery. There were rows of stalls, full of pretty Arab ladies in colourful *tobes*, who sold saddlebags, whips, saddle-pads, ropes and hobbles. Waterskins hung in colonies from the roofs, with rich sheepskins, carpets and belts. Everywhere the air was pervaded by the savoury odour of fresh leather, and everywhere it reminded me that Darfur was still the land of the camel.

7

THE TRACK IS MARKED BY BONES

> Now no one can be found alive who remembers
> the old trade along the Arba'in.
>
> Ralph Bagnold, *Libyan Sands*

We sat in the ruins of Old Kobbay and watched some Tungur children watering their donkeys. There was only one well, encircled by a wooden rim into which, over the years, the well-ropes had cut deep grooves. The children poured the water into a trough made of a hollowed-out log. One small girl, with a round black face, her plaited hair covered in dust, held her stick protectively over a pregnant she-donkey which drank from the trough. Occasionally another animal would push through for a drink, only to receive a short, sharp whack on the snout from the little girl. Lost in their own small world, these children were probably unaware that the overgrown plain which surrounded them was once the site of a legendary town. For here had stood the southern terminus of the great Forty Days Road, once the Sudan's most vital artery of trade with the outside world.

Now there was nothing left of the streets and market squares except the dark patterns of their foundations left on the earth. The houses had long ago crumbled into dust, the alleys which had once swarmed with men and camels now lay under thickets of *lalob* and *sayal* trees. Kobbay had become a dead town, peopled only by these few children who now toiled away at a single well where there had once been many. I had wanted for some time to see the place from which the great trade caravans to Egypt had set out. Although my attempt to travel up the Forty Days Road had been unsuccessful, the old caravan way still fascinated me. For this reason I had made the two-day journey from El Fasher with my colleague Donald Friend and a pair of borrowed camels. That there was little to see here did not disappoint me. I had learned much of the history of this area since I had first arrived in

Darfur armed only with some hearsay stories which were fallacious and inaccurate. The knowledge I had gained brought the dead town alive for me. I knew that the wealth of the Kayra sultans, who had controlled Darfur up to the death of Ali Dinar in 1916, had been founded on the trade flowing up and down the Forty Days Road. For centuries the chief commodity had been slaves.

Men, women and children had been taken from the south of Darfur in their thousands. Armed slave-raids were a full-time occupation of the Muslim tribes, who would often surround and capture entire villages. Only the children, the women and the younger men would be taken, and frequently the remainder would be slaughtered. The captured slaves would be brought here, to Kobbay, and sold to merchants in the thriving market. The slave-caravans would leave the town at irregular intervals, sometimes with several years between them, sometimes with many departures in the same year. Each caravan may have comprised up to two thousand camels, and taken up to a thousand slaves in addition to other merchandise.

Only one European is known to have travelled on this route. In 1793, an English traveller named W. G. Browne arrived in Kobbay having made a journey by camel of almost one thousand one hundred miles from Upper Egypt. Browne left Assyut, the northern terminal of the *darb al arba'in* (as the caravan route was called in Arabic) in April of that year. He set out in the company of some Egyptian and Maghrebi merchants and about a hundred and fifty men and a guide from the Fur tribe. Most of these men had left the Sudan in the previous year, and had spent the winter in Egypt. It was the hottest season of the year when they left the Nile. Both camels and men suffered from thirst and exhaustion. So many camels died, in fact, that at the oasis of Selima, just within the present borders of the Sudan Republic, some of the merchants had to bury their goods for collection later. From Selima the caravan had passed to Bir El Malha, the present-day El Atrun oasis. Browne noticed that then, as today, the oasis was renowned for the production of rock-salt, which was used in the manufacture of snuff. He also mentioned that the wells were likely to be infested by a people he called the '*Cubba-Beesh*', whom he describes as: 'A wandering tribe who, mounted on the swiftest dromedaries, rapidly traverse the desert and live by plundering the defenceless.'

Browne arrived in Kobbay in July, having spent almost four months crossing the Libyan Desert. He found here a medium-sized town of mud houses, which could boast a mosque and five Islamic schools, and was populated by Arab merchants from many parts of northern Africa. Browne remained in Darfur for some time as the guest of the local king, Malik Ibrahim. He noticed that, when a caravan was being prepared for departure in Kobbay, it engaged the attention of the entire country, even forming a kind of chronological peg by which people could reckon.

As I sat in what remained of the old town, I tried to imagine what it had been like in Browne's day. I pictured the streets full of roaring camels and a flux of voices speaking many different tongues. There would have been fair-skinned Egyptians, Libyans and Tunisian merchants and traders of the Jellaba Arabs from the east. There would have been black soldiers in chainmail and armoured helmets, the cavalry of the Kayra sultans who ruled the region. There would have been Baqqara Arabs bringing in trains of slaves, and veiled Tuareg from Aïr riding their short-legged camels. On the days preceding the departure of the caravan, there would have been great excitement in the town: the slaves would be prepared for departure, the squares full of camels laden with ivory and copper, rhino horn and hippopotamus teeth, ostrich feathers, gum arabic, pimento and tamarinds, parakeets and monkeys. There would have been pilgrims from the Hausa and Fulani peoples of West Africa, about to embark on the most hazardous section of their journey to the holy shrines of Arabia.

Before them lay a trek of more than a thousand miles in one of the least hospitable areas on earth. As they set off north, the camels moving in scores of separate convoys, the slaves and strangers would have been amazed to see how the vegetation became scarcer, and finally disappeared, leaving them in a stark, mysterious wasteland. The slaves probably walked freely in columns and squads, for in this pitiless landscape there was nowhere to run, and safety lay with the caravan. If the slaves became sick the caravan-masters would goad them on, with sticks if necessary, for the caravan could slow down for no one, obsessed as it was by the necessity of reaching the next source of water. A valuable slave who was unable to walk might occasionally be allowed to ride on a camel's back. But the camels were precious, heavily burdened by goods and weakened by thirst and the lack of grazing. More often the exhausted slave would have been left to die in the open desert while the caravan continued on its relentless way north. How many human beings perished in this way, pushed beyond the limits of their endurance to leave their rotting flesh for the carrion birds, will never be known.

From Kobbay, the first halt on the journey was El Atrun, within two hundred and fifty miles of which there was no permanent water-source. All provisions for slaves, camel-men and merchants had to be carried by the camels. Water was conveyed in great ox-skins of the type I had seen in Umm Ruwaba, two to a camel, and food consisted of a paste made of millet flour which could be mixed with water and drunk without cooking. This paste is still in use amongst some tribes today. The slaves would probably have been fed like animals from communal bowls, though the caravan-masters would have seen to it that they did not starve, for a thousand miles is a long way to walk on an empty stomach, and the caravaneers had every reason to protect their investment.

From El Atrun, the caravan passed north-east through the oasis of Laqiya Arba'in to Selima. This was the most dangerous section of the journey, for not only were water-sources far apart, the route was also dogged by bandits of the Kababish, Bedayatt and Gor'an tribes who were particularly apt to strike at caravans travelling south to north, since they knew that many of the merchants were likely to have sold their Egyptian-bought firearms in the lucrative market in Kobbay, and thus be unarmed except with spears and swords. The Gor'an, a black Saharan tribe, had a base at the oasis of Nukheila, north of El Atrun, not seen by any European until 1925. From here they would sally forth in raids as far east as the Ghab wells near Dongola. But threat though they were, these bandits were never a prohibitive force to the trade caravans, the masters of which were far more afraid of the levies likely to be charged them if they passed through the more comfortable reaches of the Nile valley. As Browne himself noted, this empty quarter of the Libyan Desert could sustain neither 'wandering tribes nor ferocious animals' for long.

There were other threats to the travellers, however. The caravan had to face hot winds from the north which cast a scourge of sand into their eyes and dehydrated their waterskins. Occasionally sections of the caravan would be lost, only to be found by other travellers years later, a nest of skeletons and twisted hide. Over the centuries the caravaneers piled up stones into small cairns which marked their way, but more significant were the thousands of skeletons of camels which had expired in the desert, and which lay like grotesque and unearthly insects amongst the rocks. Of such importance as signposts did these

become that the 1946 survey of the Sudan noted one stretch of the old
route as being 'A track about one mile wide marked with white camel-
bones'.

From Selima, the caravans moved north through the oases of Shabb
and Abul Hissein until they arrived at the string of settlements at
Kharja, where they came into Egyptian jurisdiction. Here they encountered local officials who assessed the revenue payable on their
merchandise, so that before arriving in Kharja, the caravan-masters
would hide the smaller slave children in the empty waterskins in
order to avoid payment of taxes. The officials soon grew accustomed to
this ploy, however, and would walk along the lines of camels beating
the skins with their sticks, and listening for a cry of pain from inside.

The two-hundred-mile stretch from Kharja to Assyut was relatively
easy. One can picture the scene of the caravan's arrival at the end of its
journey: the vast columns of camels appearing suddenly out of the
empty desert, moving towards the town with their unfaltering, un-
stoppable pace. The onlookers would be wild with excitement, but as
the caravan slowly emerged from the vast landscape, they would
become aware of the toll taken by that merciless void which it had
recently crossed. The camels would be thin and weak with hunger,
some of them staggering on feet covered in sores. The slaves too would
be in the last stages of exhaustion and malnutrition, looking on with
eyes misted with fatigue and despair at the place which marked the end
of their ordeal.

Exactly how long the journey took is uncertain. It is likely that the
title 'Forty Days Road' referred only to the actual marching time,
which might have been divided up into forty equal stretches of a little
less than thirty miles each, the average daily marching distance of a
camel. Browne's journey from north to south lasted far longer than the
prescribed forty days, and it is likely that the south–north caravan with
its contingent of slaves took even longer. The bulk of the time would
be consumed in watering and grazing the animals and in stops for
much-needed rest.

Little is known of the early history of the route. It may be that the
Egyptian explorer Herkuuf came this way with his trains of donkeys,
many centuries before the birth of Christ. It is unlikely though that
there was regular traffic south of Kharja before the introduction of the
camel to North Africa in the first few centuries AD. The lack of
grazing on the southern sections of the route would have rendered it
unsuitable for less hardy animals. Old maps of the area show the passage

of a route south of Kharja through Selima, though this route rejoins the Nile a little below Dongola. It may be, therefore, that the Darfur section of the way is a more recent innovation. More definite, however, is the knowledge of the ceasing of traffic along the *darb al arba'in*. During the wars of the Mahdiyya, between 1883 and 1898, the British built military posts at Shabb and Wadi Halfa, in order to halt trade between the Sudan and Egypt. When the Sudan was recaptured by the British at the battle of Omdurman in 1898, slave-trading was forbidden. Without this lucrative commodity, the caravans were no longer profitable, and eventually ceased. Many of the old guides and camel-men had died during the Mahdist wars and the last of the Kayra sultans had been killed by a British soldier in Darfur. Kobbay was depopulated and its water sources began to dry up. Within a few generations, the ancient way of the caravans was forgotten. Even the exact route which the caravans took between Kobbay and El Atrun is no longer known.

Nomads of the Kababish, Bedayatt, Meidob and Zaghawa still range across this vast area, but none of them now knows the meaning of the *darb al arba'in*. Some of the peoples of North Darfur and Kordofan apply the name to quite a different route which skirts around the fringes of the desert, running west to east from Darfur to Omdurman. The desert beyond El Atrun has been left to the gazelles and the desert foxes, the creatures whose domain it was before the coming of man. The ancient road is forgotten, the grooves left by the feet of millions of camels are buried under shifting sands. Nothing now remains to record those centuries of human history but tens of thousands of skeletons of both humans and camels who never saw their journey's end.

8

BORDER INTRIGUE

A stranger is the friend of every other stranger.

Arab saying

Shaykh Rashid Omar was sitting cross-legged on a pile of rugs in his house in Gineina, and around him in a semicircle were a dozen Arabs of the Rizayqat, waiting for his deliberation. The shaykh had the distinctive air of a king holding court. He was an old man, perhaps over seventy, but his eyes were very sharp and clear and his skin was as black and smooth as ebony, with those unmistakable carved-mahogany features of the Rizayqat.

'Rizayqat' is in fact a collective term for five distinct nomadic tribes who inhabit the extreme west of the Northern Sudan, roughly between El Fasher and the town of Abeche, in Chad. The best-known Rizayqat tribes are the Mahamid and Mahriyya, but each of them is divided into clans and sub-clans. They are related to the Rizayqat cattle-Arabs of Southern Darfur, who were amongst the most ferocious warriors of the Mahdi. The Rizayqat still have a reputation as fierce fighters, and are constantly embroiled in some tribal dispute or other.

The Eritrean, Hassan, and I sat a little apart from the semicircle of Arabs, on two dusty folding chairs which had obviously been brought out specially for the occasion. Slowly, the Arabs rose and left one by one, and finally the shaykh turned his attention to us.

'By the will of God you are well!' he said.

'Praise to God, we are well,' we answered. 'By the will of God, the Goodness is with you.'

'Praise to God, it is, may God's blessing be upon you.'

'May God give you peace.'

The greetings continued for many moments, in the traditionally courteous Arab way. Then the shaykh looked at me, and said, 'My son tells me you want to go into Chad with the Arabs.'

'Yes,' I replied.

'You know there is bad fighting in Chad now. The border tribes, the Gor'an and the Bedayatt are armed and dangerous. They would kill anyone, especially a *khawaja*, for they hate the French. Only the *barashoot* dare enter the country now!'

Hassan explained that *barashoot* meant smugglers.

'Perhaps you can help me to travel with them?' I said.

'I?' he said as if aghast. 'What would I know of the *barashoot*?' Then he smiled, a white-toothed, engaging smile which reminded me at once of a hyena I had seen in Kordofan. I suddenly sensed why this man was feared and respected, why he had the reputation of a vicious adversary, quite capable of smiling and stabbing someone in the back at the same time. I remembered the stories about him in the market, how he had obtained his wealth by raiding, smuggling and double-dealing. I recalled too, the words of Hassan when he had first told me about the shaykh. 'His house is like a port,' he had said. 'You will find things there that you never see in the market. They come across the desert by hidden ways, and sooner or later they make their way here.'

His words struck a chord in my mind. Already I had spent some time travelling with Arabs on such hidden ways. I had found in the desert a world which had never grown old, where life continued as it had been for centuries. Arab tribes and others still roamed with their herds and flocks, raiding, feuding and smuggling without much regard for international boundaries. The shaykh's house on the edge of Gineina, on the border between the Sudan and Chad, on the line between the desert and the Sahel, and on the route of ancient caravan ways, east, west and north, seemed ideally suited as a repository of illicit goods and information coming from all directions. Indeed it was a port, a place that almost smelt of intrigue and subversion, a world beyond the jurisdiction of governments, where the camel-man was king. Now, with one of my camels couched in the shaykh's yard, I felt again that yearning to go further into this hidden world, to leave the sedentary life of the town and set out once more for the desert where for a time I had found tranquillity and peace.

Gineina was a small settlement on the extreme western edge of the Sudan, over two hundred miles west of El Fasher. Although on the same latitude as El Fasher, its atmosphere was quite different. This area was in the Sahel belt, dressed in thick woods and smooth-walled mountains. The terrain undulated between great wadis which carried abundant water for part of the year. The wadis were decorated in places by vegetation which was almost tropical; huge *heraz* trees drooped over their banks and fruit shrubs were laden with mangoes, guavas, oranges and limes.

It was the very simplicity of the town which appealed to me the most; even in comparison with El Fasher it was like stepping back a hundred years in time. There were no asphalt roads, no electricity, no tall buildings, no running water. Camel caravans were the most important form of transport from the surrounding towns, and many of the local tribesmen rode horses. They carried sheaves of spears, swords and throwing sticks, and caparisoned their steeds with ornate harness and saddlery as if they were constantly about to ride out to war.

The marketplace consisted of rows and squares of mud-brick shops which were cracked and neglected; grass grew in their walls and roofs. These enclosed areas of wooden stalls, flimsily constructed and roofed with cane. This was the women's market, one of the most exotic places I had seen in the Sudan. It was a splash of colour and life where women from many tribes brought their wares. The air was thick with the scent of spices, of fruit and buttermilk, perfumes, fats and oils of many kinds. The *suq* was suspended in a matrix of voices, a variety of different dialects which wove around each other in a fascinating tapestry. There were women from the nomadic tribes who brought charcoal, firewood, leather goods and other animal products, elfin-like creatures with shoulder-length hair, oiled and braided, and wearing brilliantly coloured dresses which swept down to their knees, cloth head-bands and nose-rings and bracelets of gold. They contrasted markedly with the women of the local tribe, the Mesalit, who wore their hair short and decorated with trinkets and jewellery. They were dressed in wrap-round robes of coarse blue cotton which faded as it grew old.

The Mesalit were the dominant tribe in the area, which was known as Dar Mesalit. The many clans of the Mesalit owed allegiance to their hereditary sultan, Abdal Rahman Bahr Al Din, whose white-walled palace dominated the town. In the past, the Mesalit had been famous warriors, feared by the lesser tribes to the north, the Tama, Erenga and Jabal, whose culture was similar. Now they were settled cultivators akin to the Fur, who grew millet and sorghum in their fields.

Mixed in with these sedentaries were nomadic Arabs of the Rizayqat family whose territory spread north-west and east from Gineina. The largest of the clans was the Mahamid, who moved constantly between the Sudan and Chad. The Rizayqat were *abbala* or camel-rearing nomads, but there were also tribes who owned cattle in the area, such as the Bani Halba and the Messeriyya. To the east there were pockets of separate *abbala* tribes, such as the Awlad Rashid. To the north and along the Chad borders lay the territory of the powerful Central Saharan tribes such as the Zaghawa, Bedayatt and Gor'an. These semi-nomadic peoples were the Arabs' traditional enemies, and had a special reputation for wildness and rapine.

I knew immediately that I should like Gineina. It was quite unlike anywhere of comparable size I had seen in the Sudan: so inaccessible that during the rainy season it might take a lorry fifteen days to reach it from El Fasher, the nearest large town. Its position on the border meant that it was a place of secret struggles and intrigues beneath its placid surface.

The situation in Gineina was made extreme by the power struggle which was taking place between rival factions in nearby Chad. In 1980, when I arrived there, the main factions were the armies of the president, Gikoni Wadai, and the guerrillas of his former minister of defence, Hussein Habri. Gikoni was supported by the forces of Libya's Colonel Gaddafi, who had an interest in annexing Chad, and specifically in controlling certain areas in the north of the country in which uranium had been discovered. Habri opposed Libya's influence in the country and had the tacit support of the Sudan and Egypt.

Habri had armed the border tribes, the Gor'an and Bedayatt, many of whom were simple tribesmen, ill-disposed to identification with either faction. They tended to use their new weapons for projects of their own such as raiding Arab camels and attacking isolated Sudanese markets, despite the fact that the Sudanese government was supposedly supporting them. It was hardly surprising, therefore, that the Arabs of this area, who generally regarded themselves as neither Sudanese nor Chadian, but whose nomadic way of life gave them access to both countries, should be more sympathetic to Gikoni than to Habri, whose men stole their livestock with ease, by dint of the superior weapons which Habri had given them.

The travelling Arabs were well equipped to observe military movements and build-ups, and their traditional disregard of the border meant that they could easily carry such information from place to place. Thus they became useful to Gikoni as a source of intelligence, and built up an effective spy network, in which respected tribal shaykhs such as Rashid Omar were important links.

However, the Arabs were involved in the war in another way. The

Libyans had trained a force of Sudanese guerrillas, known as the *jebha*, under the leadership of the exiled politician, Ahmed Al Hindi. These guerrillas were recruited mainly from Sudanese who had left their country secretly, looking for work in affluent Libya, and many of them were from nomadic Arab tribes. The *jebha* were trained to re-enter the Sudan covertly, and to take up ordinary jobs as labourers, butchers or waiters, under the command of a local paymaster. When the strategic conditions were right, they would receive orders to pick up weapons from caches all over the country, and go into action against important government posts.

The Arabs played a vital role in establishing these secret arsenals of weapons, especially along the north-western borders of the Sudan. Arab caravans would rendezvous with Libyan convoys on the Chadian side of the border, and load up their camels with rifles and ammunition which they transferred to a hiding place on the Sudanese side of the border, to await collection by the guerrillas.

It was this world that I brushed shoulders with during my visits to the house of Shaykh Rashid Omar and I soon became a regular guest at his home, partly through my connection with the shaykh's son, an intelligent youth whose name was the reverse of his father's, Omar Rashid, and who was a pupil of mine.

Hassan, the Eritrean, a small man with Abyssinian features and a mop of wiry hair which sat on the back of his head, was another guest. He was a refugee with secrets of his own to protect. Hassan pretended to be a Muslim, but he was in fact a Christian named Michael, and had arrived in Gineina only two years before. He had fought with the Eritrean Liberation Front in their war against Ethiopia, but had been arrested by his own side when he disagreed with some of their policies. Later, he escaped and walked into the Sudan, finally reaching the capital, Khartoum. He worked as a tea-boy and a labourer, and slowly formed a rough plan to move to the west of the Sudan, from where escape would be much easier.

Arriving in El Fasher, he met by chance another Eritrean who called himself Yagub, and who had left the war several years before. Yagub, whose actual name was Jacob, and who was also pretending to be a Muslim, was well set up in the town with a wife, children and a small business. However, he was forced to leave the town after seducing the young daughter of a neighbour, and the two men fled west to Gineina.

At first, things had gone quite smoothly. They had established themselves as radio-technicians, repairing wireless sets. Gradually, however,

Yagub took to drink and spent more and more time in local brothels. Hassan, who was a most careful and circumspect man, prepared to work patiently towards his goal, grew tired of giving Yagub the money which he had been carefully saving against the time when he could make good his plans. He and Yagub had a flaming quarrel, and afterwards never spoke to each other. Yagub lapsed into alcoholism, and I met him many times in the town, usually drunk. He had a dynamic personality, and was intelligent and quick-witted, though his senses had been clouded by the insidious raw spirit which he drank, *up-chachumba*, which destroyed the liver and the brain. He had abandoned all ideas of escaping or of returning to his own country, and he pretended to scoff at Hassan's plans. He often said, 'We will all die, all of us, white or black, rich or poor. You are not different from me: we are all the same!'

However, Hassan continued to plan his escape, and this had brought him into contact with the mysterious John Bosso. No doubt acting on the maxim 'A stranger is the friend of every other stranger', Hassan had introduced him to the house of Rashid Omar.

Bosso was a medium-sized, chunky negro, dressed neatly in jeans, tee-shirt and sports shoes, and at first I took him and his slimmer, less talkative friend Alex for modishly dressed Mesalit tribesmen. It soon transpired that the two men were Ugandans from the Buganda tribe. They had left Uganda, he said, as a result of the recent invasion by Tanzanian troops. Bosso spoke English with a commanding, persuasive style, and with a perfect accent. He was a lively and interesting conversationalist, and he told me that he was a lecturer at the Institute of Fine Art in Khartoum, specializing in ceramics. Alex, who spoke no English, was Bosso's assistant. They were preparing a thesis on local art, and they had decided to tour the area by camel. Rashid Omar agreed to find two good camels for them, and an Arab guide.

One day, Bosso told me that he was unable to continue his research because his cameras had been stolen, and his project could not go on without photographs. I offered to lend him my own camera, since I knew that he would be returning to Gineina in a few weeks. I also gave him a letter of introduction to a colleague of mine, Donald Friend, a teacher in Kutum.

Bosso left alone one night, riding a camel. Alex had decided not to go with him, and so had the guide which Rashid Omar had provided. The weeks passed. Alex sold his camel and returned to Khartoum. Still Bosso did not return.

The next time I saw Donald Friend, almost the first words with which he greeted me were: 'You've got a lot to answer for, bringing John Bosso here!'

Bosso had arrived in Kutum, on his camel. He had stayed with Don, who was the only European then living in Kutum, on the strength of my recommendation. He presented himself as a research student studying local pottery, and he duly began to ride off on his camel to visit nearby sites of archaeological importance. However, before long Bosso managed to involve Don in a complicated web of secrecy about an archaeological 'find', the upshot of which was that Don was accused of a conspiracy to defraud the local people and forced to leave the town where he had been well respected.

At the same time, Bosso quietly disappeared. He sold his camel to a friend of Don's, 'Ali Atim, for a bargain price. 'Ali had paid a large proportion of the amount, when Bosso asked if he could borrow the camel once more to visit his site. Needless to say, no trace of Bosso, the camel, my camera or any of the other things which people had lent him were ever seen again.

I eventually got Hassan to confide in me. Bosso and Alex had approached him with the idea of escaping from the Sudan into Libya, a highly forbidden action for refugees, who were closely watched by National Security.

'You cannot do anything when you are a refugee,' he said. 'They watch you like hawks. I myself first came to Gineina with the idea of escaping into Chad or Libya, but they watch you so closely, and this was the first chance I found. We went to see Rashid Omar to get camels to cross the Libyan Desert, and a guide. "How will we make the guide take us to Libya?" I asked Bosso. "When we get out into the desert, we'll kidnap him, and force him to take us!" he said. Well, I couldn't go along with that: the guide was an Arab, who knew the desert, he could have left us to die at any time! Alex thought so too, that's why he pulled out.'

'But the guide didn't go in the end?' I said.

'No! That Rashid Omar is a wily bird! He must have known that something was wrong. He told the guide not to accept the job in the end, and Bosso went off alone. I'd like to know where he is now, wouldn't you?'

I would have been fascinated to know. Had Bosso reached his destination, or had he expired somewhere in the wastes of the Libyan Desert? A discussion about politics that we had once had flashed through my

mind. Bosso had spoken in defence of Idi Amin, the bloodthirsty
ex-president of Uganda, who had been expelled after the Tanzanian
invasion of the country. If Bosso had been one of Amin's men, he
would have fled to the Sudan to escape retribution at the hands of the
Tanzanians, and would be heading for Libya, which was at that time
sympathetic to Amin.

'Bosso was a lecturer in Khartoum, wasn't he?' I asked Omar, my
pupil, one day.

Omar raised his eyebrows. 'No!' he said. 'He was the manager of a
cigarette factory.'

Hassan was undeterred by the failure of the escape plan with Bosso,
and he had made many contacts in the town. One day he came to my
house to inform me that he had finally decided to make his move.

'I've met some men in the market,' he told me excitedly. 'Mahamid
Arabs, they are, *barashoot* who go across to Chad. I will go with them,
disguised as an Arab. No one will find me!'

When the appointed day came, Hassan left Gineina after dark with a
smuggler's caravan.

It was Yagub who related the end of the story to me. Hassan reached
the capital of Chad, N'Jimeina, and looked for work. He found this
difficult, however, as the country was in such turmoil, and he began to
travel back to the Sudan. He had bought with his savings a Kalashnikov
rifle, hoping to sell it across the border at a considerable profit. At the
town of Abéché he was searched, and the rifle was found. The Chadians
immediately shot him dead.

Yagub said, 'But we will all die, in Sudan, in Chad, in England, it's
all the same.'

9

LOST ROADS IN DAR ZAGHAWA

North of Gineina, the landscape rolls and folds through valleys where water-courses meander like golden snakes, lush with subtropical vegetation. Huge *heraz* trees, their canopies like green parachutes, rise above brakes of lesser shrubs: *lalob, kitir, nim, umn sayal, gamez, ushur* and *mukhayyit*. These valleys are rich agricultural land, where the farmers of the Erenga, Tama and Jabal tribes grow fields of millet, sorghum and groundnuts. The grass-hut villages of these tribes nestle amongst the trees and the tall grasses as they have done for generations. Beyond these rich lands, however, the terrain becomes more arid: wastes of red sand and multi-coloured rock carpet the floors beneath the crags of the mountains. This, the most remote region of Darfur, is the land of the Zaghawa, an ancient tribe of the Sahara.

The Zaghawa are the largest Sudanese section of a family of tribes whose homeland is probably the central Saharan massif of Tibesti, on the borders of Chad and Libya. The family includes the Tubu, Gor'an, Bedayatt and Berti tribes, who speak related Central Saharan dialects, and whose origins are shrouded in mystery. Some scientists believe that these races represent a fusion of Mediterranean and Negro peoples which may have taken place while the Sahara was still fertile, around 5000 BC. If so, they may be the oldest surviving inhabitants of the Great Desert.

The Zaghawa are semi-nomadic, keeping cows as well as camels, growing some crops. Though they claim descent from an Arab ancestor, their forefathers probably lived along the eastern edges of the Sahara before the coming of the bedouin.

In December 1980, Dar Zaghawa was in a potentially dangerous state of turmoil. Across the border, in Chad, the Bedayatt and Gor'an tribes were heavily involved in the civil war. They had been armed, but instead of putting all their efforts into the war, in which many of their kinsmen, the Tubu, fought on the opposing side, they occupied themselves in raiding across the Sudanese border. They attacked not

Camel herd watering on the Nile

Herdsmen on the bank of the Nile

Preparing a meal
below left Herdsmen building a sun shelter at the midday halt
below right Herdsman hobbling a camel

Camel herd on the move near the Wadi al Milik

Herdsman folding a blanket as padding for a pack saddle

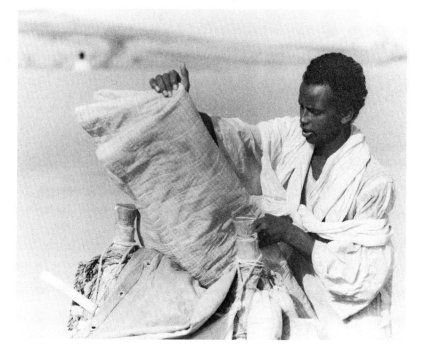

Kababish nomad

below left Michael Asher

below right Nomad women fetching water

Arab boys bringing a goat to slaughter

Nomads celebrating at a circumcision ceremony

Nomad woman

Nomads dancing at a circumcision ceremony

Nomad girls wearing traditional ornaments
below left Father and son, with traditional coxcomb of hair
below right Nomad playing the *zambara*, the herdsman's pipe

Camel drawing water from a deep well in North Kordofan

Kababish tribesman

their cousins, the Zaghawa, but the nomadic Arabs, whose lines of migration passed through this territory, and who were the traditional enemies of the Saharan tribes.

My ambition was still to travel along the ancient Forty Days Road, though in the four weeks which I had at my disposal in that winter of 1980, I knew that I should never get farther than the watering-place of El Atrun, which was 'first base' on the old route. Nevertheless, I was determined to reach this oasis, even though I might have to travel alone for some of the way. I made the mistake of forgetting the companions, and thinking only of the way. My direct route to the oasis lay through Dar Zaghawa, and though I received many warnings of the delicate situation there, I was driven on by lack of time, and secretly by a desire to see this inaccessible region in which few Europeans had travelled.

It was to the shaykh, Rashid Omar, that I turned for advice in this matter, for I knew that anything he said would not be affected by the attitude of the official authorities. I decided not to consult the police, since I was certain that they would refuse me permission to travel at this hazardous time. I knew that between Gineina and the Zaghawa 'capital', Tina, about a hundred miles north, there was little but remote sparsely inhabited country, where old tracks and pathways lay hidden under gorse and thornbush, overgrown and obscured through disuse. I asked Rashid to find me a guide with whom I could travel at least as far as the borders of Zaghawa country. The shaykh introduced me to Adem Ahmed, a tribesman of the Zaghawa, who had walked to Gineina from his camp near the village of Kulbus, to seek advice from Rashid about his eight camels which had been stolen by a raiding party. I agreed to meet Adem in a few days' time near Jebel Kundebi, a lone knoll which stood outside the town.

I spent those days preparing my camels and equipment. I had recently acquired two fresh camels. One was an immensely strong bull, which was inclined to be bad-tempered, as all adult males are, and the other a small four-year-old of the type known as *hiq*. As I might be travelling alone in the desert, I intended to use the calf for carrying extra water. I laid in a good supply of flour, tea, spices and dried meat, as I expected the journey to El Atrun to take fifteen to twenty days, and I took with me a light hiker's tent, two blankets, which were more useful in the desert than my old sleeping-bag, and two full-sized waterskins which I had obtained from Rashid Omar.

Shortly before I left, Rashid's son, Omar, visited my house, bringing with him a .22 revolver which he insisted on my taking. I objected at first, remembering the heavy responsibility which firearms imposed. 'Everyone in that country is armed,' he told me. 'And they will be after your camels. You must have protection.' Eventually he persuaded me that he was right, and I accepted the weapon.

I left Gineina on 4 December, leading my small caravan. I wore Arab dress, a thick headcloth wound around my face so as to prevent too much attention being drawn towards me. I hoped to be able to slip away from the town quietly, with as little fuss as possible, for I had already learned that it took very little to excite the townsfolk, and that a crowd of onlookers would gather at the least excuse.

Soon I was clear of the town, climbing out of the depression in which it lay. I couched and mounted the large bull, and as he vaulted up, a current of elation swept through me. I was back in that wilderness which I craved. Now it seemed that I had never been away. That night I camped with some Mahamid Arabs in the dry watercourse under Jebel Kundebi, in which I had arranged to meet my *rafiq*. The Arabs had with them seven camels which were suffering badly from the mange. They had been to Gineina to visit my old acquaintance, Awad Al Kariim, the vet, who had recently been transferred there. Awad had prescribed some antibiotics, and the Arabs asked me to translate the instructions on the packet, which were written in English.

Not long after dawn the next morning, Adem Ahmed arrived at the camp. He was a slim, knobbly man with polished black skin, dressed in a short Arab shirt and a white headcloth. He carried over his shoulder three spears: a long stabbing weapon, six or seven feet in length, and a couple of light javelins. After drinking tea we saddled the camels and set out into the *qoz* with the Mahamid. The Arabs and the Zaghawi chatted amiably, for generally the Arabs do not hate the Zaghawa as they do the Bedayatt, and anyway it was the custom to be courteous to a travelling companion, no matter to which tribe he belonged. We ascended the wind-worn slopes of the mountain, from which the magnificent panorama of Dar Mesalit could be seen: a land of sweeping downs and corries, decked in russet, green and saffron. There was no single thing in the landscape that belonged to the twentieth century.

Soon the Mahamid turned off to their camp, and Adem led me through cultivated fields to Wadi Sirba, which coiled through a cleft in the hills. For three days we followed the line of the wadi, passing through the territory of the Erenga and Tama tribes. Our path led us into deep ravines filled with tropical lushness, along yellow hedgerows blazing with grasses, punctuated by the twisted trunks of giant acacia trees. We rode through fields of grass, like prairies of wheat, where columbines grew amongst the stalks, mixing with the maroon red of *kirkadea* and the brilliant yellows and pinks of flowers whose names I never knew, like jewels amongst the ranks of green and buff. Negro girls of the farming tribes worked in the fields, or drew water at the boreholes in the wadi. They were black as ravens, with smooth, shiny skin and firm, rounded bodies. Their hair was cut short in braided locks, glittering with silver coins and pendants, and their bodies, covered only by loincloths, were decorated with nose- and ear-rings, and metal bracelets which rattled on their wrists and ankles. Around them played scores of naked, pot-bellied children, chattering happily.

It was harvest time here, and often we would come across areas of hard-packed sand where men and women were threshing the millet with wooden flails. Sometimes Adem would stop and help the local villagers in the threshing, while I continued with the camels. Once he came back clutching five freshly cut ears of corn which, he said, were lucky. I guessed, though, that his real reward had been a bowl of *merissa*, the local beer, which the farmers drank as they threshed.

Occasionally Adem and I would walk with the camels, descending into the deep creek beds, enjoying the golden prelude to the sunset, as the coolness poured down upon us from the north. After dark, we would camp in the wadi, lighting a fire in the cool, soft sand, eating *'asida* and drinking tea, while Adem talked away in his strangely accented Arabic.

It seemed a lost world, young, innocent and beautiful. Travelling here, on a road which no one in a car or truck could ever find, was valuable for its own sake, not merely for exploration, or to meet the local people, but also to get away for a time from those hated engines and live in the peace of an unspoiled land.

Adem spent much of his time in the evening involved in his prayers. This was because he had been too tired to perform them in the heat of the day and believed he could make good by doing them all together at night. The Zaghawa are generally fairly religious, like the Arabs, though the Bedayatt and the Gor'an have a reputation for neither praying nor fasting.

Throughout these first days I continually had trouble with the large bull. His behaviour got worse as we moved north, almost as if he were reluctant to leave his homeland. Several times he turned his head and tried to bite me as I rode him, a rather daunting experience, as a fully grown camel has sharp canine teeth and could easily crush an arm or leg with a single bite. Eventually, I allowed the Zaghawi to ride him, though even Adem found him impossible to control.

'By God, but he's bad, that camel!' he said. 'You'd better change him in Tina, or he'll kill you!'

After eating in the evenings, we would talk for a short time. I asked him if the Bedayatt were as treacherous and godless as the Arabs said. Adem considered the question, then said, 'Indeed, some of them do not know God. Some do not fast, some do not pray, some even don't believe in the Prophet. It's said that they will kill for no reason, and that they steal camels: that is also true. But some of them are very good people, and there are bad men in all tribes, even the *Ingleez*!'

On the third day we met a great caravan on its way back from the village of Kulbus. There were fifteen bull camels tied head to tail, and each animal carried two fat saddlebags filled with grain. Kulbus was a centre of the millet trade, and caravans travelled to the village from all over North Darfur. This one was being led by three men of the Gimmar, a small tribe of whose territory Kulbus was the capital. We stopped to greet the cameleers, and after the usual formalities, Adem asked about the news from the north.

'Last week four men of the Gimmar were travelling to Kulbus from the north, by camel. Some Bedayatt came across the border and attacked them. They hit them with bullets and all were killed. Then the raiders took the camels and went back into Chad.'

'Upon you be the Prophet!'

'By God, it's true! I advise you not to go into the land of the Zaghawa at the moment. The road to Tina lies along the border, and it's very dangerous!'

'By God, you're right!' said Adem.

We thanked the Gimmar and carried on, but their words haunted my mind. Indeed, it seemed that what had been said about this route was true. North of Kulbus, I should be alone in what sounded like very dangerous country. I began suddenly to feel very glad of my small pistol.

Early the next morning we passed through a rocky gorge, from the exit of which we could see a wide valley. Here, Adem pointed out to me the green wedge of Kulbus. It looked peaceful that day, slumbering in the cool of the morning. Within a year that village was attacked by repeated bombings from the Libyan airforce, and had become the home of thousands of Chadian refugees.

Adem invited me to stay at his camp, but explained that he would be delayed in the village for some time on business. I thanked him, but said that I would rather press on as my time was limited. I preferred not to tell him of my apprehensions about the small police post in Kulbus, and the three Camel Corps troopers who he had informed me were permanently on duty. I had no wish to be stopped at this stage in the journey, especially as I had no permission to travel.

As we descended into the settlement, I cursed the bravado which had induced me to enter the place, rather than avoiding it, despite the complicated explanations this behaviour would have warranted to my *rafiq*. I was not keen to expose the clandestine nature of my journey to the Zaghawi, since I was not sure that he could be trusted inside his own territory. I knew the ethics of the Arabs, but the Zaghawa were not Arabs, and I was not certain that they would behave in the same way. We parted on the outskirts of the town.

'Watch out for the Bedayatt,' he told me. 'Once you get to Tina you will be safe, but don't sleep alone on the border road. Go in peace!'

'Go in peace!'

I watched the lean Zaghawi as he stalked off towards the grass huts, his spears sloping over his shoulder. Then I wrapped my headcloth carefully around my face, and led my camels into the main street. There was the usual row of rotting stalls and dilapidated mud shops. Luckily the place seemed almost deserted. Three youths sat in the sand and eyed me sullenly as I passed. A single trader wished me *salaam 'alaykum*. At the far end of the street, I passed the tiny police post, and just as I did so, a man wearing the green uniform of the *shorta* came running out, and shouted to one of the sullen youths, 'Hey! Mohammed! Bring us three teas. With milk. Be quick, by God!' He cast not a single glance in my direction, so familiar must the sight of camels have been to him. I carried on steadily, not looking at him, and trying not to seem hurried. Out of the corner of my eye I saw him re-enter the building. Only then did I release a great sigh of relief beneath my headcloth. If the trooper had known I was a *khawaja*, I would certainly have been stopped, and had he but glanced at me, he would surely have noticed my white hands and feet. I had escaped by the skin of my teeth, but I had escaped.

Just outside the northern limits of the town, I found a wadi shaded by *heraz* trees, in which some tribesmen of the Gimmar had collected to water their cows. I couched my animals in the wadi and asked some women to fill my waterskin. They were friendly and hospitable, but I found myself unconsciously parrying their questions about my tribe, my destination and my origin. I saw that this attitude was making them suspicious and I hurriedly loaded my skin and mounted.

As I climbed out of the wadi, the way stretched before me: sand, thornbush, rock and more sand. This was the border path to Tina, a comfortless, shelterless landscape, supreme in its bleakness. There would, I knew, be a few Zaghawa villages dotted about, though how much I could rely on their protection, I was not sure. If I was caught in open country by the Bedayatt, I could expect no quarter. I was a stranger, in a remote corner of the world. Behind me lay threat of discovery by the police, and before me the dark menace of the Bedayatt reared like a spectre. I remembered Omar's words, 'They will be after your camels!' and the story told by the Gimmar. I halted the bull, and extracted my pistol from the bottom of the saddlebag, loaded it and placed it in a canvas holdall, which I slung from the saddle horn. Now this weapon seemed nothing more than a toy.

Some time later I made camp for the afternoon by a narrow water-course. As I sat cooking my *'asida*, a pretty girl came out of the scrub, driving two cow camels with a stick. From her peach-gold skin and luxurious, uncut locks, I knew she was Arab.

'Hello!' I said as she walked by.

'Welcome and peace!' she replied softly, and as she disappeared into the brush I heard her humming a light melody. Shortly after this, a man appeared from the direction in which she had gone. He was unusually fat for a tribesman, wore a singlet of cotton and carried a woodcutter's axe slung over his shoulder. The man had small, mean eyes, and even as he greeted me I could feel the suspicion in them. He said that he was an Arab of the Erayqat, a branch of the Rizayqat.

'What is your tribe?' he asked.

'*Al Ingleez.*'

'Do the *Ingleez* ride camels?'

'This one does.'

'Where've you come from?'

'Gineina.'

'What's your work there?'

The questions went on, and I grew irritated by the blunt manner in which he asked them. I began to saddle my camels as he spoke, but disliked the threatening way he stood over me as I did so.

'Are you going to Tina?' he asked.

I replied that I was.

'You should not go alone. The route is very dangerous. Don't you know the Bedayatt are raiding the borders? Only last week they killed four men of the Gimmar. If they find you here, your life won't be worth a shilling!' His words seemed to take the form of advice but his manner was belligerent, as if he were threatening rather than advising. 'If you sleep alone they will find you by your fire. They will come upon you silently and kill you. What can you do?'

I murmured something intended to brush the man off and prepared to mount my camel, when suddenly he grabbed my arm.

'Hey! Where did you get that camel? It has Erayqat brands.'

'I got in in Gineina market.'

'How do I know you're not a bandit?'

I began to feel glad that my inquisitor was alone, and I was armed.

'I have the paper here,' I said. 'I'll show you it.'

I unzipped the holdall which carried my pistol, and slowly took out the weapon, stuffing it into the ammunition belt at my waist. Then I removed my yellow certificate of ownership and waved it before the Arab's nose. His eyes fell first on the pistol, then on the paper.

'I got this camel from Rashid Omar,' I said, before he could speak. 'Look, this is his seal.' I showed him the ink-mark of the shaykh's signet ring. 'If anything happens to me or my camels, Rashid will be very angry. He is my friend.'

I took the headrope of the large bull and led the camels off, hoping that the man would not follow. I saw him watching, his axe in his hand, until his plump figure was obscured by the thorn trees. I moved on as quickly as possible, for the man had unnerved me considerably. Now I knew I was really alone in this no man's land, for even my potential friends the Rizayqat were hostile and suspicious. I thanked providence for my pistol, but wished sincerely that I had brought with me only one camel. I had discovered now that the animals did not travel well together. If I was riding, the bull would constantly shy away into the acacia trees, trying to turn south. The calf squealed and moaned continuously as if he were about to be butchered, and several times the rope which strung the two together snapped, giving me enormous problems. Often I was forced to lead them by hand, but even this was difficult, for the bull continued to hang back and often I had to lean hard on the headrope as if I were dragging a heavy weight up a steep incline. These difficulties slowed my progress tremendously, and I realized that this was the worst possible situation in which to discover the inadequacies of my transport. Even if attacked I could not rely on my camels to ensure a speedy retreat.

That afternoon, however, I met a small herd of camels belonging to some Erayqat, driven by a toothless old shaykh and his son, who rode horses. These Arabs were friendly, and stopped to talk. The old man was delighted to find I was English, and began to talk about Guy Moore. As many others had, he enquired if the *Ingleez* were coming back. The Arabs told me that they were still moving south on the *mowta* migration which they had begun late that year. I asked the shaykh if the Erayqat had had trouble with raiders.

'We haven't seen any this year,' he said. 'But the Mahamid have been eaten by the Bedayatt. They are dogs and sons of dogs! Last week they killed some Gimmar near Kulbus, by God, did you hear?'

'Yes.'

'This is a dangerous road for one alone, where is your *rafiq*?'

'I was travelling with a Zaghawi.'

'The Zaghawa are all right. At least some of them are. But they're all one kind. You can't trust them. Anyway, there aren't many villages between here and Tundebay. Once you get there you'll be safe, for they've sent a troop of border guards on horses to watch the road between Tundebay and Tina.'

His words gave me little comfort, for I had almost as much wish to avoid the border guards as the Bedayatt, and I hoped that there would be some way of avoiding a meeting with them without exposing myself to any other dangers. Tundebay, however, was two days away at my present rate of progress, and in those two days anything could happen.

As night came I was alone, travelling through a petrified thorn forest which extended for mile upon weary mile. The bleached-grey bones of the trees seemed to hide all manner of menace within the deep pools of their gathering shadows. The camels sensed this too for they were nervous and recalcitrant, and after almost a day of heaving them up hill and down dune I was exhausted. I swore at the camels and at myself, but kept my pistol ready. I told myself that if I was seriously threatened by anyone I met, I would shoot to kill. Then I laughed at these thoughts, for it would have been too easy for someone to have approached me in a friendly way, and strike while I was unguarded. The pistol was a toy, really intended for practice-shooting, and no match for the Heckler-Kochs and Kalashnikovs of the tribesmen.

Still I pressed on through the ethereal world of the darkness. All was still and soundless, but the silence was oppressive, as if something evil and predatory was waiting to strike.

Eventually I was too tired to continue and led the camels away from the track deep into the bush, where I couched and unloaded them and laid out my camp. I was reluctant to light a fire, remembering what the aggressive Arab had said, yet I was hungry and my hunger won out. I made 'asida and tea and doused the flames immediately. I found myself listening in the darkness, my two camels forming a wall around me. I was afraid, but resolved to take on whatever came. I knew that this corroding fear was born of loneliness, and had I had a companion all would have been well, though the danger no less. Eventually, with my pistol beneath me, I lay down to sleep but I got little rest. Every time the camels shifted or groaned I was up and ready, staring into the darkness. And so it continued until dawn came like an injection, creeping soft and cold amongst the grotesque framework of the bush.

The next day the camels went even more slowly and I made agonizingly little progress. By mid-morning, however, I broke out of the forest and it was a relief to see open acres of sweeping grass prairie before me once more. Moreover, in the clearing was a chain of Zaghawa villages, which stood like fairyland castles on the top of a ridge of dunes, ancient hill-forts which commanded a view for miles over the open country. Around them were corrals, fenced in by hedges of thornbush, in which the Zaghawa camels grazed, and my own beasts fretted to join their unladen fellows. Soon I came to the fringes of another thorn forest, and stopped for the afternoon rest. For the first time I began to consider whether I should go back to Kulbus. My progress was so slow that I began to doubt if I could reach El Atrun. I decided, however, that I must press on to Tina, no matter what happened, and change my camels there. As for the border guards, I should have to take my chance with them. For the second night I camped alone in the forest with the bushes curling vicious and hostile around me, like Arthur Rackham illustrations, and it seemed almost as if I was living in some hallucinatory dream world beyond the reality I had come to know.

The morning was crisp and sharp like a spring day in England and the mirkwood seemed endless and unforgiving. Once again, though, I broke out into the refreshing light of a clearing overlaid with a stubble of grass. Not long after, I heard the sound of hoof-beats on the hard sand and turned to see three riders approaching from the east. They wore thick headcloths and old blue greatcoats buttoned up to the neck, and one of them carried a shotgun across the horn of his stallion's saddle. Their horses looked swift and sleek, and their faces dark and inscrutable. A warning-bell sounded in my brain, and I recoiled. Couching the large bull, I crouched behind his shoulder with my hand on my pistol. If this was the enemy, then I was ready to fight.

The men approached me at a trot, and halted a few yards away, greeting me with *as salaam 'alaykum*.

'Where are you going, *khawaja*?' one of them shouted.

'To Tina,' I answered.

'You shouldn't be on this road. This road is dangerous. The border is near and the Bedayatt come across this way all the time.'

'What's your tribe?' I asked them.

'Zaghawa of the Ango clan,' the speaker said. 'Listen, this area is bad for strangers. You should not travel alone. Go to Tundebay, our village, and visit the sultan there, Sultan Hissein. He'll give you a guide to Tina.'

The knowledge that I was near to this village came as a great relief, until I remembered that the border guards were there. I was ready, though, for a trick from these supposed Zaghawa whom I did not trust. However, the spokesman continued, 'We're going to Tundebay, you can follow us.'

For a few moments I mulled over his words. On the one hand these men might be Bedayatt, trying to take me off guard. They spoke in heavily accented Arabic, though I knew that the speech of the Zaghawa and Bedayatt was the same. On the other hand, they were riding horses, while the Bedayatt were more likely to ride camels, since horses were used for local transport only, and none of the tribesmen was carrying food or water. I decided that they were telling the truth. The problem remained, however, with the border guards. If, as they said, they were travelling to Tundebay anyway, they would report my coming as a matter of course. Whichever choice I made there were problems. 'All right,' I said, at last. 'You go on, and I'll follow.'

The three men rode off at walking pace, and I followed on at a safe distance behind, wondering what the next few hours would bring.

About an hour later, we arrived in Tundebay, a fortified village dominated by a huge *heraz* tree, like a fantasy scene from *Lord of the Rings*. My camels were couched in the corral and I was escorted inside the walls of the stockade to the hut of the sultan. This was the first time I had been inside a Zaghawa settlement, and I saw that it was quite different from the villages of the Mesalit and the other farming tribes to the south. The huts were larger and constructed far more solidly. Each house was surrounded by a series of courtyards, large and small, which opened into one another in an intricate system of access.

The sultan was an unusually tall man wearing a sweeping white *jellabiyya* and headcloth. He greeted me graciously and ushered me to a rug beneath a small shelter. Very soon four or five men wearing police uniforms appeared. They sat cross-legged on the rug and, though they were both friendly and polite, began to ask questions about my nationality and business. By the greatest of luck, however, they did not ask me for a letter of permission, but told me that I must report to the police post in Tina as soon as I arrived there.

'The road between Tundebay and Tina is safe,' one of the guards told me. 'You've passed the most dangerous part, but you must report to the police chief in Tina, who is responsible for travellers.'

I knew that I had not escaped the clutches of the law, for there was no way I could avoid Tina now if I wished to re-equip for my journey to El Atrun, and it would be there that my real problems would start.

For the next day and a half I travelled over grassy downs, clotted with acacia from which scarlet crags of rock jutted like the teeth of some predator. The camels went badly, but I felt more at ease in this open landscape, resigned to the problems I was going to face in Tina. Sometimes I came across places where the poor soil had been leached away, leaving only red sand and defiles of sharp rock. Only a few years ago, this country, like other parts of Darfur, had been savannah woodland, teeming with animal life, giraffe, zebra, lion and leopard. The landscape was now no more than the dry bones of its former richness, inhabited only by gazelle and wild chicken. Years of drought had sheared away the vegetation and driven the wildlife far south. Soon, I knew, the land would be too poor to sustain the cows and sheep of the Zaghawa and the tribesmen would follow in the wake of the many who had fled to the towns, such as El Fasher, where the Zaghawa already composed almost half the population. These patches of rocky ground, which would never again be fertile, heralded the approach of the deadly *kataha*, the drifting sands of the Libyan Desert which every year move further and further south. Within ten or twenty years, unless drastic measures were taken, this area would be absolute desert, capable only of supporting camels. The Zaghawa of the Ango and Kobbe clans who inhabited the tiny settlements in this area had moved here in living memory from the north, which had already become too dry to support their herds. Before long they would be forced to move on again, and then there would be no alternative but to abandon the traditional way of life from which this Saharan people had lived for centuries.

On the morning of 10 December I saw Tina in a depression below me. Beyond it the landscape lay rolling and open for hundreds of miles, but the town was centred on a narrow watercourse called Gar Hajjar, which marked the border between the Sudan and Chad.

The town was set on white dunes, and there were no trees except on the banks of the wadi itself. I saw that the Zaghawa had constructed their houses from chunks of red rock, in the absence of cane and grass, and this gave the settlement an unusually solid appearance, like an imperfect imitation of a Cotswold village. My arrival in the town caused a great stir, for, as I learned later, I was the first European to have been there for some years, and certainly the first to have arrived dressed like an Arab and leading two camels. A crowd of fascinated children gathered around me shouting *khawaja! khawaja!* but I was rescued by a local teacher, Tijani Bashir, a wiry, rather gruff-mannered Zaghawi, who led me to his house and helped me to unload the camels.

Soon I was visited by Ibrahim Khalil, a young Zaghawi of the Kobbe clan, whom I knew from Gineina. He took charge of my camels, finding a herdsman to mind them, and later Tijani took me to the house of the hereditary sultan of the Kobbe clan, Sultan Dowsa. The Kobbe were the tribe which inhabited Tina and its surrounds, and they regarded themselves as a distinct branch of the Zaghawa family, akin to the Bedayatt. Their sultan was an old, old man, who had been famous at the time of British colonial rule. At his house, however, I was told that he was ill and was unable to see me. Instead, I was introduced to his eldest son, Bishara, who was himself a man of over sixty. He told me that his father was reputed to be well over a hundred years old and had scores of children, grandchildren and great-grand-children. He was one of the Sudan's old-style tribal monarchs, who still employed a man upon whose back he stood while mounting his donkey. Bishara was a tall, spare, thoroughly gracious man, who offered me tea and talked about Guy Moore, within whose jurisdiction Tina had been during British rule.

'Sultan Moore came to Tina every month to preside at the court,' he told me. 'By God he was a hard man, but absolutely honest. You could tell the time from his punctuality. Whether he came by car or camel he would arrive at exactly the same time. He had no excuses: everything was exact in those days.'

Later we walked through the streets, which were almost deserted, for the market was held only twice a week. A chilling wind blew from the north, giving the town a stark, spartan feel, yet there was deep beauty in its bleakness. The town seemed to stand like a fortress against the desert: the last outpost of the Sudan, beyond which lay the wasteland, ancient, brooding and empty.

The wind became a blizzard, blasting razor-edged particles of sand across our faces, slashing into the streets, where figures, their heads shrouded in cloth, bent into the savage assault. Suddenly a shadow loomed across our path, a stocky man wearing a long white cloak and a tightly wrapped headcloth. Tijani introduced him to me as the local police commandant, and as he loosed his headcloth, I saw a wizened, rat-like face, the colour of a dried prune. He shook hands brusquely, then in the irritating Sudanese custom, began talking to my companion about me as if I was not present. I knew that this was not intentionally impolite, but it never ceased to irk me.

'Your friend has just arrived in the town?' he asked. 'He is *khawaja*, isn't he? British? Ah, a teacher. I see. Tell him to come to my office first thing tomorrow. Don't let him forget!'

With that he was off again, enveloped by the whiteout of the wind which snaked and coiled about his robes. It was with some disappointment that I discovered that the next market day would be on 14 December, a delay of four valuable days. I knew, however, that before making any decisions I must wait and see what the police had to say.

When I arrived at his office the next day, with Ibrahim Khalil, the officer received me formally and politely. He was dressed smartly in his green uniform, and I felt rather conspicuous in my ragged Arab clothes. At once I saw that this was going to be a no-nonsense meeting.

'You are English? Yes? Where is your permit to travel from Gineina?'

'I have none.'

'No one is allowed in this region without papers. There is a war on. You should have asked for them in Gineina. There is no alternative but to return.'

'I'm a teacher in Gineina,' I protested. 'Everyone knows me there. This man Ibrahim knows me. This is unreasonable.'

'Nevertheless, you must return.'

'But I am a teacher there, I work for the government.'

'I believe that you are a teacher. If I did not I would make you sell your camels and have you sent to El Fasher.'

I could see that the man was adamant. There was no point in protesting further. I decided that discretion was the better part of valour and kept my mouth shut, but I left his office resentfully. The meeting had realized my worst fears. And to cap it all, I had to return to Gineina by the same dangerous route by which I had come.

Ibrahim noticed my silence and said, 'Don't worry, *ustaz*. That man knows nothing. There is a way. The nomad way.'

I could guess his meaning. I knew that outside these settlements, the police could exert little authority. The country was in many places too rough for motor vehicles, and there were few Camel Corps. This was a town on the very edge of a great desert, beyond and around which lay wild, unknown country, where the people were a law unto themselves. I knew, however, that should I commit myself to the anarchy of the desert, I could expect little support from the authorities if I found difficulties.

For the next two days the wind ravaged the town, and the temperature plummeted. Whips of sand thrashed the bald dunes, bent the stunted bushes and poured with icy force into the sheltered yards where the people sat huddled, swathed in their robes and cloaks. Meanwhile, Ibrahim and I explored the area together. We crossed Gar Hajjar into Chad and visited Hill Gaynor, a tiny settlement of the Bedayatt composed of dome-shaped cabins of brushwood, inhabited mostly by women and children, whom Ibrahim spoke to in the tongue of the Kobbe, which was close to that of the Bedayatt. Later, back in Tina, we ate at the house of Ibrahim Abdallah, the man who controlled sales of camels in the town, sitting on rich carpets, whilst his son brought in legs of mutton roasted on spits and sliced them with a dagger. While the other guests spoke together in their own language, I drifted into thoughts of my own about the 'nomad way' and what I should do next.

On the 14th, things looked up. The wind-storm dropped slightly, and we went out early to watch the people coming into the market. The shallow, concave scoop of the *suq* was soon full of Bedayatt camels, couched in lines, the sand littered with saddlebags full of rock-salt from Chad. The cliff behind the marketplace was covered with sheep and goats attended by Kobbe shepherds, their heads wrapped in cloth against the piercing *haboob*. Beyond them lay a phalanx of camels bearing the brands of the Kobbe and Ango clans, with piles of saddlery. Men in greatcoats and white turbans sat in tight groups, and Bedayatt tribesmen strode across the sands, their eyes glittering from beneath their headdress. They looked stern, confident and majestic, and I realized how wrong I had been to think of the Arabs alone as being masters of the desert. These people were as old as the desert itself and its ways were no mystery to them.

For some time we watched the endless strings of camels crossing Gar Hajjar from Chad, unloading their wares in the *suq*. Then Ibrahim and I fetched my two camels and took them to join the others which were for sale. Here the stock seemed of far better quality than that in Gineina, and I recalled what the Zayadiyya had told me about the desert fringes being the best country for camels. Almost all the camels in the market had Bedayatt brands. Eventually I sold the two camels to a Bedayi from Abeche in Chad, and bought a huge grandfather of a bull which seemed ideal for the desert. After the selling and the mutual congratulation were over, Ibrahim led me to a low thatched building which was full of the smells of cooking meat and coffee.

'There are some Bedayatt going to Umm Buru tomorrow. They say you can go with them.'

'Bedayatt! Brother, they're robbers!'

'They are. But they are also my relations. They will not harm you. These are all right, and it's your only chance.'

'What about the police?'

'They won't know unless someone tells them. I will say that you have returned to Gineina.'

I thought long and seriously about this proposal. This was the nomad way. I knew he was right. The police would never find me with such people. But to commit myself to the Bedayatt would be to put myself at their mercy. I could not, however, face the idea of abandoning my expedition to El Atrun, so I whispered to Ibrahim that I accepted and arranged to meet them outside the town the next morning.

10

THE ROVING ARAB

O turn the roving Arab back,
Who tyger-like infests the way
And makes the traveller his prey.

Eyles Irwin, *Ode to the Desert*

I met the Bedayatt early the next morning at their camp in a wadi
outside the town. Ibrahim Khalil and I had been up before sunrise.
We saddled my new bull and slipped away in the cold shadows of
daybreak.

There were four of the tribesmen there when I arrived, sitting
huddled around a fire upon which a blackened kettle rattled. The men
were wrapped in thick cloaks and woollen shawls, for it was still unusually cold. To me, these Bedayatt were indistinguishable from the
Kobbe Zaghawa, except that they wore their headcloths wound over
the lower parts of their faces in a distinctive style. This custom had no
doubt developed because of its practical value in an environment which
was constantly choked by dust, and had been accepted as a convention
of dress. However, it was not forbidden for a Bedayi to show his face as
it was for some Berber tribes such as the Tuareg.

As Ibrahim and I couched our camels in the watercourse, I noticed
that there were eight bulls grazing along its banks. Some of these bore
the complex star, lightning-flash and twisted-rope symbols which
marked them as Bedayatt camels, whilst others had the less conspicuous
double-line brands of the Arabs. The men stood up to greet us speaking
in heavily accented Arabic, which they spoke as a second language. We
were shown to a place near the fire and Ibrahim introduced me to his
relation, 'Ali Ahmed, who he said was a camel-trader, taking animals
from Tina to sell in the markets of Mellit and Kutum. I wondered
secretly if 'camel-trader' was a euphemism for 'camel-thief', but I
checked myself for my prejudice. All the stories I had ever heard

about these Bedayatt were bad but I had learned to let the actions of people speak for themselves, knowing that stories of rapaciousness and dishonesty were often born of jealousy and resentment.

The Bedayatt were tall men, perhaps a head above most Arabs, but with the same whiplash leanness which is the mark of desert peoples. They were darker than the Arabs, their skin that shade which with typical perversity the townspeople called *akhdar* (green), and the Arabs *azraq* (blue). They wore specially tapered *sirwel* like cavalry breeches, and the knee-length, sideways-slashed shirts called *conflets* which I myself was now wearing instead of my Arab shirt. All of them were wearing daggers and 'Ali Ahmed was carrying a rifle in a leather case.

The Bedayatt were once regarded as a subsection of the Zaghawa, renowned as raiders who pillaged the desert as far east as the Nile. They now occupy a large part of the country between the Darfur mountains and the hills of Tibesti in Chad. They are nomadic and semi-nomadic people who possess camels and goats. They have no tents or palanquins as the Arabs have, but live mostly in cabins of brushwood of the type Ibrahim and I had seen in Hilla Gaynor, across the Chad border. Many are devout Muslims, but some of the tribe have never adopted Islam, and still follow the animistic practices of their ancestors. They have never been a rich race, for the Libyan Desert and the western Sahara in which they live is the harshest part of the North African desert, though since the time of French colonialism in Chad they prospered. Some of them served in the Camel Corps of the French army, and not only profited financially, but also learned new methods of warfare which they practised on their old enemies the Arabs. Since the civil war between Gikoni and Habri had broken out, many had volunteered to fight in Habri's forces, but by that December the fortunes of war had gone badly for them: many had been pushed out of their homes and had lost their livestock.

I watched as the Bedayatt couched and loaded their riding-camels. I had chosen to use the less comfortable pack-saddle on this trip, since I was carrying a great deal of baggage, but they were using neat riding-saddles padded with costly furs and slung with hide saddlebags, worn shiny with use. Their camels looked as lean and powerful as leopards, and I wished, not for the first time, that such superb animals were available in the market. I knew, however, that such camels could not be bought: the Saharan peoples reared their riding-camels from their own herds, and trained them carefully from birth. Besides their mounts, my bull seemed like a great cruiser beside a flotilla of fast frigates.

Soon we were moving north, pushing the four loose camels before us, across a bleak winter landscape where the cruel blast of the desert winds slapped our faces. We moved through graveyards of brush and tree, where not a leaf was to be seen and where there was no sound but the soft crunching of the camels' percussion-padded feet on the crystalline sand. I knew that I had left the last settlement of any size in the Sudan, and was approaching that wilder world of the desert, beyond the fringes of civilization, that young unruly world where there was no law but the law of nature.

We halted at Khazan, where there was a water-pool consisting of black flats of mud on which a light film of water shimmered silver in the winter sun. Some Zaghawa camels were drinking at the water's edge and women were drawing water in buckets and filling waterskins. We asked them to help fill our skins, then three of the Bedayatt asked our leave to go. They were travelling to their camp near the Khazan, whilst 'Ali Ahmed and I were heading north-east towards Umm Buru with his four camels. The two of us moved on, crossing interminable wastes of sand which nursed occasional beds of dead camel-thorn and the blond stubble grasses. For hours we crossed these featureless flats, until in the early afternoon we discovered the deep red wound of a water-course where a steep cliff of sand gave us protection from the tyrannical wind. We turned the camels out to graze on the sparse vegetation along the edges of the wadi. I began to make 'asida while 'Ali Ahmed went off to watch the camels.

After eating we sat back in the sand and examined each other's weapons. 'Ali's was a locally made shotgun, which nevertheless looked well-built, and 'Ali told me that he often shot gazelle. He said that he travelled on this route constantly and usually alone, and because of this it helped to have some protection.

'Are there many robbers?' I asked.

'Ali smiled a broad, good-humoured smile. 'A few,' he answered. 'Sometimes you have to be careful.'

Unlike most tribesmen to whom I had addressed this question, he did not immediately accuse other tribes of stealing. This, I thought, was indicative of two things: either he was an unusually fair man, or he knew who the real thieves were. I had no way of deciding which of these was correct, for I had been completely thrown by the personality of 'Ali Ahmed. Tales I had heard of the Bedayatt had led me to expect some kind of uncouth barbarian, but I found instead a man with what the Arabs called *ahsas*: instinctive politeness and a natural ability to inspire trust.

'Ali told me that as he usually made this journey alone, he was very glad of my company, for the road to Mellit was long and lonely. Later we set off, driving the free camels into the icy wind, padding through pillowed creeks of sand along the banks of which goats were grazing, over plunging downland the baldness of which was broken only by the stunted stubs of old thornbushes. Night came, but the sunset brought no cheer in this cold wasteland. The camels seemed to hate the cold, hanging back and moaning, and once when they got the scent of a wood fire began to move instinctively towards it. I tried to steer my bull away, but he became very nervous, bucking and pulling on the headrope. The intense cold which now set in, and the resistance of the camels, brought to mind a verse from T. S. Eliot:

> The ways deep and the weather sharp,
> The very dead of winter,
> And the camels galled, sore-footed, refractory,
> Lying down in the melting snow.

Hours later we arrived at a creek sheltered by the boles of *heraz* and *lalob* trees, which were still in leaf. We made camp by a tall cutting where the water had sheared a smooth wall of soil and sand at the side of the wadi bed. We turned the camels out into the trees and ate *'asida*. Thousands of stars were out above and 'Ali Ahmed began telling me the names of the constellations in his own language. After some time, I noticed, looking around with my torch, that my camel was no longer in sight. I mentioned it to 'Ali, suggesting that we should bring the camels into the camp for the night as was normal practice. He disagreed, preferring to let them feed a little longer. Finally, however, he said that he would help me look for my own animal. We moved through the thick foliage of the wadi in silence. Five minutes passed, then ten. The animal was nowhere to be found. I became worried, and hoped I had not made an error in tying the *qayd*. 'Ali stopped suddenly and began listening hard in the starlight. Somewhere behind us the other five camels chewed on oblivious. Then came the distinct sound of a camel's groan in the darkness. We knew that this could mean only one thing, for a camel will not usually groan unless approached by a man. Immediately the Bedayi unslung his shotgun. 'Quick,' he whispered to me. 'Get your gun!'

I hurried back to the camp and collected my pistol, wondering what was afoot. Quickly I returned to where 'Ali stood, by a low bush. Now we both stared outwards into the night trying to give form and substance to the grotesque shadows which spread out before us. Again there came the roar of a camel. 'Who is it?' 'Ali called out, in Arabic.

It was then that I heard the sound which I recognized instantly and which made my hair stand on end. It was a sound I had once spent my entire waking life listening for: the cocking of a rifle.

Almost instinctively 'Ali and I dropped, expecting a shot to ring out in the darkness. Both of us brought up our weapons, although we had neither direction nor target at which to aim. I knew that at the faintest move I would squeeze the trigger, for behind that small chain of muscle lay all the pent-up fears and tensions of the journey so far. Then a voice cracked the shell of the tension; a man's voice speaking in a language I did not recognize. 'Ali answered immediately in his own tongue and as I watched, two shadowy figures emerged from the blackness, their forms thickening as they approached.

'It's all right, they're Zaghawa,' 'Ali said.

We shook hands with the two men in the darkness. They wore greatcoats of some dark material and headcloths piled up in the Zaghawa style. One of them carried an automatic rifle which looked like a Heckler-Koch. At once 'Ali began to speak to them in a quiet, though forceful manner, and I guessed he was dressing them down for sneaking up in the night. The man with the rifle spoke with equal conviction, assisted at intervals by his companion, and I assumed that he had some good excuse. The unarmed man disappeared suddenly, but reappeared a few minutes later leading two camels through the underbrush. He pointed further down the wadi, and said something to 'Ali.

'That's your camel,' said the Bedayi, 'through those trees.'

Relieved, I went to collect the fugitive and drove him back to our camp, where I found the others seated around the rekindled fire with the kettle on it. I couched the camel with the others, which 'Ali had evidently brought in, and went to join the men at the fire. They were still chattering away in Zaghawa, but by interjecting here and there, I managed to ascertain their story. They were Awlad Diqqayn Zaghawa, nomads from the Libyan Desert to the north. About a week before, some raiders had stolen four of their camels. They suspected Rizayqat Arabs, but were unsure. They had followed the tracks of the raiders,

but finally lost them in the Tagabo Hills. Now they were doing a
desperate sweep around Dar Zaghawa. They had come upon this wadi
in the night and, spotting my camel in the bushes, had gone to investigate. The story sounded rather shaky to me, for this area was a
long way from the Tagabo Hills, but 'Ali Ahmed seemed quite at ease
with them, and since he had more to lose than I, I gave up worrying and
got under my blankets. Still, as I did so, I felt thankful for my deliver-
ance from what could have been a nasty situation. My puny .22 was
no match for the rifle of the Zaghawi, and I was glad things had not
come to a fire-fight. I had come too far to leave my bleached bones for
the ants in this desolate world beyond the fringes.

The next day, at dawn, the Awlad Diqqayn rode off south. 'Ali and I
carried on north-east, passing over rocky ridges with hard gravel
underfoot, where the wind whistled stinging and sharp, drawing back
its lips from the jagged canines of the rocks. We descended through an
ox-bow of a wadi where a deserted village stood, a ghost town of
rotting huts, scattered and broken.

'See that, brother!' 'Ali said. 'All gone! That was a Zaghawa village.
Now there's not a single tribesman left in the place. They had to go
when the water finished.' I remembered what the forester Farah Yusif
had told me about the desiccation of this area.

A little further on, we came across the temporary huts of some
nomadic Zaghawa, who had made a winter camp inside the bed of a
wadi. These people had only camels and a few goats: this, I suspected,
was the shape of things to come.

As we reached the top of the valley wall, I saw in the distance the
Libyan Desert: a fragment of orange sand shining far beyond the re-
entrants of the mountains. Immediately before us lay another wide
valley, like the overture of the desert. It was a saucer-shaped hollow,
rimmed with ragged black rock, where great reptilian ridges rose out of
beds of bright sand. In the very centre lay a tiny patch of pure green,
the village of Kornoi, and towering over it like glistening black fangs,
the pinnacles of Hajar Kadu. As we picked our way down the valley, a
freak wind hit us and I shivered violently. It was approaching noon,
yet the temperature was not far above freezing. Remembering the heat
which had been my most awesome enemy the previous summer, I was
astonished that the desert could be so cold during the day.

On the valley floor we joined a track which led to Kornoi. On the
road was a Zaghawa caravan carrying bags of rock-salt into the village,
the camel-men muffled in their headcloths and their thick greatcoats.

Neither 'Ali nor I had any wish to enter the town, however, and we bypassed it, following the track which led to Umm Buru.

The next two days were the coldest I had experienced in the Sudan. We traversed many valleys, assaulted by the desert wind which cut into us like a scimitar on their high tops, but we were rewarded by the splendid spectacle of Dar Zaghawa. It was a mountain landscape of spinal ridges of polished granite, sculpted by the scathing wind over millennia into a grisly scaffolding of rock. My camel hated this stony, steep going, and twice he went berserk, running off at the gallop, with me desperately clutching the saddle. He was every bit as bad as the bull I had exchanged him for in Tina. On the morning of 18 December we reached the village of Umm Buru. This settlement reflected the changes which had taken place in the area in recent years. It had once been an important and flourishing community, and Guy Moore had kept a house here in the 1930s. Now it was on the decline, mainly because water-sources had dried up, and water had to be brought from far away.

'Ali and I parted outside the village. He was taking the eastern route to Mellit, whereas I was turning north into the Libyan Desert, still hoping to reach El Atrun despite the delays I had suffered. 'Ali told me that my way lay through the tiny outpost town of Muzbat, which had a small section of Camel Corps. I made a mental note to avoid the settlement.

I watched the Bedayi as he drove his camels away to the east. If anyone criticized the Bedayatt again in my presence, I would tell them of this man, who was one of the most agreeable companions I have ever travelled with, without the constant suspicion I had experienced amongst other people.

That night I camped alone near Umm Buru. A freezing *haboob* whipped down from the hills to the north, and I erected my tent for the first time, since there was no wadi for protection. In the morning I set my compass, and walked with my camel up the winding side of the valley and into the scarlet hills. As I reached the top of the valley and prepared to mount, an astonishing sight met my eyes. Forty or fifty camels were tied head to tail in the largest caravan I had ever seen, led by men on horses who were cloaked in white from head to foot, with only their eyes showing through the slits in their cloaks. The camels moved silently and swiftly almost as if they were not touching the ground, and the strangely spectral figures of the men gave the caravan the atmosphere of a ghostly visitation. As it came nearer, I hailed the men. They were Awlad Diqqayn Zaghawa from Muzbat and were travelling to Kulbus to buy millet. They pointed out to me the direction of Muzbat and began to disappear into the valley. I wished suddenly that I was travelling with them, rather than taking this lonely road without a companion.

Just before sunset on that day I spotted a village, set on the crest of a knoll, and suddenly, smelling wood smoke, my camel bolted. I fought to bring him under control, and as we neared the village, an old man came out, grabbing my headrope and forcing the camel to kneel.

'That's a bad camel, by God the Great! He's strong all right, very strong, but he'll throw you one day,' the old man said. 'He wants the company of other camels; he's a fully grown adult. He seems afraid of the cold too. You be careful of him!'

I looked around at the village, and saw to my surprise that most of it was in ruins, like the ones I had seen previously. Only the old man's house seemed to be in good repair with a freshly made stockade of grass.

'Where are all the people?' I asked.

'Gone!' he replied. 'All gone off to Libya, or south to the towns, to El Fasher or Kutum, or Mellit. I'm the only one left now, me and my daughters. I was the shaykh of this place. I could leave like the others, but I've been here most of my life.'

'God is generous.'

'Yes, God is generous.'

He told me again to be careful of the camel, and disappeared into the house for a moment, reappearing with a steel chain device, known as *silsil* in Arabic. It consisted of a V-shaped piece of iron which fitted over the animal's head.

'This will do the trick!' the old Zaghawi said. 'They don't like it, and it keeps them quiet.'

He began to show me how to fit the contraption over the camel's jaw. I thought it cruel, as it worked on a principle of squeezing the animal's jaw. I knew that no Arab would be seen dead using one of these, since they said it was only used by those who were 'afraid' of the camel. I decided to humour the old man, however, as I could always remove the device later, and certainly the animal seemed more docile after it was fitted, though he screamed and fretted as it was being put on. I understood why some tribes in the Sudan rode the female instead of the bull. Fully grown bulls are strong and hardy, and mine was exceptionally so, but they are also inclined to be wilful, and can be dangerous.

I was hoping that the old Zaghawi would offer me hospitality that night, but for once, it seemed, he had become fond of his splendid isolation, and still lacking the gall to impose myself, I pressed on, riding fast into the gilded glow of twilight. Not long after dark I made camp alone in a wadi.

In the morning I carried on towards Muzbat. The weather was still sharp, but had warmed a little as I crossed another chain of intersecting valleys. In the early afternoon I emerged from a wadi clothed in *ushur* shrub, when a leather pad dropped from my saddle. Grumbling with irritation, I dropped from the camel's back and bent to pick it up. Just as I did so, two camel-riders broke from the wadi behind me. They were riding loose-legged calves and moving fast. Both were dressed in old blue greatcoats and headcloths, as most tribesmen wore in winter, but I noticed that each had a Heckler-Koch automatic slung from his saddle. So unexpectedly had they appeared that I was taken by surprise. My pistol was way out of reach, in the canvas holdall attached to the saddle. My heart sank as the distance between us narrowed. If this was the 'enemy' – and I could not believe anyone but bandits would sport their arms so openly – then I was lost. As the riders halted their camels near me, I saw that they were young men, with the dark, rounded faces of the Saharan tribes. One of them, a rather cheerful-looking youth with a smooth, open face, greeted me, then said, 'Where are you going?'

'Why do you want to know?' I answered aggressively, not willing to drop my guard merely because of appearances.

Suddenly the other rider unbuttoned his coat, and beneath it I caught a glimpse of a green uniform. 'Because we are the Camel Corps,' he said.

'Ah,' I said vaguely, not knowing quite what to do next, wondering whether the revelation was good or bad for me. I hoped sincerely that these troopers had not followed me from Tina. 'I'm going to Muzbat,' I said.

'That's where we're going,' said the broad-faced man. 'We can go together. Come on, ride!'

I had little alternative but to join them. As we rode the troopers chatted away amiably, but between the bouts of conversation, I found my mind wandering to the possible consequences of being asked for my certificate of permission to travel. I had not even a passport or an identity card. I had left Tina illegally, and for all I knew there could be a warrant out for my arrest. If so, then neither of the troopers seemed aware of it. The broad-faced man, whose name was Medani, pointed out to me places of interest, telling me the names of mountains and valleys and the various small animals which scuttled across our path. If it had not been for the fear of detection hanging over me, I should very much have enjoyed this journey. Medani was of the Berti, and the other trooper, more silent but no less friendly, was called Hassan, of the local Awlad Diqqayn clan.

We arrived at Muzbat that afternoon, coming pell-mell down the ridge that overlooked the settlement. It was very much as I had expected: a wide wadi of soft sand, along the side of which stood a few cracked and yellowed plaster buildings. Beyond them the razor-edged wind blew over a bleak and empty landscape which stretched to the horizon on every side. The wadi was full of camels, of every possible size, shape and colour. They were being watered at boreholes in the sand by some men, almost the same colour as myself, who wore thickly matted wavy hair and long beards, and whose rough clothing told me at once that they were Arabs. Medani told me that they were Kababish of the Atawiyya clan. There were other tribes in the wadi too, dark-skinned, beardless men of the Bedayatt and the local Awlad Diqqayn Zaghawa. It was fascinating to see these two races, the Arabs and the Saharans, working shoulder to shoulder at the wells, both races descended from peoples who had been at home in this environment for millennia, yet who were quite distinct in manner, language and culture. I understood why they were such deadly enemies. The Arabs and the others kept apart from each other, although here at the wells there seemed to be a truce whilst each tribe went about the work of watering.

If Tina had been the last of civilization, then Muzbat was a desert crossroads. El Atrun was only six days from here, and Wadi Howar, the outer limits of the Rizayqat migrations, only two days. Medani, Hassan and I couched our camels outside the almost derelict shell of the police post. Although I was still waiting for the bomb to drop, the troopers treated me like an honoured guest. When I asked where they had been on their camels, Medani told me that they had been scouring the area for a camel thief of the Bedayatt, whom they had had secure in their one cell. The man had apparently escaped in the night and disappeared into the desert. When Medani showed me the tiny window near the roof from which he had escaped, I guessed that he must have been a man of some determination, or a great deal of money!

Luckily for me, the senior rank in Muzbat, a sergeant called

Mohammed Ja'ali, was not present, and neither Hassan nor Medani were keen on paperwork. I imagined that the situation would change when he returned, and I was anxious to continue to El Atrun as soon as possible. I stayed with the troopers that night and the next day found in the wadi some Awlad Diqqayn who were travelling to the desert wells at Malemal Hosh, two days' journey away. I had wanted to travel to the wells at Wakhaym instead, since this was on a direct route to El Atrun, but I could not afford to delay longer in case of discovery.

That evening, therefore, I set off with the Awlad Diqqayn, who were driving four fat cow camels in milk. They were smooth-faced men in the typical Zaghawa mould, wearing elaborately piled head-cloths and long white shirts. The Zaghawa seemed always to dress as if they were going to a banquet, whereas the Arabs dressed roughly. I preferred the Arab style, for to me riding a camel in a *jellabiyya* was like riding a motorcycle in a dinner suit. All the Awlad Diqqayn carried rifles, though they were careful not to take these out of their specially elongated saddlebags until they were well outside the town. Three of them were brothers, Jiddu Mahmoud Biddi, and his brothers, Mohammed and Atayeb; the others, Juma Mustafa and Esa Abdallah, were cousins. Jiddu was the most talkative of the five. He told me that Bir Biddi, a small oasis in the desert near the Libyan border, was named after his grandfather. If this was true, then he was the descendant of the most famous of all Bedayatt guides, Biddi Audi.

We rode for only about two hours, and in the moonlight came upon a huge circle of camels. In the centre of the circle stood a single tent, from which came the glow of a fire. This was the encampment of some Atawiyya Kababish, who had watered that day in Muzbat. We did not enter the camp directly, but found a comfortable place at a polite distance from the camp, where we unpacked our equipment and made a fire. I was surprised that, with all the wide desert to choose from, the Awlad Diqqayn should prefer to camp so near to another group, but I discovered on subsequent journeys that it was always the custom to camp near others, even if they were enemies. It was a two-way thing, for it allowed each party to keep the other in his sights; far more to be feared was the raider who came secretly in the night.

Soon after we had made camp, the Arabs came out to greet us. There were five of them, all brothers, and with a striking family resemblance. They had fair skin, with large semitic noses and long, unkempt hair which was 'soft' like that of Europeans. They wore thick, uncut beards, *sirwel*, and a motley array of tattered shirts and waistcoats. Each wore a dagger and carried a rifle. Most of these, I noticed, were British Lee-Enfields .303, one of the most accurate rifles ever made, and for these conditions probably better than some of the automatic weapons. The Zaghawa carried the Belgian FN, similar to the SLR I had used in the army, though there were other automatics. Both tribes seemed to love weapons, constantly examining them and taking them apart. I amazed the company by stripping down an FN in a few seconds, a thing I had done so many times I could literally have done it blindfold. I grinned when I saw that the inside of the weapon was filthy: Zaghawa arms drill evidently did not include cleaning.

'It's filthy, brother!' I said to Juma, the owner of the rifle, trying to reproduce my arms-instructor voice. The man looked at me in amazement, but said nothing. I guessed that if he tried to fire it in this state it would jam after the first shot. The Arabs were wiser with their bolt-action rifles, which were less likely to jam.

The Atawiyya brought us bowl after bowl of fresh camels' milk, and we ate their rough *'asida* with camel-milk gravy, while the two tribes chatted away. It interested me to watch these two races interacting at such close quarters. They had a great deal in common, though much of what they said was tribal one-upmanship; for instance, they compared current bride-prices, the Kababish saying that they must pay nine camels and the Awlad Diqqayn immediately answering that they had to pay twelve. I astonished both sides by saying that my tribe paid nothing. Towards the end of the evening, the Arabs entertained us with their musical poetry, known as *dobbayt*. The songs spoke of everyday things – camels, grazing, the desert, beautiful girls. I realized that what I was hearing was a direct continuation of the oral tradition which had flourished amongst the Arabs since pre-Islamic times, the finest flowering of language amongst a people who could neither read nor write.

Some time later, the talk as always shifted to bandits and camel-stealing. The Awlad Diqqayn pooh-poohed any suggestion that there should be camel thieves in this area. After the Atawiyya had left, I asked Jiddu if it would not be better to bring the camels into the camp, for they had wandered out of sight, and would be easy prey for raiders.

Jiddu laughed and said, 'Don't worry about raiders! The Awlad Diqqayn are the only raiders here! Your camel has Bedayatt markings, no? No one will steal that, or any camel with Zaghawa brands.'

At the time I was affected by the jocular way in which he said this,

but had I considered it more carefully, I might have had some pre-
monition about the events of the coming day.

As we set off in the morning, the desert opened like a book on all
sides: hundreds of miles of boundless sand punctuated by rocks and
the occasional clump of trees. Again, my camel was difficult to control.
It would not respond to my tugs on the bridle, and continually pulled
against me.

Jiddu noticed that I was having some trouble, and said, 'That camel
is no good for riding. It will throw you!'

I could not help thinking he was right, in view of some of the
hair-raising experiences I had suffered near Umm Buru.

'It's a *sadiis*, your camel – a fully grown male. It's ready for breeding.
It wants to be with other camels, that's why it's so tricky. Why don't
you try mine instead? This one is younger, a *raba'*, it would be better
for you. Why don't you try it?'

I looked at his camel; it was young and sleek, like one of the fleet
beasts that the Zaghawa raised in their herds. I guessed that my camel
was worth more than the *raba'*, and I felt reluctant to make the exchange
without being absolutely sure I was getting a good animal. However,
Jiddu was very persuasive. 'Just try it for a short time,' he said. 'And if
you don't like it, never mind.'

I reluctantly agreed to try it, and during that afternoon's rest, we
exchanged saddles. As we set off, I rode the *raba'* while Jiddu rode my
camel. After a few minutes, I realized that the camel was too weak for
my purpose; it had looked swift when Jiddu had ridden it, but I
supposed that his saddlebags were empty, whereas I was carrying food
and water. Meanwhile, Jiddu was talking quickly to his companions in
Zaghawa.

'This camel's no good for me!' I told him. 'It's too weak to carry my
things!'

Suddenly, Jiddu spun around on the saddle, and waved his rifle at
me. 'The camp of my friend is near by,' he said. 'I'm going off to see
him! I'll see you later!' And whipping the camel's flanks, he charged
off at speed.

For a few seconds I was too startled to understand what was happening. Then one of Jiddu's brothers said, 'We're not going to Malemal
Hosh. We've changed our minds. We're going to our camp first, then
we'll water at the wells. Go in peace!' The four Awlad Diqqayn wheeled
around, pushing before them the loose cows, and rode off fast in the
opposite direction from the one Jiddu had taken.

I watched dumbfounded as they became dots on the edge of the landscape, and it was only when I was alone that the full horror of the situation became apparent. Jiddu had stolen my camel in what appeared to be a deliberate and calculating manner. I had allowed myself to be lured into a false sense of security. Knowing that to Arabs travelling companions were inviolable, and after my agreeable experiences with the Bedayatt, I had assumed that these Awlad Diqqayn were also trustworthy. But there was more to the situation than the loss of the camel. I was now beyond the fringes of the Sudan, in a country where people knew no law except the law of the tribes. I was in trackless, waterless desert, and since I had been relying on the local knowledge of the Awlad Diqqayn to guide me, I had no idea of my position. I was lost and friendless. Perhaps I could have found my way back to the camp of the Atawiyya, but there was no guarantee that they would still be in the same place, even if I found it, and anyway, to have gone back would have been to give up all chance of seeing my camel again. The camel I now rode would not take me to El Atrun, neither would it take me back to Gineina. My evasion of the police had rendered me undeserving of their assistance, and I could not return to Muzbat for fear of arrest. My only chance was to find Malemal Hosh alone.

I still had a few cards in my hand. In Muzbat, I had taken a rough compass bearing on the wells from directions given by the Awlad Diqqayn. I could not check this, as the Hosh was not marked on any map I had, but I hoped at least that it would take me in the right direction. I had food and some water, and I knew the names of all the Awlad Diqqayn I had travelled with, for by chance I had noted them in my diary. I knew that the family were from somewhere near the Hosh; I also knew that it was the only well in the area, and that sooner or later Jiddu Mahmoud Biddi would be forced to water there. When he did, I hoped that I should be waiting for him.

However, the immediate problem was to get there. I was alone in the emptiest quarter of the North African desert, searching for a tiny dot on the landscape, using a compass bearing I was unable to check, and riding a camel which was already faltering. It was the most perilous situation I had encountered on my journeys, and I knew that in the next two days my powers of survival would be tested to the full.

I halted just after sunset that evening in a great wadi under a cliff of sand. I thought it better not to blunder around at night, despite the moon, and I had no wish to exhaust the camel further, knowing that the animal was my only lifeline. Without my camel, I could not carry my water, and without my water I could last no more than a day in this, the driest of all North African deserts. I ate *'asida*, using the water sparingly, and thanked providence that I had brought two skins of water rather than one, though I remembered how the Awlad Diqqayn had laughed when they had seen them. After eating, I scrambled up the wadi bank, to spy out the landfall. I gazed out over unbroken miles of desert bathed in its casement of moonlight. Here and there the shadows were drawn in around a clump of thorn trees, but nowhere was there any sign of humankind. Sitting there on the edge of nothingness, I felt as if I were the sole survivor of a devastating holocaust. There seemed not the slightest connection between myself and any other living being.

The first thing I saw on waking that morning was a gazelle. It had ventured inquisitively into the wadi, to within a few yards of where I was sleeping rolled up in my blanket. Instinctively, I picked up my pistol and aimed. Then I remembered my predicament and chuckled, as the animal darted out of the wadi. Food was the least of my worries. However, I found the presence of the gazelle comforting in some way. Many Sudanese had told me that this animal could live for months without water, though frankly I did not believe this, and could not help but feel some sense of relationship between myself and this other warm-blooded creature which had made its home in this least comfortable of the world's environments.

My greatest problem that day was the camel. It seemed subdued and exhausted now it was separated from its companions. It refused resolutely to move at a reasonable rate, whether I rode or walked. The sun came out like a sledgehammer, and the morning's journey seemed to go on without end as I crossed flats of pale sand, and patches of *heskaniit* grass which embedded their sharp caltrops in my *sirwel*. I whipped and cursed, whispered and coaxed, but still the camel refused to budge from his reluctant drag. And meanwhile it seemed as if the desert looked on and laughed at my progress.

Once I saw a giant vulture in a thorn tree. It gazed down at me with a chilling glare, not at all perturbed by my presence. The bird was so large that I wondered what I would do if it tried to attack me, though I knew that vultures are only supposed to attack the dying and the dead. The thought brought to mind the caption of the well-known comic poster, depicting two caricature vultures, which read: 'Patience be damned, I'm gonna kill something!' Despite the amusement, the brooding, watchful, fearless presence of the bird reflected in my mind the relentless sands in which I was now travelling. Should I not reach my destination, I might well be leaving whitened bones to be picked clean by such as this. Still I followed the compass bearing, keeping myself in check by the knowledge, gleaned long ago in the depths of military training, that the compass must be right. There was cold comfort in knowing that if I missed the wells I should be lost in waterless desert without much chance to retrace my steps.

I drank little water, not knowing when I should find more, and my throat was constantly parched. I noticed with growing apprehension, however, that my waterskins were getting lighter, as if some phantom drinker were consuming the liquid. I realized that there must be some tiny leaks, but though I sought them feverishly, I could not pinpoint them. The outer surfaces of the skins stayed wet, and the sun evaporated the precious fluid. To prevent this further, I covered them with a blanket. So the day wore on, and I saw no other living person, nor the tracks or spoor of animals. Once I saw before me a hollow where water glistened silver, but as I approached, the liquid vaporized into thin air and I knew I had been duped by a mirage.

The hours passed, and the sun dropped down behind me. Soon after, I made camp by a patch of *heskaniit* grass. I was still intensely aware of the need to preserve the strength of my camel, so I turned him out to grass, while I cooked myself some '*asida*. I tied the *qayd* tightly, knowing that should he wander off I would be lost. After eating, I took stock of the situation. Unless my bearing was completely wrong, I must be very near the wells, I knew. I refused to consider the possibility that I had missed them, for although the place was tiny, I was sure that there would be animal tracks leading there. I found in the bottom of my saddlebag the old RAF desert survival pamphlet which I always carried, but rarely looked at. Thumbing through it in the light of a torch, my eye fell on the section entitled: 'Natives'.

> With a few exceptions the natives are friendly. They know the country, its trails, food and water sources, and can be the means of your being speedily returned to civilization. In short, they are your best help, but it all depends on how you approach them.
> ALWAYS BE TACTFUL, PATIENT AND HONEST.

If, at that moment, there had been any natives about, I should have been as tactful, patient and honest as I had ever been in my life.

For a long time I sat looking out over the moonlit sands. Once I thought I spotted the flicker of a camp fire, and I was gripped by a mad impulse to run towards it. But as I looked again, it disappeared like an enticing will-o'-the-wisp, leaving me alone with the awful quiescence of the stars.

On waking the next morning, I found to my horror that most of my water had leaked from the skins, leaving no more than three or four pints. My survival manual showed me that, moving at night, I could cover about thirty miles with this amount, though there were no figures for daytime movement. If I didn't find the wells today, I thought, I might as well lie down and invite the vultures to a feast. If anything, the camel was even more uncooperative than the previous day, despite the lighter load and the grazing; I was now walking with him, but he hung back, pulling on the headrope and making the work exhausting. The land was undulating dunes, with a little rough grass and a few trees in places. Passing up the steep slopes of the *qoz* was difficult work, and I noticed that the camel's legs trembled with weakness. I almost hauled him bodily up a particularly steep incline, panting with exhaustion.

As we broke over the ridge I saw that the dune was crowned with a few *hejlij* trees, and beneath them about thirty camels huddled away from the sun. No sooner had I taken this in than I heard a savage roar. Suddenly a large white bull camel came charging towards me out of the tight ranks of the herd, blowing an obscene pink bladder from his mouth and leaving behind him a trail of froth. This I knew was a sign of sexual maturity, and I guessed that this animal was the *naib* or leader of the herd, coming out to defend his territory. As he closed with us, I slashed at him with my whip, but could not drive him away, and I found myself dodging and ducking away from the madly dancing, snake-like head with its gnashing canines. There was no doubt that the camel was in season, and I knew that in this state camels would kill or maim. Finally, the bull bit my camel on the rear leg, and the younger animal let out an ear-piercing screech.

Suddenly a dark figure appeared on the ridge overlooking the area: it was an Arab carrying an automatic rifle, who shouted out a challenge. I waved at him frantically, hoping that he would realize that I was not trying to steal one of his camels. I was relieved, nevertheless, that I had at last found someone with whom I could share the loneliness of this sea of nothing. I began to climb up to the ridge. The Arab was no more than a boy, and behind him, in the shade of another tree, sat two younger boys.

'Peace be on you,' I said.

'And on you be peace,' he replied. He led me to the tiny camp, telling me that they were Arabs of the Awlad Rashid, a tribe I had heard of but not encountered before. They laughed when I said I was English, saying that from afar they had taken me for an Atawi because of my red face and beard. They told me that the Rashid were watering their herds at Malemal Hosh and that their particular family was waiting its turn at the wells. Those Awlad Rashid boys will never know how grateful I was to find them, or how delicious the camel's milk which they offered me. They said that the Hosh was only a few minutes' journey away, and that many tribes were watering there at present, especially the Awlad Diqqayn, the Mahriyya Rizayqat, and the Zayadiyya. I thanked the Rashid with all the patience, tact and honesty I could muster and gave the eldest boy my lace skullcap, which he had examined with interest.

A short time after leaving them, I came over the ridge of the dune, and saw the wells below me, laid on the cracked brown bed of a wadi. A pall of dust blew across the surface of the valley, obscuring the little clutch of houses which marked the place. I descended the dune painfully and led my camel towards the well compound, outside which many camels were tethered to posts or couched in the dust. I looked for my own bull, but did not spot him, though I saw many with the distinctive brand of the Awlad Diqqayn. I was greeted by some Arabs standing near the gate of the enclosure: they were Zayadiyya tribesmen, one of whom, Rabi', was responsible for the wells. He showed me to a tiny stone-built house and helped to unsaddle my camel. After I had eaten and drunk, I related to him and another Zayadi, Harara, the story of my stolen camel. They listened silently, shaking their heads, and finally Rabi' said, 'What's the name of the one who stole your camel?'

'Jiddu Mahmoud Biddi of the Awlad Diqqayn.'

'I know him well. He's a rascal that one. He'll come here sooner or later, in fact his father watered some goats here today. His father's a good man. We'll have a word with him.'

I warmed to the attitude of these Zayadiyya, for I had been apprehensive that my story might not fall on sympathetic ears. Later, Rabi' took a careful look at the camel I had been riding, and again he shook his head, 'By God that Jiddu,' he said. 'Look at those brands, they're Arab marks, Ribayqat Kababish. I would say that camel is stolen. Have you got the paper? No, I thought not. I think you would have trouble trying to sell this animal.'

'Stealing from the Kababish is one thing,' said Harara, 'but robbing a guest in our land is another. A serious matter.'

'Yes,' replied Rabi'. 'But he'll be here in a few days, I'm sure. Then we'll have him, by God!'

It seemed suddenly that those two days of desperate travelling had been worthwhile, and I had had the luck to fall in with these gracious and right-minded Zayadiyya, who were able to help me.

I stayed at Malemal Hosh for four days. It was a mini-sized settlement with only four houses, which were inhabited by the Zayadiyya who looked after the well and their families. Each day huge herds of camels were brought into the well from the sparse grazing on the *qoz*. Rabi' took me to visit many of the nomads of his own family, the Awlad Jerbo Zayadiyya, and we would sit and drink tea and camel's milk while they talked of their journeys in the desert. These men had the largest herds I had ever seen: one single family I met had two thousand head. Each day I awoke to the sound of roaring and braying and went to join the men struggling at the metal troughs amongst the piles of excrement on which the well seemed to have been built. Always herds of camels waited on the dry mud-flats of the wadi, like soldiers on parade, and dust rose from the great squadrons of animals as the Arabs drove them into the wells. The Arabs of the Mahriyya, Zayadiyya and Awlad Rashid I met here seemed affluent in comparison with other tribes, judging by the richness of their saddlery, which was often worth far more than the camel. They carried Zayadiyya saddles of polished wood and studded leather, draped with costly sable furs, hand-decorated saddlebags, expensive curved scimitars and automatic rifles. I knew that I was in one of the finest camel-rearing areas in the world, and amongst some of the most successful camel-breeders of all time. In the evening more herds would descend from the surrounding dunes, which were known as the Qoz Al Hor and Tawaanis; the wadi filled with the thunder of their hooves and drapes of dust rose around them, hanging in the golden light of the dying sun.

On the second day, Rabi' introduced me to an old man who was watering some goats in the iron troughs.

'This is Mahmoud Biddi,' he told me, 'Father of Jiddu.'

Rabi' explained to the old Zaghawi about what had happened. Mahmoud Biddi lost none of his composure, but he nodded and said that he would come to the Zayadi's house to discuss the matter. He arrived later bringing with him some relations, among whom I recognized Mohammed, Jiddu's brother. I was tempted to give vent to some of my pent-up anger towards him, though I managed to suppress it, thinking that I would gain little. We ate *'asida*, and sat cross-legged in a circle on the floor of Rabi''s house, and many more of the Zayadiyya and Mahriyya came up to join us out of pure curiosity.

It was Rabi' who held the floor. He spoke with the fluency of an orator, explaining my plight, and representing me as a visitor to this area, who would no doubt be making reports as to the hospitality of the people here. He waxed eloquent about my personality, sometimes claiming that I was a 'poor, unfortunate person' who knew nothing of the desert or its ways, and others as a 'person who knows everything about the desert and camels'. I hoped that the apparent contradiction here would go unnoticed in the flow of his rhetoric, and so it seemed, for when he had finished it felt almost as if we should all stand up and applaud. Mohammed Mahmoud, Jiddu's brother, then apologized for the behaviour of Jiddu and of himself and his brothers, but explained that Jiddu had returned to Muzbat, an assertion which I did not believe. His father, old Mahmoud, cut in, however, speaking in a dignified, respectful manner. He told us that he had once been a desert guide for the British like his famous father and had the greatest of respect for them. He regretted the 'misunderstanding' and assured me that the camel would be returned directly.

Sure enough, the next morning Jiddu turned up at the wells with my camel. He approached me with a grin on his face, as if to say, 'It was only a joke, it's all over now.'

I felt like punching him in the teeth, but remembered the words of the survival manual: 'Tact, patience, honesty.' It was, after all, good advice.

'I told you that I'd see you later!' he said. 'Didn't I?'

'Yes,' I answered. 'But you forgot to tell me the way to the wells.'

'God is Generous!'

'Praise be to God.'

I was satisfied just to have retrieved my camel, and I knew that I owed the Zayadiyya a great debt. Now, at least, I could continue my journey to El Atrun, which was only five days away. I was already well behind schedule, but I was determined to push on as fast as possible. I prepared my equipment, ready to leave for El Atrun the next day. As I was doing so, Rabi' came up and said that a group of Zaghawa had arrived with some news for me.

I squatted down with the three men, and Rabi' brought us water.

'Are you the *khawaja* who came from Muzbat a few days ago?' one of them asked.

I replied that I supposed I was.

'We've just come from Muzbat,' he went on, 'and the Camel Corps told us to look out for you. You must return immediately.'

I was very sceptical, and believed that the Zaghawa had mis-understood the true message.

'Listen, *khawaja*,' the tribesman went on, 'this is serious talk. Mohammed Ja'ali has come back. He told us himself that he wants to see you. It would be better for you to do as he says.'

My heart sank as I realized the import of his words. Evidently the police chief had returned and discovered that in his absence I had been allowed to slip through. Perhaps he had even had a report from Tina. For a moment I considered going the 'nomad way', but I sensed that this time it was impossible. I could not evade the authorities for ever if I wished to remain in the Sudan. I told the Zaghawa that I would return to Muzbat the next day. For the rest of the evening I felt depressed and disappointed. After all the difficulties and problems I had overcome and the hardships I had experienced, I was still not to reach my destination. I had been robbed, cheated, subjected to danger and abandoned in the desert, only to be stopped on the last stretch of the journey.

11

CHRISTMAS UNDER GUARD

The next morning I set off back towards Muzbat. I had taken careful directions from the Awlad Diqqayn and having traversed the distance once, I felt sure now that I could find my way back without difficulty. Travelling on my large bull, I could make much faster progress than on the *raba'*, and I expected that it would take no more than two days to reach the outpost.

I set off over the hard-packed mud of the wadi, the camel going at a fast trot as his feet moved like feather dusters over the flaky ground. I was heading for a lone acacia tree on the skyline, which was on my compass bearing, and was one of the few landmarks I could see. Despite his speed, the camel groaned and complained. I should have taken more notice, but I was consumed with irritation at being forced to return, and I put the complaints down to bad temper.

As I neared the tree, the camel pulled heavily on the headrope, tilting his head downwards, which I knew was the prelude to some wild behaviour. The animal bolted towards the tree, plunging in under its branches with full force, like a burning man plunging into water. One of the low boughs struck me across the chest, knocking me out of the saddle. Unfortunately I was wearing a long Arab shirt, which caught on the saddle horn, and for a horrific moment I was suspended from the camel's back, swinging helplessly above the ground as the camel rubbed the saddle against a thick branch, trying to knock it off. I remember thinking, 'This is it then!' For I knew that with one forward kick of the animal's rear leg my back would be broken. Just then the front saddle horn cracked. There was the sound of rending material as my shirt tore, and I landed on my face. The beast sat down almost at once, and I was able to seize the headrope.

I must have been a sorry sight, my hands and face bruised and bleeding, my shirt ripped down the whole of its length, my headcloth still suspended somewhere up in the thorns. I coaxed and pulled the animal out from under the branches. Then I saw what was wrong. He was still wearing the iron chain which the old Zaghawi had given me. Rabi', the Zayadi, had helped me to saddle that morning and had set the chain a notch too high so that it was pinching the camel's chin. I cursed the good intentions of others, and swore that in future no one would saddle my camel except myself. I knew, however, that I myself had fallen short by failing to notice the fault earlier. In my travels, I had often experienced the tricks of camels, but this had been a deliberate and calculated attempt to destroy me. The thought was a sobering one.

That day I pressed on and on, seeing no one, and after darkness fell I found myself in a great black basin, leading my camel by the headrope under the glimmer of the stars. I realized suddenly that it was Christmas Eve. At home there would have been beer and sherry and good cheer, bells ringing in the villages of my native Lincolnshire, carol services and parties, fairy lights on the trees and presents wrapped in coloured paper. Here I was in another dimension, with one hand leading a camel which had that day tried to kill me, and holding a compass in the other. My party that evening was just for two, myself and my reluctant four-footed guest, whom I treated to all the dry grass he could eat while I sat by a camp fire, wrapped in my blanket, and drank sweet tea.

Christmas morning was cold and raw, like the *'asida* I ate to celebrate its coming as I moved off over the plain. After some hours I saw a herd of camels and some goats, and as I approached I noticed that they were being guarded by three young boys who rode tiny, immature camels. They were of the Awlad Diqqayn, and told me that Muzbat was close, then gave me a bowl of camels' milk to drink. They asked for tea and sugar, which I let them take from my saddlebag, then, remembering that it was Christmas, gave them each a small sum of money, and rode away rather pleased that I had had the opportunity of giving someone a Christmas present.

Within the hour I was sloping in under the *heraz* trees of Wadi Muzbat. The place seemed almost deserted, as I couched the camel by the broken-down police post. At once Medani appeared, and with him a stout, rather simple-looking man who wore the chevrons of a sergeant on his sleeve. We went through the usual greetings. The sergeant, whom Medani introduced to me, was Mohammed Ja'ali, chief of the *shorta* in Muzbat. I told him that his message had reached me in Malemal Hosh.

'The situation is this,' Mohammed Ja'ali explained. 'An officer arrived from Kutum on a tour of inspection, and heard about you. He gave orders that you should go to Kutum immediately.'

'But Kutum is the opposite way from Gineina. I will be late for my work if I go there.'

'His orders were clear.'

'You mean I must go?'

'You have no choice.'

'Then I'm under arrest!'

'Yes.'

I looked at the good-humoured, broad-faced Medani, and wondered how much of a rocketing he had received for letting me go. Mohammed Ja'ali took me to his office, and I stood before his desk looking awkward, and feeling humiliated. Mohammed explained that I had no means of identity and no permission to be here. The officer suspected that I might be a spy or a guerrilla of some kind from Chad, the border of which was only a few miles away. Then he told me something I did not know. In the last week, Habri's forces, the ones supported by the Sudan, had been pushed out of Chad by a combined army of Chadians, Libyans and foreign mercenaries. Gineina, Kulbus and Tina were full of refugees: in Gineina alone they numbered eight thousand, and Habri had set up an emergency HQ there. I had, by pure chance, become involved in an international situation. Mohammed Ja'ali added that if it made me feel any better, he did not believe that I was a spy, but orders were orders.

He explained that we would leave the next day for Kutum, and would travel with a guide of the local Awlad Diqqayn, named Ahmed. That evening I saddled up and, accompanied by Hassan and Medani, travelled down the wadi to some wooden cabins, which were the winter quarters of some Awlad Diqqayn. Here we found Ahmed, who welcomed me avidly. In other circumstances I should have enjoyed talking to this spirited man. As it was I could not avoid a slight sense of resentment at being a prisoner. After eating, I was shown to a place to sleep inside the brushwood cabin, and the two troopers lay down on either side of me, with rifles near at hand. I could not suppress a feeling of amusement that all this was intended for me. Nevertheless I wrote in my diary that Christmas night: 'Christmas under guard. In a nomad's cabin in Wadi Muzbat. Outside the wind is blowing off the desert. Tomorrow being escorted to Kutum. Merry bloody Christmas!'

I had been in the situation of being a prisoner only twice before:

once when I had been caught speeding on my motorcycle, during student days, and the second during a 'resistance to interrogation' exercise in the Special Air Service Regiment. Both had been humiliating experiences, the latter worse than the former, despite the fact that it was only simulation. I had been punched and kicked, pushed into cold water, made to stand on tiptoes for hours with a sack over my head. The four days I spent under guard of the Camel Corps, however, bore only the faintest resemblance to these previous experiences of custody.

First of all, Medani and Hassan were the most considerate custodians one could have asked for, and gave the impression that they were performing an odious, yet necessary duty. Secondly, our way was lighted by the presence of Ahmed's sister, a pretty girl called Hawa, who wanted to go to the market in Kutum. She was a slim-limbed creature, black as a firepot, with a full, rounded figure and short braided hair, smeared with butter. She had flashing white teeth, bright eyes and a lively manner, and was evidently excited by the prospect of visiting the 'big town', which was the only place of any size which she had seen. Ahmed asked if she could ride with me, as my camel was the strongest, and when I assented, she brought out a small leather sling which she strung from the rear horn of my saddle. Even my ill-tempered bull seemed to lose some of its wildness, as if it were aware of the delicateness of this jewel of a girl. Her presence eased the tensions of the journey, and I was much taken by her, as were the Camel Corps men, for they lost no opportunity to talk to her.

We spent almost all the first day searching for the troopers' camels, which had been taken out into the *qoz* to graze by some Awlad Diqqayn. This meant that Ahmed and I had to carry their saddles while they walked, scouring the desert for two animals with government brands. It was almost sunset by the time they were found and saddled, and we set off towards Kutum.

At nights we camped in the *qoz*, and the delectable Hawa would make *'asida*. Always, though, she slept apart from the men, and ate alone out of her own bowl. Slowly, we moved higher into the hills which surrounded Kutum, through Wadi Jinaiq, a twisting watercourse which ran through a shallow valley, ringed by black rock walls, where the mountains had been sculpted by time into strange phallic shapes. In the lush greenery of the wadi bed, hundreds of camels were grazing, 'Like locusts!' Ahmed said. Most of them belonged to the Mahriyya, whose tents we often saw nestled along the banks of the wadi. The area was teeming with gazelle, and throughout the journey Medani and Hassan were keen to shoot some meat. Whenever someone sighted gazelle, one of the troopers would dismount and run towards them with great excitement. Some time later, a salvo of shots would ring across the desert, but each time he would return crestfallen and empty handed, saying, 'They were too far away!' or 'They moved too fast!' I could not disguise my grin on one occasion when Medani returned in this manner. He began to clear his weapon. Suddenly there was a sharp crack and a bullet whistled past my ear. The grin was wiped off my face, like a wet rag on the chalk of a blackboard.

'God! Careful!' I said.

'Rifle jammed, by God!'

After that I was most circumspect whenever the men handled their weapons, and made sure that I was at a safe distance, out of the line of fire.

The landscape became steadily richer as we approached Kutum, and I saw that the wadis were alive with acacia and tamarisk, mango and lime, and even the tall, haloed trunks of date palms. We passed through the villages of Desa and Khereir, and on the fourth day, very early in the morning, joined with a caravan of the Zaghawa which was going into the town of Kutum.

I found it a place of beauty. It was set on the banks of its wadi, which was clothed in trees. On the northern side of the creek were the grass huts and houses of the townspeople, and on the opposite side stood the yellow government buildings of the administration, which had stood here since colonial days. We left our camels in the wadi with Ahmed, and I was escorted to the police station for questioning. My worst fear was that I would be repatriated. I was guiltily aware that I had behaved irresponsibly in leaving Tina secretly, but I knew that if I always allowed myself to be governed by bureaucracy, I should never be able to travel in the remote areas that I craved.

The cell had one window, barred and covered in mosquito-netting and through it, in a blaze of sunlight, I could see an expanse of sand and a thick acacia tree. Two boys were playing beneath the tree. They were as black as pitch, and their clothes in ragged shreds. Their game, as always in the Sudan, seemed to consist of a competition to make the most ear-piercing screech.

Beyond the children, up the steep slope of the wadi bank, I could make out the squat outline of the old British colonial headquarters, its shock of home-counties thatch looking grey but intact. This very building, I knew, had been used by those two almost legendary characters of the Sudan's recent history – Guy Moore and Wilfred Thesiger. I wondered ruefully and very unfairly if my reception in Kutum, a town I had often longed to visit, would have been different had these two still been in office.

Now, sitting in my cell, I felt suddenly apprehensive about what was to come. My guards had not warned me what I should expect. Though I was not in physical fear of the forthcoming interrogation, I was worried that this might mean the end of my wanderings in the Sudan.

'*Min wayn inta?* Where are you from, you?'

My interrogator spat out the last word as if it were something distasteful to him, and I watched the small fleck of spittle which accompanied it as it landed on the table in front of me. He was a lean, spare man, very black but with finely chiselled features and a mop of frizzly hair which sat like a cap on the back of his skull. He wore the uniform of a captain of police, immaculately pressed. I guessed from his features that he was not a local Darfuri, but from one of the Arab-Nubian river tribes who are almost a ruling élite in the Sudan.

'*Shaghal shinu inta?* What do you work at?'

I answered that I was a British teacher, based in Gineina, but my Arabic stumbled out, and he gave me no chance to complete the sentence.

'What have you come here for? And why did you come by camel? *Khawajas* don't ride camels. If you are British, show me your passport and visas.'

I had no papers, I argued, the police in Gineina had given me none. My passport was in Khartoum, to have the visa renewed. The captain regarded me disbelievingly.

'No one is allowed to travel without papers. It is forbidden. Now, where are your papers?'

'I have no papers.'

And so it continued with interminable monotony. I felt sure that the officer must realize that I was telling the truth, for I mentioned the names of people I knew, and described places with which I was familiar. Still, I had no papers. He seemed unduly keen on extolling the possible punishments for spying, which seemed to include everything from incarceration to being taken out and shot.

'But you have notes,' he said suddenly. 'The Camel Corps troopers saw you making notes.'

I explained that I had a diary and some other notes in my saddlebags. 'Then why, by God, didn't you bring them? You knew you'd be questioned.'

He sighed and called to a trooper who had been waiting outside. The man shuffled in, his tattered and ill-fitting uniform in marked contrast with that of his superior. He saluted sloppily.

'Take this man to his camel and bring back his papers. All of them. Understand?'

'Yes, *ya sayyidi*.'

It was a short walk to the wadi, where the Zaghawa guide, Ahmed, was minding my camel and equipment. From the police post it was a striking sight: a wide swath of pale golden sand winding beneath cohorts of huge *heraz* trees and lined with date palms which leaned over at curious angles. It was market-day in Kutum and the wadi bed was filled by literally hundreds of camels belonging to the local tribes. Between the ranks of the couched animals the tribesmen had piled their luggage, and the smoke of many fires curled upwards from the sandy floor. Scores of people from a dozen different tribes moved in ever-changing patterns around the mud-brick and timber stalls of the marketplace.

As we approached the wadi, a horrific thought struck me. My papers were in a canvas holdall inside my saddlebag, and in the same holdall was the .22 revolver. The discovery of the pistol in my luggage would do little to alleviate suspicion of my being a spy. I had thought it miraculous that the Camel Corps had not searched me, but I had virtually forgotten about the weapon since my arrest. If, as he had been ordered, the policeman took all my papers, the gun would almost certainly be found. We found Ahmed amongst the legions of tribesmen, and he stood up to greet us, shaking hands with the policeman.

'Is everything all right, Makil?' he asked.

'I've got to take some things to the captain,' I answered.

I turned to my saddlebag with a sinking feeling, when something unexpected happened. Ahmed said a word to the trooper in the Zaghawa dialect, which I did not understand. The officer launched suddenly into a dialogue in the same language. The two men greeted for a second time, touching each other on the shoulder as was the custom amongst close friends or relatives. I guessed that they had discovered a family relationship, for they continued talking animatedly. While they were occupied in this way, I seized my chance. I quickly found the holdall, opened it, removed the diary and a sheaf of notes and replaced it without hesitation.

'Right, got them,' I said.

Without even a glance at the documents, the trooper began to say farewell to Ahmed, and a few moments later we started back together up the steep bank of the wadi. Not for the first time I thanked providence for the closeness of tribal ties in the Sudan.

Back at the police post, the captain and another officer examined the papers sternly, asking questions about places I had visited and dates. They seemed amazed that I had managed to get so far without being stopped by the police. I did not explain that I had only managed to evade them by subterfuge on two occasions. Eventually, the captain closed the book and laid it on his desk. He drew his hands together and regarded me rather as I might have regarded a wayward pupil.

'In this country we respect our teachers,' he began. 'We think you are telling the truth. We could punish you for having no papers,' he paused to let this sink in, 'but I have decided not to.'

A flash of relief shot across my brow. After all, there was to be no humiliating repatriation, as I had feared. But he continued, 'But listen to me well. You must give up these foolish ideas of travelling in the desert on a camel. What can a *khawaja* know of the desert? You will die of thirst. Or the Arabs will get you, them or the Bedayatt. There are men who will kill anyone for a camel.'

'Yes, I understand,' I said, as meekly as possible, not wanting to endanger my position by explaining that I had already crossed thousands of miles of desert with the Arabs, or that the Bedayatt, with whom I had travelled, had been my means of escaping the police only a few weeks before. I stood up and prepared to leave, but the captain waved me back.

'And one more thing,' he said. 'There is a lorry going to El Fasher the day after tomorrow. Be on it!'

I realized then that there was to be no triumphant return to Gineina on my camel. I must sell the animal and go back by detested motor transport. The police, after all, had laughed last. I walked out feeling disconsolate, trying to gauge the import of my punishment. As I left the police building, my eyes settled again on the old house of Thesiger and Moore, crouched fortress-like in the sloping sand. I felt a sudden surge of envy for them. In their day, the world had been different, a simpler world with fewer borders or restrictions. Or had it? Had the government, now in the 1980s, any greater hold on the desert than they had had in the

1930s? The world I had seen out there was one where the law was the law of the tribes, where the people acknowledged not overlords but God and the desert itself. I determined merely to make sure I avoided the police more efficiently on my next journey into the sands.

12

THE HUNDREDTH NAME

Only the camel is great.

Arab saying

For the first months of 1981 I chafed at my tether in Gineina. I felt like a captive in my classroom, itching to escape once again to the more primitive world I had discovered out in the *qoz*. My only contact with this other world was the cattlemarket, out on the very edge of the town, where each day Arabs of the nomadic tribes, the Mahamid, Mahriyya, Awlad Rashid, Bani Halba and others congregated with their animals. They mixed with camel-breeders from Chad, the Gor'an and the Bedayatt, who ran their small herds in from across the border, where the country was in chaos.

These two elements, the Arabs and the Saharans, with their traditional rivalries, gave the market an atmosphere which was vibrant with electricity. Usually a truce was declared on this neutral ground, though occasionally there were fights and verbal exchanges. It was there that I felt most strongly the sense of timelessness which was now a familiar sensation to me, and which I had come to crave like some narcotic, and I arranged my work so that I could visit the place as often as possible.

My old acquaintance, Shaykh Rashid Omar, was the dominant figure in the market. With the other shaykhs and *umdas* or senior shaykhs of the nomadic tribes, he controlled much of the sale of camels, horses, cows and sheep. When I met him there, about a week after returning from El Fasher, he embraced me as if I were a prodigal, and led me off to an enclosed shelter, where eight or nine other distinguished-looking Arabs were sitting cross-legged on the floor. Rashid introduced me to them as the shaykhs of the Umm Sayf Al Din, Awlad Iid, Awlad Zayd, and Shenabla sections of the Mahamid, and the *umdas* of the Bani Halba and Messeriyya. After we were seated, he told me that he had heard about my arrest by the Camel Corps, and questioned me carefully about all I had seen and done in Dar Zaghawa and the desert.

'By God, but you were lucky to reach Tina!' he said. 'Just after you left some Gor'an came across the border and attacked the Messeriyya, as Shaykh Abdallah Janumma will tell you.' He gestured to a rather mischievous-looking man with over-large ears, who took up the story.

'Yes,' he began. 'We made a big camel-camp near Wadi Sirba. The Gor'an came by day, about forty of them, riding camels. They all were armed with automatics, by God, and you know where those came from! What could we do? They lifted a hundred camels, and took them off into Chad.'

'Didn't you send a search-party?' I asked.

'Yes, by God, we picked up their tracks at once and went after them on horses, twenty of us armed with rifles. They were travelling fast, but the herd slowed them down, and we caught up with them after a few hours. We could do nothing, though, for their rifles were better, and they knew how to fight. Only eighteen of us returned. And no camels. Two of my brothers died.'

'God have mercy upon them.'

'The Gor'an are strong,' Rashid continued. 'Many of them fought with the French Camel Corps. They steal camels because they love it, and they fear no one.'

It seemed that these raids across the border were increasing. The Gor'an and Bedayatt, dislodged from their homelands by government forces, were finding the Sudan easy prey, and they could pillage herds and even villages without fear of retaliation from any forces on their own side of the border. The reports I had heard suggested that anarchy was the order of things inside Chad, and that each tribe, now armed to the teeth, was vying with the others for dominance. Beneath these raids, though, lay the ancient feud between the Saharan nomads and the Arabs which had affected this area for generations.

Rashid Omar told me that he himself had recently returned from a journey 'to the south, on business'. I guessed, partly from the stories I had heard, that he had been into Chad, where it was reputed that he had dealings with the government defence minister, Asiil, who was himself an Arab. The nomads on this side of the border favoured Asiil, simply because he stood against the Gor'an and Bedayatt who were harassing them with increasing force.

In such a lawless situation, tribal *damins* such as Rashid and his friends were extremely important. If any tribesman wished to sell an animal, he must first ask his *damin*, a kind of guarantor, who then recommended the tribesman's character to the buyer. The *damin* was then responsible, should the stock turn out to be stolen, for finding the vendor and bringing him to justice. His authority depended on the consent of the tribe, and therefore his position was strong only as long as he did his job well. Each *damin* had a signet ring, with which he endorsed the certificate of sale. The ring was a symbol of his position, and was handed down from father to son, unless the rest of the tribe disagreed. Some *damins* such as Rashid were famous all over the region, and were responsible for many tribes, although often I heard it said that the *damins* were far more dishonest than any of the people they were asked to represent.

Later the same day, Rashid invited me to eat at his house. The house was full of people who had come to consult the shaykh about disputes over the ownership of animals and debts. Many nomadic families profited by herding camels which belonged to rich merchants, farmers of the settled tribes or townsmen. The Arabs were not paid in cash, but in animals: a certain number of camels each year in proportion to the number they were herding. This often went on for many years. The problem was that the herdsmen could easily claim that a camel had been stolen, or died, or simply that a female had not given birth, when in fact she had. It was difficult for the owners to prove that the nomads were lying, though the custom was that if a camel died, its skin with the appropriate brands should be shown to the owner. This then absolved the herdsman from blame. Thus, although a townsman might expect his herd to increase over the years, more often it became depleted, and I heard of one case in which Rashid's own family had herded a mob of three hundred camels which over fifteen years had been reduced to no more than twenty.

At his house Rashid asked me about the two camels I had bought from him, and sold in Tina. I told him that I had not been happy with them. 'They were badly behaved,' I said, 'and the large bull kept trying to bite me. I lost money on them in Tina.'

'It is not possible for a camel to be badly behaved,' the shaykh told me. 'They are not humans. They don't have manners! No, the rider is to blame if the camel is uncontrollable.'

Although I respected the shaykh, I knew that this was partly to defend himself from any suggestion that he might have caused me to buy bad camels. I knew from talking to other Arabs that some camels *were* more badly behaved than others, for there were even special words for their different traits. I knew too that the Arabs were honourable men in almost every sphere but that which lay closest to their heart: camels. I was no longer the gullible *khawaja* I had been when I had first met the shaykh, and now I felt angry, because I could see that the Arabs took advantage of their special knowledge of animals to defraud not only strangers like myself, but also anyone who was not a nomad as they were. I did not blame them for this: it was their livelihood. But I was determined that I should never again be cheated over a camel. This meant that I should have to set myself the task of learning everything I could about these odd animals, which, like the Arabs, I had come to love.

Some weeks later, I watched one of the *damins* selling a camel to a Mesalit tribesman. The prospective buyer was a small man with the good-humoured, rather childlike features of his tribe. The little man stood amongst a jostling crowd of Arabs, all talking at once to him and to each other about the superb qualities of the camel he was considering, which of course belonged to their family. The *damin*, Amir Ahmed, a young man with fair skin and smooth features, was examining the camel.

'By God, brother, he's strong,' he was saying. 'Look at his legs, no extra fat on them. And isn't his hump fat? He doesn't look too old, either. Let's see the teeth.' He parted the animal's jaws with a deft movement. 'Look! Not got his upper teeth yet! Plenty of work left in him!'

The little Mesalati seemed unimpressed by the flow of rhetoric. 'Let's see him walk,' he said.

Amir called to an Arab lad in the crowd, and the youth came forward. He was as lightly boned as a bird, with handsome, delicate features. He took the headrope and stepped easily on to the camel's bare back, seating himself just behind the hump. He flicked the animal's flank with the end of the rope, and sent him into a sharp trot, cleaving a path through the nodding heads of the tribesmen, bringing the animal round in a tight circle and couching it at the Mesalati's feet. He jumped off lightly, as Amir said, 'How's that?', a question which brought murmurs of approval from the onlookers.

'Seems all right,' said the Mesalati. 'How much?'

'No, you name it,' said one of the Arabs. 'The buyer must name it.'

The little farmer looked at the *damin*. 'A hundred and fifty!' Amir said.

'May God open!' declared the owner.

'A hundred and fifty-five!'

'May God open!'

So it continued in the customary way, Amir offering prices and the owner praying God to open. At two hundred, the negotiations suddenly broke down. The owner flung his arms in the air, and shouted in a high-pitched voice: 'By God, Amir! You are trying to cheat me! This is a fine camel! Look at it. Is it not fine? How can you offer such a low price?'

Amir regarded the owner with a trace of aggression. 'It's a good camel. But this man wants it only to carry his goods. He is not a rich man. And is not two hundred a good price?'

'Never! May God open!'

Amir touched the little Mesalati cordially on the arm, and led him a little way from the crowd. I could not hear what was being said, as they spoke in whispers, but I could guess. The Mesalati had previously told the *damin* to bid up to two hundred pounds for him. Now Amir was 'advising' the farmer to increase the bid. I knew by now that this whole process of offer and rejection, the righteous anger, the small conference were all part of the same practised performance which I had seen enacted over and over again. I myself had been caught out many times by the same conspiracy. Amir, supposedly buying the animal for his 'customer', was actually receiving a commission from the vendors. I saw the farmer nod; the *damin* walked over to the owner, and led him away for a similar conference. I guessed that a good price had been agreed upon. Judging by previous performances, there could at this stage have been another burst of angry talk from the owner, and another round of negotiations. This time, it seemed, a good price had been reached quickly, or Amir had decided that the Mesalati had no more money.

'How much?' someone shouted.

'Two hundred and twenty!' the owner cried. 'By God, I'm letting it go for nothing!'

Indeed, it did seem cheap for its age and size, and immediately I suspected that there was something I had missed. I watched as the *damin* urged the buyer to present the Arab with a ten-pound note, the customary pledge of good faith, which he did. Then as the Arabs led the camel away towards the hut of the clerk, I saw what I and the Mesalati had missed. On the animal's left side, just above the gristly chest-pad, was a small patch of dry skin, with the slightest trace of blood upon it. It was the tell-tale sign of what the Arabs called *zabata*:

a condition in which the camel's foreleg rubbed against one side of its chest, making it a little slow in walking, and unable to carry the heaviest loads. The Mesalati was obviously a stranger to the camel-market.

I knew about this ailment of camels simply because I myself had once owned a beast which had been suffering from it, and had only found out when the time had come to sell it. In fact I had lost money on many of the camels I had bought, generally because there was something wrong with them. I had learned the hard way.

My first task was to learn the considerable terminology of the camel. There is a different name for the animal in every stage of its life, for females in different stages of pregnancy and motherhood, for different colours, traits, states and conditions. The age of the camel is judged by the development of its teeth, and the Arabs can read a camel's mouth as perfectly as I can read a book. As I slowly began to master these terms, I turned my attention to being able to distinguish between a good camel and a bad one. There are certain defects for which one had to be vigilant: flaps of useless fat on the legs, a drooping neck, bad joints at the knee or ankle, blindness in one eye or disease in the skin or chest-pad. Once aware of these, spotting them became easy, but what was far more difficult to assess in the confines of the market was the temperament of the camel. A good temperament is essential for a riding-camel, but the great problem is that the Arabs and other tribes refuse to sell any but their inferior animals, for obvious reasons. Some camels look powerful, but are 'lazy', others are highly strung and might throw their rider. Camels reared in the *qoz* are often terrified of buildings, streets and crowds, while those accustomed to human habitation are often uncontrollable outside the town. One of the most dangerous types is the *sharaat*, the camel which fears human beings and is likely to run away at any opportunity.

Camels generally do not bite their riders, which is fortunate because their powerful jaws and sharp teeth can easily kill or maim. It is said, however, that camels remember those who have done them harm and will strike back when they are least expecting it. A close friend of mine in Gineina once told me of an instance witnessed by his father, who had been a Camel Corps trooper escorting a dispatch rider through the Libyan Desert between Dongola and Khartoum. The dispatch rider had beaten his camel severely during the day, but after sunset the animal had gone well, and the man loosened his grip on the headrope and was talking amicably with his companion. Suddenly, the camel turned its head and seized him by the arm, dashing him from its back

against some rocks. My friend's father had at once shot the berserk
animal in the head, but on examining the dispatch rider, he found him
already dead. I heard dozens of stories of this kind during my years in
the Sudan.

The most dangerous time for a bull camel is when he is in season,
which is usually in the rainy season or in winter. At this time, the bull
blows from his mouth a bulbous pink bladder, like the one I had seen
on the camel which had attacked me near Malemal Hosh. When in
season, the camel is likely to attack any human being who gets in his
way, and I saw this myself during 1982, in Gineina market.

It was January, and the weather was still relatively cool, and some
Bani Halba had brought in a large bull camel from the *qoz*. He was one
of the biggest camels I had ever seen, and from his superb condition I
judged that he had been kept as a stud. I walked past the place where
he had been couched and hobbled, and remember noticing the strange
gurgling sound which he made and the froth which dripped from his
jaws, a sure sign that he was about to inflate his mouth-bladder. I had
gone over to greet some Mahamid Arabs whom I knew, when I heard a
piercing scream and a great commotion around the area of the great
bull. Turning to look, I saw a crowd of Arabs gathered, and some
sticks flailing in the air. Dashing over, we were just in time to see a
young Mesalit tribesman being dragged from the dripping maw of the
camel. His *sirwel* was torn and bloody, and the curious angle of his leg
suggested that it had been crushed. As the Bani Halba pulled the
victim clear, they beat the bull ferociously on the head and neck with
their staves. He heaved and roared, trying to dodge the blows, and at
the same time to sink his teeth into his assailants. I hoped sincerely
that his hobbles would not snap, for he was a mighty creature, and
could have done a great deal of damage amongst us. Eventually, though,
the Arabs managed to fix a rope over his head, and then a *silsil* chain.
Once he was well strung up, five or six Arabs gave him a tremendous
thrashing with whips and sticks.

I asked later what the Mesalati had done to deserve such an attack,
and one of the Bani Halba told me, 'Nothing. He was just walking past
and the camel grabbed him. Rose on his knees, stretched out his neck,
and grabbed him – would not have let him go if we hadn't beaten him.
A mating camel will attack someone without any reason!' When I
remembered that I had walked past the bull a few moments before the
tribesman, I thought myself extremely fortunate.

It was a hard battle to get myself accepted in the camel-market as a serious camel lover. The Arabs were willing to sell me camels, but at first found it very amusing that a *khawaja* should want to ride one. It was even harder to get them to teach me about the animals, and I sensed that this was partly to do with the fact that they wanted to preserve their own mastery of the mystique of the camel, just as they saw mystique in the European's mastery of things mechanical, though I myself had no such skills and hated machines. It took me a long time to break down this cultural barrier, but eventually I managed to learn enough about camels to talk to the Arabs intelligently about them. The greatest hostility came from Arab children, who at the age of nine or ten knew more about camels than I probably ever would. Often, when I rode about on my camels, these kids would shout out, 'Hey, *khawaja*! Your camel's got no balls!' This was a terrible insult to the Arabs, who identified with the virility of their camels. The first time I heard it, though, I dismounted to see if it were true as soon as I was safely out of sight.

The Arab sense of superiority came out in their claim that the *zurqa* were afraid of camels. The Mesalit had many camels, though some of the settled peoples were afraid of them. These people tended to buy the most docile animals, and to use them for carrying. The Arabs loved spirited animals which would jump up and run at the slightest touch, since these were useful in raids or pursuits. For a riding-camel, they preferred a *raba'* over short distances, as these immature bulls ran very fast and were extremely light of foot. The fully grown adult males were preferred in the desert itself, or for long distances, since they had more stamina. The best camels came from the Butana in the east of the Sudan, and were reared by tribes such as the Bishariyyin and Shukriyya. These were a special breed, known as *bishari*, and it was said that one could place a cup of water on their shoulders, and so smooth was their step that even at a gallop it would not spill. They were imported by Arabia and the Gulf States as racing camels and were the most successful in the world. It was always my ambition to own one of these dromedaries, though there were none in the west of the Sudan.

Apart from the negro farmers, the other important buyers of camels were the *samasra* or merchants, who built up their own herds and exported them to Libya and Egypt. Originally, Libya had been the best market, as the Libyans paid in hard currency. In 1980, however, the Libyans closed the route to the Sudanese, because of the tension over Chad, and the merchants turned to Egypt, which had been importing Sudanese camels since the 1930s. The Sudan had replaced

Arabia as the most successful camel-rearing country in the world. There were officially estimated to be three million head of camels in the country, as opposed to six hundred thousand in Saudi Arabia, though the Sudanese figure, at least, may have been only a third of the actual number.

At first, years before in Dongola, I had regarded the camel merely with interest: nothing more than an extension of my two feet, which unaided were inadequate for the purpose of desert travel. By now, however, I had begun to see the animal as the Arabs saw it, as a figure of beauty and grace. Most Europeans think of the camel as an ugly or comical beast, because they are not acquainted with its qualities. They tend to judge its shape against that of the horse, with which they are familiar. The Arabs have revered the camel's beauty for centuries, and much of their early poetry is devoted to this animal: the camel is mentioned in the Holy Koran as an example of God's wisdom. It is said that only ninety-nine of God's names have been revealed to man. The camel smiles because he knows the hundredth.

As my visits to Rashid Omar's house continued, the shaykh's presence there and in the market became less frequent. Often his son Omar told me he had gone 'south'. Once, I saw him in the main market of Gineina, riding his black stallion, with his kinsman Baraka Mubarak and some other Arabs. He looked a magnificent sight and he stopped to greet me, his great turban piled up like an exotic crown and his white robes flying behind him.

'Where are you going, Shaykh?' I asked him.

'South,' he replied.

I watched the group of horsemen as they disappeared into the market crowds. That was the last time I saw Shaykh Rashid Omar alive.

Throughout the first part of 1981 the incursions of the Gor'an and Bedayatt into the Sudan continued. The Awlad Janub sub-clan of the Mahamid lost three hundred camels in a single day to fifty Gor'an who came armed with machine-guns and automatic rifles. The Gor'an were Habri's guerrillas who needed the camels for food. It was rumoured that the Libyan Polisario fighting in Chad were not Libyans but Sudanese who had been working in Libya. Habri himself could be seen in Gineina from time to time, organizing offensives into Chad, while his men were organizing offensives in the opposite direction: into the Sudan.

By July 1981, the situation had become even worse. The Libyan airforce was bombing Kulbus and Tina, and there were forays over

Gineina itself. Two Libyan Jaguars were shot down by the guerrillas right over the school, and of the crews which baled out, one was found to be a Sudanese pilot, recruited in Libya. There were rumours that Sudanese *jebha* working for Libya were infiltrating the Sudan, and there were many arrests. An Arab of the Mahamid was arrested in Khartoum, trying to blow up Habri's HQ there with a device given him in Tripoli.

One day in November I noticed that Omar, son of Shaykh Rashid, was missing from my evening classes, in which he was a student. No one knew where he was, but later in the day I happened to walk past the town police post. The station had an external lock-up, like something out of the Wild West: it had a barred door through which the felons could be seen peering at any hour of the day. On this day, I realized with a shock that it was Omar's face which was peering out at me. I went over to ask what was wrong and he told me sheepishly that he and his father had both been arrested in connection with the war in Chad. I asked the police captain if I could bail him out, but the officer told me politely that it was a security problem, for which the secret police were responsible.

A week later he was released without punishment, and he told me that he had been arrested at the border, trying to get into Chad to join the Libyan forces. His father had been arrested at the same time. I had long suspected that the shaykh was a recruiting agent for Asiil, but the full story did not become apparent until that December, when I heard that Rashid Omar had died. He had gone 'south' once too often. His business trips, as I had suspected, were illegal journeys into Chad, where as an Arab who had once moved in and out of the country constantly, he knew all the secret routes and safe areas. On several occasions he had brought home to his Arabs news of the Libyan Polisario, the troops fighting in Chad against Habri's Gor'an and Bedayatt. Many of these soldiers were Arabs of the Rizayqat. After one trip, he returned saying that the Arabs in Libyan service had been pressed into the army against their own will when they had gone to Libya to find jobs. However, Asiil was prepared to release the sons and husbands of the Rizayqat families, if a certain amount of money was paid. Rashid was charged to collect that amount.

He duly collected the money from the tribes and transported it secretly across the border. Some months later, he returned. None of the sons of the Rizayqat were with him. He said that Asiil had taken the money, then refused to release the fighters. Then Rashid really had gone south: down to the Mahamid *damr* in Wadi Habila. It was here that he had met his death, stabbed and beaten by the angry Arabs whom he had either cheated or failed.

It seemed almost a fitting end for one who had lived by cunning as he had, yet I could not help regretting the death of the most colourful character I had met in the Sudan. As I watched his son Omar, who at the age of nineteen took responsibility for the entire family, women, goats, camels and cows, and accepted the responsibility of his father's signet ring, the symbol of his new position amongst the Arabs, I could not help feeling intensely curious about the nature of the future *damin* of the Mahamid.

13

SEASON OF MIGRATION
TO THE SOUTH

From Gineina I decided to set out into the ranges of Dar Mesalit. Although I had travelled in the desert, I had never seen anything of the family life of Sudan's nomadic tribes, and now my plan was to find the nomads who were at that time on their annual migrations to the south through the Dar Mesalit. Luckily, I had made a friend in Gineina: a fellow teacher named Mohammed Hissein Mukhtar, himself an Arab of the Zayadiyya tribe, who agreed to travel with me as a *rafiq*. We left Gineina riding my two camels, an old bull, strong but slow, and an excitable five-year-old.

As we drew out of the rows of grass huts which made up the town, I felt the old familiar excitement welling up inside me: the freedom and exhilaration of the desert. For two days we travelled in Mesalit country, crossing occasional cultivated fields of millet, descending into watercourses and passing below the peaks of mountains. The witches' caps of Mesalit villages peered at us over the tall grasses, and we passed bare-breasted women toiling in the fields while their menfolk sat in the shade and drank the local beer, known as *merissa*. Though alcohol is forbidden in Islam, *merissa* drinking was a Mesalit tradition going back to the times when the tribe were renowned as warriors. It seemed to me, though, that the women, who worked in the fields, cooked, reared the children and built the houses, had an extremely hard life. Mohammed thought so too.

'For the Mesalit men, buying a wife is like buying a tractor,' he said. 'If you have four wives, you have four tractors! You are a wealthy man!'

Everywhere we asked for news of the nomads and then, by chance, in the third day, we almost rode into a family of Arabs of the Mahamid section of the Rizayqat. I will never forget the sight which met my eyes as the Arabs came towards us. There was a small herd of camels, being marshalled by some oldish men on horses, but the herd was led by a gigantic male camel, carrying on its back a black litter. This was almost like a small house or shelter, built on a special frame, which fitted over the saddle. The frame was draped with skins and cloth and around it were attached all kinds of baskets, leather and wooden vessels, which represented all the nomads' worldly possessions. The camel was decorated with a headdress of jet-black ostrich feathers, and a variety of plaited leather necklaces, from which streamers of hide cascaded, decorating its head and neck. More ornate streamers tumbled from special saddlebags at the animal's flanks. Within the depths of the litter, known in Arabic as the *howdaj*, I could make out the thin pale face of a woman. The whole pageant was a magnificent and spectacular sight, and Mohammed and I halted our camels to watch it as it drifted towards us across an open plain of desert.

The Arabs stopped to greet us as the procession passed by, and told us that they had been far north, into the country of the Zaghawa, and were now returning to their winter grazing grounds around Gineina. This southern movement they called *mowta*, and it was the custom amongst the Rizayqat tribes that the women and children moved with the men, leaving only the very old and the very weak in the semi-permanent summer camps. These Arabs were grumbling about the Mesalit, whose territory they were now crossing. As often happened, the harvest had come late this year, which meant that on their way south, the camels had to pass through unharvested Mesalit cultivation. For every camel which entered a Mesalit field, the Rizayqat were obliged to pay one pound, though often they would refuse and this sometimes led to clashes. Only a few years ago there had been a full-scale war between the Mesalit and the Mahamid, resulting in a number of killings. The Arabs maintained that these were their traditional lines of migration, dating back centuries. The Mesalit, of course, had an equally strong claim to the land on which their livelihood depended. The Mahamid told us that the whole of their clan was travelling on this route, though the main body of them had already passed south. If we continued north, they told us, we would find the tail-end of the migration.

Sure enough, that evening just at sunset, right on cue it seemed, we came across a Mahamid family camped in the bed of a watercourse. As soon as they saw us, the men came running out, and as we couched our camels they clasped each of us by the hand, saying, 'Welcome! Welcome!' over and over. Though by now I was accustomed to Sudanese hospitality, I was bowled over by the openness with which these men received us.

They had built an overnight camp in the shade of two trees, where the women had erected a tent. The men sat on rugs in the bed of the wadi, and produced glasses of strong, black tea on a metal tray.

'Why do you stay here, brothers?' Mohammed Hissein asked.

'One of our calves is ill, by God! Don't you hear the *naqa*?' said an old, old man, whose face seemed to have been wrought with hammer and chisel rather than formed from flesh and bone. It was only then that I became aware of a piteous wailing sound, and the old man directed my gaze to the base of one of the trees, where a large cow camel stood fidgeting nervously around a light bundle of fur stretched out on the ground.

'She has just given birth,' continued the old man. 'But the calf is ill. Perhaps it will live. God knows!'

After drinking tea, we turned the camels loose on the wadi banks to graze with the Arabs' small herd. I stood on a high point and watched the last embers of the sun burning out, taking in the camels, lumpy shapes moving in the grass, goats bleating, the moan of the distressed *naqa*, the women, grey ghosts amongst their piled-up saddlery, pounding spices in huge mortars carved from wood. It seemed to me a scene of perfect beauty and peace, an age away from the town, with these people whose entire worldly possessions were now laid out under two trees in the gathering darkness. And what I felt for the lives of these men was envy. I knew that somehow I wanted to be like them, to embrace their way of life: yet at the same time I knew that no matter what, I could never be completely accepted by them. I was still as far removed from them as a visitor from another planet.

We met again in the wadi to eat *'asida* and drink more tea. Mohammed explained to me that in a camp such as this, the men would always sleep and sit apart from the women. As we ate, we talked of the migrations. The Mahamid said that they had begun to move north in June, at the beginning of the rainy season, and like the Mahamid we had met earlier they had been north into Dar Zaghawa.

I asked if the whole tribe always moved at the same time, and one of the Arabs said, 'Yes, we all travel on the same day, unless something prevents us. That's because of raiders. This route is a very dangerous one, by God the Great! And it's getting worse!'

'You mean raiders from the Mesalit?' I asked.

'Never!' the man scoffed. 'It's the Bedayatt and the Gor'an we have to be careful of. They have many weapons because of the war in Chad, and they know how to use them! A small family on its own in that area would be eaten, by God!'

I asked how long they would stay in one place during their migrations.

'Not more than five days or a week usually,' the old man said. 'Then we move on for a few hours or a day, until we find another good place.'

The Mahamid explained that some of their number were fighting on both sides in the Chadian war, though most of them were supporters of Gikoni Wadai, the President of Chad, merely because their enemies, the Gor'an and Bedayatt, supported his rival, Hissein Habri. They told us that they were neither Sudanese nor Chadians. 'We are Arab,' said one of the men. 'And our enemies are the *zurqa*, especially the Gor'an and Bedayatt.'

They were curious about me, and though they were familiar with the word *Ingleez*, they said that undoubtedly my people were Arabs. 'In fact,' said the old man, 'you *Ingleez* are the nobility. It is said that the father of the *afranj* was Abu Jahil, one of the noble Quraysh, who was born in the days before the birth of the Prophet, may prayer and peace be upon him. He travelled to the land of the *afranj* and married one of their women. He forgot the noble tongue of the Arabs and began to talk in a strange tongue, as you do.'

I was both surprised and a little embarrassed by the story, although I did not wish to insult my host by contradicting him in what was evidently considered a compliment. But I was tempted to smile when Mohammed whispered to me in English, 'Rubbish!'

Later, the men brought us a bowl of camels' milk. It was steaming hot and the Arabs had added a little flour to the liquid, giving it the consistency of thick cream.

The next day we left the Arabs in their camp and went off in search of the main body of the tribe. We followed the meandering course of the wadi until it narrowed into shallow creeks which were overshadowed by the canopies of *nabak* and *heraz* trees, hung with bunches of catkins and wreathed in white butterflies. We passed occasional Mesalit settlements, and once saw a camp of the Bani Halba cattlenomads, whose houses were hemispherical huts of matting, like straw igloos, quite distinct from both the tents of the Mahamid and the beehive cabins of the Mesalit. Around the village was gathered a large herd of cattle, black, white, red and brown. I was surprised to find the Bani Halba so far north, for I knew that their homeland was south Darfur. Mohammed told me that recently they had begun to move further into Dar Mesalit, and to acquire camels instead of cows.

Later that day we arrived at some boreholes in the wadi bed, where a group of Mahamid were watering horses. They greeted us warmly and immediately invited us to stay at their camp, which lay in a nearby thicket of thornbush. It was the largest camp I had seen, consisting of twenty or thirty tents, divided into family groups. Each family seemed to have its own small area. Our host, Abdal Kariim, was shaykh of one of the families. He and his relatives helped us to unsaddle our camels and showed us to an area of rugs and canvas sheets, at some distance from the tents.

As we sat, drinking water flavoured with buttermilk, many men and youths came up to greet us with tremendous grace. They were obviously unaccustomed to seeing skin as fair as mine, and many jokes were bandied around about my having come to collect taxes or to take someone away. It always seemed curious to me, on my travels, to be associated with the government – a leftover from the days of Turkish, Egyptian and then British rule when the government had been in the hands of white men. Some of the tribesmen I met in remote areas of the Sudan seemed quite unaware that the government had changed hands.

Soon, however, the attention of the Mahamid was turned to Mohammed Hissein. They questioned him closely about his origins, in a rather suspicious way. Luckily, although he normally spoke in the standard dialect of the towns, as I did, he was able to switch to the distinctive patois of the nomad, and I saw that they were soon satisfied with his Arab status. Mohammed himself was intensely proud of his Arab background, and regarded the Mahamid as being related to the Zayadiyya.

As this was my first experience of a camp of this size, I was interested to see how the Arabs arranged their lives. The tents which they used were elaborate affairs, consisting of thick sheets of canvas hoisted over wooden frames. In the past they had used skin tents, but this canvas had become available due to recent trade with Libya, and had replaced the old-style shelters. I admired the way in which the Arabs had only accepted that facet of progress which was adaptable to their way of life, rather than adapting their culture to new developments.

At sunset the camels were brought in from the fringes of the wood and gathered around the tents, where they were hobbled. Mohammed and I brought in our own camels, and hobbled them by the fire in the men's area, the *dara*, couching them with their heads towards the fireplace.

'They always like to see what's going on,' Mohammed told me. 'And it's the custom to let them face the fire.'

After dark we ate more *'asida,* and the Mahamid gathered in the *dara* to talk. They were discussing the next day's move, and though Abdal Kariim was the head of the family, the decision as to where and when to move seemed to be taken communally. Even small boys aged no more than nine or ten had a part to play in these discussions, and were listened to politely when they spoke.

Amongst these nomadic Arabs, a boy became an adult at his circumcision, which might be performed at the age of eight or nine. The event was marked by a great celebration, for which all the relatives and friends would gather. Animals would be slaughtered, and all the children would be dressed in new clothes. Usually the operation would be performed on a group of boys, who would be brought forward in turn to sit on a upturned water-container. The cutting was usually done with a sharp knife by a skilled man of the tribe, though the process could be long and painful, taking up to thirty minutes. During this time the boy was expected to remain mute, and to encourage him the girls and youths of the family would sing traditional songs such as, 'Ox, son of the ox, an ox remain!' It was considered a great disgrace to cry out, and the boy who let his parents down in this way would be shunned and branded a coward. With such a social stigma at stake, of course, it was rare for a child to break down. After the operation had been successfully completed, the Arabs would fire off their rifles and celebrate with a great feast. From that moment on there would be a change in the boy's status in the tribe. He would be considered capable of defending the tribe's camels and womenfolk, and as a sign of his manhood he was allowed to wear a dagger.

Amongst these tribes there was a tremendous feeling of family unity, each man being considered an important part of the workforce of the tribe. Old men were respected for their age, but generally a man's standing in the tribe depended on the number of camels he owned. The women were considered to be inferior and were not allowed a part in the decision-making of the tribe. In practice, however, most of the men listened closely to the advice of mothers and wives. A wife could be chosen for a boy soon after his circumcision, and it was customary to choose a first cousin. The marriage would be celebrated, and con-summated several years later, by which time the boy would be in a position to pay the bride-price. Traditionally amongst the Arabs this was one female camel, though in recent years even camels, it seemed, had been subject to inflation, and up to nine or ten camels might now be paid.

When the Mahamid had finished their discussions that evening, they began to talk to Mohammed and me. They were interested to know why I had come to see them, and why I was riding a camel.

'Why don't you work in an office?' asked one of the younger men.

I grinned to myself, and wondered what this young man with thousands of acres of desert and semi-desert in which to roam would think of spending his life in a few square feet of stifling space, crowded with millions of other humans within a few square miles of ground. I was tempted to say that the Arabs had everything in their lives, though they did not know it. Then it suddenly struck me that perhaps they were quite aware of the quality of their lives.

I learned later, indeed, that the Arabs called their migrations 'the glory of the Arabs', and considered them to be an important part of their lives. Before each move, they would meet as they had done on this night, to discuss future moves. They told us, though, that as the next day was a feast day, the 'Feast of the Sacrifice', they had decided to postpone the move for two days.

That night we slept in the *dara*, and woke in the morning to the sound of roaring camels and bleating goats. Already, the sunlight was tilting through the trees, and the horses of the tribesmen were stamping impatiently at their tethering-posts. Soon Abdal Kariim's son, Hassan, a lad of about twenty, lit a fire; the morning was cool and crisp and it was a pleasure to stretch our limbs before the blaze. One by one, those Arabs who had spent the night in the tents came to join us, and since today was a feast day, they greeted us with a special formula, 'May goodness be with you all the year!', to which we answered, 'And may you have health and peace!' Apart from this, however, the day seemed no different from any other. We ate *'asida* from a wooden bowl, and I watched as Hassan milked a female camel and brought us the milk still warm from the udder.

Amongst the tents, I could see the women moving around in their brightly coloured dresses, and a little later Hassan called one of them over and introduced her as his wife, Zirqa. She was a beautiful, plump girl who looked no more than sixteen, her hair braided in the Arab style, known as *mashat*. As I had expressed an interest in seeing the women's area, Hassan escorted me around the family tents where more women were making buttermilk in large urns slung on short tripods, which they swung to and fro. Another woman, Hassan's grandmother, with skin like dried and wrinkled leather, was grinding corn between two flat stones.

'This is the Arab mill,' Hassan told me. 'We carry the grindstones with us when we move.'

Later, the men of the camp took the herds off to the wadi for watering, and left Mohammed and me in the camp. Although I had heard stories of the Arabs' jealous regard of their women, they obviously had no qualms about leaving us alone with them. Zirqa came to ask Mohammed Hissein if he would slaughter one of their camels for the feast. Arabs will not eat meat killed by a woman or an uncircumcised boy, and since none of their men were in the camp, Mohammed had to perform. He took my dagger and we walked over to the tents where some girls were holding the doomed animal, a young camel which was suffering from some illness. The Arabs rarely slaughtered their camels unless they were worn out or ill. I watched as Mohammed stabbed the calf in the shoulder, letting the blood spurt from the main artery, then making a clean cut across its neck.

'We're honoured,' he said to me, wiping the blade of the knife. 'This camel is for us. I've never had a camel killed for me before. It is written, "If you live long you will see the camel slaughtered!" I never thought I'd be doing the slaughtering!'

We ate the camel that afternoon: the meat had been cut into strips and roasted over wood-chips in a brazier. After we had eaten, Abdal Kariim called together some youths and dispatched them as scouts to survey prospective sites further on. Grazing in this area, Abu Wishdera, had become sparse, and a move was needed very soon. Then Mohammed and I accompanied Abdal Kariim on a tour of the camp, greeting members of each household. I was reminded of a military commander inspecting the state of his troops before a push.

At night, after the herds had been brought in, we again sat in the *dara*, and were joined by many visitors who wanted to meet us, the guests. Night clouded over the spiky canopies of the trees, and Hassan built up a fire against the chill. I sat contentedly amongst the Mahamid as they crouched by the hearth in their woollen *tobes* and furled headcloths, recounting tales in the customary way. Hassan said that he had heard some strange stories about Mohammed's tribe, the Zayadiyya.

'For instance,' he began, 'I heard that there is a Zayadiyya woman who dresses like a man! It is true, brother?'

'Yes,' replied Mohammed. 'But there's a good reason. She was once young and beautiful. One day two men, they were from the Berti, *zurqa*, they tried to rape her. Her father and brother caught the Berti, and they killed them there in front of her. Stabbed them to death with their daggers, which was only just, was it not? From that day she wore a man's clothes.'

'By God, a strange story! But they were just, they were just!'

By way of return, Mohammed said that he had heard about the trouble between the Mahamid and the Bedayatt on their recent migrations.

Hassan answered, 'One of my uncles was herding some camels with his son, a boy of not more than ten. They were north of Tina. Some Bedayatt came on them suddenly and demanded his camels. He refused, so they beat him with clubs, and when he was lying senseless on the ground they took the boy and broke his arm. Then they escaped with the camels. But they are animals, by God! We soon made up a search-party, though!'

The other Arabs present shook their heads in remembrance of the deed. Hassan continued, 'We made them regret it, we killed two of them!'

'How did it happen?'

'Well, I'll tell you, brothers . . .'

As the Arab spoke, I could imagine how it had occurred. Six or seven Mahamid on their finest horses, with automatic rifles slung over their shoulders, tracked the Bedayatt for miles across the open *qoz*, through acacia groves, into gullies and over rocky escarpments, pushing deep into Chad. Just before sunset, they spotted a long blue wisp of smoke which marked a camp fire. Hidden by thorn trees, the Arabs dismounted and saw their own camels grazing near the fire. The Bedayatt, deep within their own land, seemed to believe themselves safe. But as the Mahamid moved nearer, the crack of an automatic rifle rang out across the *qoz*, then another. The Bedayatt had posted a sentry. The Arabs opened fire with chilling accuracy: the sentry fell dead, his skull crushed by a 7.62 millimetre round from an Arab Kalashnikov. The other Bedayatt leapt on to their camels and dashed away, but one of the Mahamid brought down a Bedayatt with a single shot, fired from almost three hundred metres, and the man crashed into a cairn of boulders and lay still. The stolen camels scattered at the sound of gunfire, and while some of the Arabs rode off to round them up, the others went to inspect the dead.

I tried to picture the scene as Hassan spoke, imagining the Arabs standing silently around the limp, bloody figures of the fallen raiders, as the flies settled in swarms on the open wounds and the blood slowly coagulated in pools in the grey sand.

As I gazed round at the pacific, nodding heads of the Mahamid, I found it difficult to imagine that these generous, hospitable people could kill with such merciless abandon. Yet, savage as these laws of retribution seemed, such deaths were the price of freedom in a world without a date or time, where no policeman or soldier had real jurisdiction, and men considered themselves free of interference from any except their own kinsmen.

The next morning Abdal Kariim's scouts returned on their horses and reported a good patch of grazing about five hours away. The Mahamid began to saddle their stallions and to round up the camels and goats. About an hour later the animals began to trickle out of the thorn groves towards their new camp site. The remaining men and the women then started to dismantle the tents, which gave me a chance to examine the Arabs' possessions. Their beds were constructed of wooden laths, bound together by uncured hide, which could be easily rolled up and tied on to the camels. The food and cooking gear was packed into a variety of containers made of straw and leather, often brightly decorated, and the unmilled grain was carried in bulging leather saddlebags. All the household items, the millstones, the carved wooden mortars, the utensils and the furnishings were carried on the *howdaj*, which the Mahamid called the *'utfa*. The water was carried, not in skins, but in great pots mounted on wooden frames and carried either side of the *'utfa*.

While the beautiful Zirqa collected the household goods, Hassan began loading the tent-poles and posts on to a large camel fitted with a special saddle, known as a *jongola*. Suddenly the camel lurched up, roaring and spitting: it threw off its load and scattered lengths of wood everywhere, causing us to dodge and duck out of the way. I watched as Hassan grabbed the animal's headrope and tied it to a tree. Then, to my surprise, he picked up a tent-pole and began beating the camel savagely on the neck, hitting it so hard that it collapsed. I had never seen an Arab mistreat a camel before, but Hassan said that occasionally an animal must be taught a lesson so that it would not repeat the felony in future. I noticed, however, that Mohammed Hissein shook his head in silent disapproval.

When the *howdaj* was prepared, Zirqa brought down the great camel's head with a tug of the bridle, and stepped lightly on to its neck.

As the animal lifted its head she twisted herself effortlessly into the litter. It was an impressive picture with its black plumed headdress and its rich tassels of leather tumbling from its throat, neck and flanks. The nests of basketwork vessels presented a brilliant display of colours, and the litter itself was draped with costly materials, silk veils and thick hand-made carpets with intricate designs. Hassan and the remaining men then mounted their little stallions, slinging their rifles across their shoulders, and urged on the baggage-camels, now laden with tent-frames, boxes and equipment. The old woman whom I had seen grinding corn climbed into the saddle of another bull camel, but without the colourful trappings: the 'utfa was evidently reserved for the young married women and tiny children.

As we broke from the trees, many other families emerged from their camps, as if on some unconscious signal. There were a dozen litters containing women and children, which now formed into a caravan, a dazzling pageant of colour and ostentation. The baggage-animals followed on, and within an hour we had caught up with the herds and flocks which were now driven behind the caravan. The occasion took on the quality of a formal procession, each link of which had its individual splendour, as it moved grandly across the plain. Mohammed and I rode behind the women, and as far as we could see was a coiling serpent of finery: ostrich plumes were ruffled in the slight breeze, the ornate leather strands fluttered. The sunlight gleamed along the furrowed ridges of the men's headcloths, glittered on the tips of the javelins which they carried, and sparkled on the jewellery of those women who rode without shelter. Behind us the camels rippled forwards, shuffling through a smokescreen of dust, and behind them a wall of sound from the goat flocks seemed to force them onward. I was overwhelmed with the grandeur of this sight, for I knew that I was witnessing one of the world's last nomadic Arab tribes moving with all their possessions and livestock on their annual migration. I felt intensely privileged to be here, seeing an event whose historic continuity was unbroken, and whose roots proably went back to the legendary sons of Qahtan who had migrated in just such a manner before the time of Mohammed, or Jesus, or Moses, or even Abraham.

Some time later we moved into a valley where the way was obscured by thorn scrub. The procession was forced to break up, and we lost sight of Abdal Kariim and his family, travelling for a while next to an old man with a flock of goats. Further still we came to a wadi, where some Mahamid girls were filling water-pots. Mohammed and I stopped to water our camels, and helped the children to lift the heavy jars from the boreholes. Then we took it in turns to stand ankle deep in the muddy borehole water and fill a dish for our own animals.

In the afternoon, we returned to the acacia thickets, which were full of Mahamid. We were unable to find Abdal Kariim, so we spent the night at the tents of an older man, Amin Yusif. His tents were pitched on a rocky shoulder overlooking the scrub, and he arranged a *dara* for us outside the perimeter of the camp, as was the custom, and lit a fire. After we had drunk tea and camels' milk, we settled around the fire for the usual storytelling and exchange of news, and several young men came up to hear the talk.

On this night it was Mohammed Hissein who held the floor spell-bound with his comparison of the customs of the Mahamid and his own people, the Zayadiyya. It was when he began to compare methods of camel-rearing that the others became really interested. As I had remarked on my journeys in Zayadiyya country, that tribe had some fine herds, far out of proportion to its population. Mohammed explained that this was because the desert fringes where the Zayadiyya lived were far better suited to camel-rearing than the sub-Saharan zone of the Mahamid.

'In our country, there is dried grass and thorn trees,' he said, 'which camels prefer. They like it better than the wet grass which you find in this place. Of course the camels here are big, but they are not hardy, not like ours. They have to drink often, because they are used to softer conditions. Our camels may be smaller than yours, but they are more healthy. Many of your calves die, but few of ours do.'

The conversation passed to another favourite topic of the Arabs: guns. Mohammed told the Mahamid that the Zayadiyya had many guns, often obtained from refugees from the war in Chad.

'By the life of the Prophet, we have plenty too!' said Amin Yusif. 'But the police don't like it. Last year they raided us and tried to collect all our weapons. They said we were fighting the Bedayatt and Gor'an who were friends of the government. Friends! When they steal our camels!'

'That's unbelievable! Did they find any?'

The old man's face creased into a boyish grin, 'Never! We knew they were coming, of course, and put them in the ground. They found nothing!'

We talked until late at night, bathed in the soft light of a bloated moon which illuminated our shelf and the grazing camels which belched and gurgled happily in the thorn trees. As the flames of the fire faded and the chill of the winter night set in the Arabs retired one by one, leaving us alone with the splendour of the desert stars.

The next day we set off back to Abu Wishdera. The woods were still full of Mahamid and some Bani Halba, whom we greeted as we rode. Before nightfall we reached a chain of spurs from which we could see the green oasis of Gineina, like a jewel against the pastel-coloured *qoz* which surrounded it. As we approached the town, I felt a twinge of disappointment. Previously, it had seemed primitive and exciting; now, after a few days with the nomads, it seemed like any town, anywhere in the world.

14

SANDS OF UNRULINESS, SANDS OF SUBMISSION

What a difference in substance between the sands of unruliness, and the sands of submission.

Antoine de St Exupéry, *Wind, Sand and Stars*

It was March. I was watching the days pass and the weather get slowly hotter as the season drifted towards high summer, fretting at the steadily increasing temperature, mindful that in a month's time the desert would be a far from pleasant place. I had begun to lay the foundations of my next attempt to reach the elusive Forty Days Road and I wanted to visit the oasis of El Atrun, but I knew that the way through the remote reaches of Dar Zaghawa was barred to me. Instead I planned to trek north-east to Kutum and Mellit, and then north into the Libyan Desert. I had been warned by the police not to attempt this again, but I saw no reason why they should object to a journey to Kutum and Mellit. Besides, I had made a friend in the secret police in Gineina, and with his help I obtained written permission to travel as far as Mellit. From there onwards, I would have to take my chance with the authorities.

My friend Mohammed Hissein advised me strongly not to begin the journey in Gineina.

'Even if you have permission, it will be dangerous,' he told me. 'Between here and Kutum the country is as wild as in the north. There are Bedayatt and Zaghawa all over the mountains. Remember what happened to your camel! And there are the Umm Jallul Arabs who live in these mountains. They are well known as robbers. It would be better for you to go from Mellit: at least there are few Bedayatt in the desert!'

I thanked him for the advice, but told him that such threats did not disturb me. This was not bravado: I merely felt that as I had accepted the sheer joy and freedom of travelling in the nomads' dimension, then

I should also accept the hardship and danger. I never expected my journeys to be easy. On this particular trip, though, I had good reason to remember Mohammed's words.

Mohammed helped me to find a superb riding-camel in the market. It was a tall *sadiis*, strong, sinewy and even-tempered. I then set about trying to find a companion. Mohammed himself declined to go with me and eventually I managed to find some Hamar who were taking camels from the market back to Kordofan. Unfortunately, though, when I arrived at the *suq* one afternoon to meet them, I discovered that they had already left. Therefore I left the town alone on 9 April, wearing Arab dress, carrying a full complement of food and water, and armed with my pistol and a walking-stick. I had no companion, but at least I was on the way.

I crossed Wadi Kajja which looped in a semicircle around the town, and at once pressed my camel into a victorious trot. The animal braced himself, surging forward like a cruiser into the swell, his legs pumping like greased pistons, his feet tripping lightly over the sand as if they hardly touched it. My whole body was charged with excitement, and it was as if the camel and I were one, a merged unit of power, crossing the short time-warp between the city and the *qoz*. For several hours I rode like this, following the track which hugged the wadi bank, tunnelling through thickets where the leaves glistened silver on the thornbush and red knolls of rock rose steeply from the other side of the track.

The vegetation here was the skeletal remains of its former glory. Fifteen years before this had been savannah woodland. Water-buffalo had rutted in the thickets and lion and leopard had stalked the tall grass. Herds of elephant had moved through the woods like tanks, feeding on the rich greenery. Only fifteen years ago, Sultan Abd Al Rahman of the Mesalit shot an elephant on this very track. Now there were no elephants north of the Bahr Al Arab, a hundred miles away. Desiccation had crept into the valley like an evil spirit, withering the trees and driving out the animals. All that was left of that teeming fauna were a few red monkeys playing in the mango trees near the wadi's edge, and a family of small crocodiles dammed up in one stretch of the wadi which held water all year round. Soon, perhaps, they too would be gone.

Just before sunset that day, I met a shaykh of the Mahamid, like an ageing Don Quixote on his bony stallion, his old sword hanging low in its sheath, and his spear held ready.

'Where are you going, *khawaja*?' he said. I told him that my destination was Seref Umra, the nearest large settlement. 'Don't go alone by night!' he told me. 'There are robbers on the road. Only an hour ago I saw a party of Gor'an. They will take a fine camel like yours without doubt! Look, over in the wadi is an Arab camp. Go there and rest.'

I thanked him and set off towards the tents which were laid like brown stones on the concave bed of the wadi. The sky was already heavy with prussian blue and grey as I sloped in amongst them. A group of women with long, braided locks were pounding spices on the far bank, and in the bushes some camels and horses grazed. As I couched my camel between the tents, two young men with keen, predatory features came out saying, 'Welcome! Peace be upon you, welcome and peace!' They shook hands warmly, then automatically began to unload my saddlebags and other luggage, carrying it to a *dara* near the tents, where rugs were laid out. They brought me water, as custom demanded, and as I crouched to drink, told me that they were Essel and Yahyah Sadiiq of the Mahamid.

They were evidently unused to seeing Europeans, for they treated me rather stand-offishly at first, and Essel asked if I were 'travelling for the government'. I hastily explained that I was not. As the remaining blue patches of sky thickened into deep grey, and stars appeared like bright badges on its coat, they performed their sunset prayers, kneeling in the soft sand. Afterwards they brought a steaming dish of *'asida* and brewed tea on the fire with the now familiar ritual.

As we drank tea, I asked them how long they would stay in Wadi Kajja.

'Until the first rains come,' Essel told me. 'Then we go north into the land of the Zaghawa. The camels hate the dampness, so we cannot stay in the south after the first rains fall.'

I asked for information about the area between here and Kutum. Yahyah said, 'It's hard country and becoming dangerous! The Bedayatt and Zaghawa have come to settle there because of the dryness in their own country, and they try to drive out the other tribes by killing and stealing. They steal from everyone, by God! But usually they steal from the *zurqa* – the Fur and Tungur, who have few weapons.'

'We heard a strange story recently,' said Essel. 'By the life of the Prophet, you won't believe it, *khawaja*!'

'What happened?'

'It was up in the mountains near Kutum. Some Tungur – there were five of them – were taking grass to Kutum market by camel. It was early morning, and some Bedayatt watched them from far away hidden on the side of a hill, in a hole they'd dug. They had automatic rifles mounted on stands, like this . . .' He drew two twigs into a 'V' shape to demonstrate. 'Then boof! Boof! Boof! They hit the Tungur from above as they came. Hit them all with bullets! Then they crawled out of their holes, ran down and took the camels. But by God, one of the Tungur was alive, he was only a boy, and he asked for mercy. But where was mercy? They shot him through the head! They have no fear of God, those men!'

'Didn't the Tungur search for them?' I asked.

'Yes, they gathered twenty men and followed the tracks for days. They found the Bedayatt camp up near Jebel Meidob. But as soon as they came near, boof! boof!' He held up a twig as if it were a rifle. 'The Bedayatt shot at them. What could they do? They had no weapons except small pistols. They had to return home without justice.'

'God destroy them, those Bedayatt!' Yahyah said, spitting.

I felt obliged to tell them of my pleasant experience with 'Ali Ahmed in Dar Zaghawa. 'Yes,' Essel replied, 'there may be some good men amongst them, Muslims who know God. But most of them are like animals. Arabs may steal, but they do not kill without purpose as the Bedayatt do!'

I saw the Arabs' point. To them, raiding and stealing was a game to be played by certain rules – a game which might bring honour and fame. The Saharan tribes, so near yet so far from Arab culture, did not play by the Arabs' rules. They were merciless and ruthless, and did not consider five deaths a large price for five camels. This was the reason the Arabs hated them so much. If the Arabs stole, they would do so in daylight, while the Bedayatt attacked at night. The Arabs would not kill women and children except by accident; the Bedayatt made no such distinction. The races would never be reconciled while they played by such different standards.

'You must be careful north of Sereyf, *khawaja*,' Yahyah told me. 'It's wild country around Kutum. You will pass through the *dar* of the Bani Hissein, who are Arab, and good people. You will find no difficulty there. But beyond that the country belongs to no one.'

I had heard of the Bani Hissein and was curious to meet them. They were a settled Arab tribe of cattle-owners and cultivators, who claimed to be *ashraf* or 'noble' Arabs, descended from the Prophet's nephew, 'Ali. Despite this claim, though, they had intermixed with the neighbouring Fur cultivators and in many cases their appearance was hardly Arab-like. Nevertheless, they had an unequalled reputation for hospitality.

It was four days later that I arrived in Sereyf, the centre of the Bani Hissein. I had passed through the crossroads settlement of Seref Umra, where tribesmen from the Fur, Gimmar, Zaghawa and Bedayatt mingled with the Arabs of the Mahamid, Awlad Rashid and Bani Halba. From there, I had travelled north across miles of semi-desert where caravans passed me on the track and nomads moved in the thorn woods. Beneath the great turtle-shell massif of Jebel Bir Kasayra, I had passed through the villages of Darai and Abu Jowra, arriving at the wells of Sereyf near sunset.

Sereyf was an austere settlement of grass huts and compounds, like an imperfect copy of the Hamar villages I had seen in Kordofan. It stood on a high flat shelf above a wadi which was filled with cows and sheep, and a score of boreholes at which dozens of tribesmen were watering. At the very first house I passed, a middle-aged man came out to greet me. He was as coal black as a Mesalati, but with the broad square features of the Arabs. He greeted me solemnly and led me into his poor house of grass stalks, saying, 'You must stay here tonight.' He told me to couch the camel outside. 'There are no robbers here,' he said. 'This is the country of the Bani Hissein.'

That evening my host, whose name was Adum, entertained me in a three-sided *khalwa dyuuf* where his aged father, a toothless old man who could no longer walk, was a permanent fixture. Chickens were killed to honour me as guest and many tribesmen came to greet me and to sit around the fire drinking tea. I warmed to the courteous yet sharp conversation. The Bani Hissein knew little about the outside world, but their minds were quick and penetrating.

Adum began to tell me about the days of British rule in Dar Bani Hissein. 'Sereyf wasn't where it is now in those days,' he told me. 'It was up near Dileyba, that was in the days of Sultan Moore. Mr Moore held a court at old Sereyf every week. He used to come by camel from Kutum along a special way, it is still called "Mr Moore's Road". That's the best way for you to approach Kutum.' Adum informed me that the next day he and his son would ride with me as far as the wells at Dileyba, in order to set me on 'Mr Moore's Road'.

It took us until noon the next day to reach Dileyba. The Bani Hissein rode the muscular horses for which they were renowned, and carried shotguns slung from their shoulders or balanced across their saddles. Dileyba was no more than a few wells set in a dry watercourse, where the sand was all but obscured by the accumulated animal dung of decades. Hundreds of full-bodied cows and bullocks were being watered by the Bani Hissein, and further along I saw seething nests of camels, belonging to nomads of the Mahamid. The Bani Hissein herdsmen welcomed us and slaughtered a goat in honour of our arrival. We drank *ajina*, a delicious drink made from millet. Afterwards, Adum and his sons escorted me to 'Mr Moore's Road', a narrow animal track which wound through thin bush.

As I wished him farewell, Adum said to me, 'I advise you to get out your pistol, *khawaja*. This is a dangerous road. There are even more bandits about than there were in Mr Moore's time! Go in peace.'

'Go in peace.'

After the Bani Hissein had gone, I did as Adum had advised me, putting my pistol into my pocket.

The prelude to what was to come happened the next day. As I climbed out of a verdant wadi in which I had been resting, I saw a single camel-rider coming towards me, and he halted his mount beside me. He was an Arab youth, with a fox-like, pugnacious face, the narrow, pointed features of which were accentuated by the skullcap which he wore rakishly on the back of his head.

'Who are you?' he demanded.

'*Ingleezi*,' I answered. 'And who are you?'

'Arab, Umm Jallul. What are you doing here alone?'

'Travelling,' I answered, resenting his aggressive tone, 'to Kutum.'

'Not good,' he shook his head. 'Not good at all. The *Ingleez* should not be alone out here. This is bad country. There are robbers here.'

'So people say,' I said, as nonchalantly as possible. 'But I haven't seen any, brother, and there are robbers everywhere!'

'I'll tell you, *khawaja*, there are Zaghawa ahead. They won't let you pass! They won't let you alone!'

'Perhaps you're right,' I said. 'But in any case, that's my business. Go in peace.' And I set off at once up the steep slope, whipping my camel into a trot. The boy had angered me considerably. Advice I much appreciated, but this patronizing attitude cut me to the quick. It turned out, though, that the youth's aggressive advice was quite sound, if a little inaccurate.

Some time later I realized that I had lost 'Mr Moore's Road'. Either it had petered out into nothingness, obliterated by the scores of animal tracks which criss-crossed it, or I had merely strayed off it inadvertently. Before me lay some very rough country, an uneven plain of rock, cut deeply by gullies and ravines, scattered with boulders and sharp outcrops, and covered in twisted brakes of acacia. It was cut off to the east by a smooth green wall of rock. I saw no alternative but to cross the plain on a due east bearing which I set on my Silva compass, hoping that I would find some pass through the mountain on the other side. It was difficult going and my progress was painfully slow, descending slippery banks of sand and shale and through narrow gorges where I was forced to duck away from the twisted boughs of the thorn trees.

Suddenly, I saw two camel-men bearing down on me. They were riding at an oblique angle on a collision course, and it was obvious that they intended to close with me. Their camels were small and fast and as the men came nearer, I could see that they were Arabs, two youths with the same streamlined features as the Jalluli I had seen earlier. Something in the purposeful way they rode ignited a warning signal in my head, and I decided to get away from them as soon as I could. But in a few moments they had moved skilfully across and stood blocking my path. I looked into the two youthful faces and was met by a slit-eyed stare. The youths were of different ages, one perhaps fifteen, the other in his early twenties.

'Where are you going?' asked the elder youth nastily.

'To Kutum.'

'To Kutum? Then why aren't you on the path? Are you alone?'

'Yes.'

'Why do you go this way?'

'I use this,' I said, showing them my Silva compass.

'What is it?'

'A compass,' I said, using the Arabic word.

'What does he mean?' said the younger to the elder.

'He can look through it and see Kutum,' the other said.

'No, no,' I began to explain.

'Where're you from?' snapped the elder, interrupting me. 'What is your people?'

'*Ingleez.*'

'What's that? A tribe from Chad?'

I tried to explain that I was an English teacher, but it seemed that these Arabs were so cut off from that world that they had no concept of what I was saying.

'What's in your saddlebags?' asked the elder.

'Food, cooking things, that's all.'

'Show us,' the younger boy snapped, and suddenly I found myself looking straight into the yawning jaws of danger, just such a danger as I had been warned about. A clot of adrenalin liquified in my bloodstream, my breathing became more rapid, my dry mouth tripping up the foreign words which I struggled to pronounce.

'Show us!' the youth said again.

'Why should I?' I said, my right hand fingering the grip of the pistol in my pocket.

'What are you afraid of? We want to see what you've got. Come to our camp and show us.'

'No, I'm in a hurry.'

'He doesn't want to go to a camp,' the young one said. 'He's come to spy out the land for others!'

And just then I noticed that he was cradling something beneath the folds of his shirt. It could only be a weapon. In those spinning seconds I was faced with the two choices with which a man in danger is always faced: fight or flight. If I fought, then someone would be hurt or killed. Then I saw a way out. A few yards to my left was the edge of a deep gully with a steep, sloping side which was covered in loose gravel, held in place by clumps of bush. Without considering it twice, I thwacked my camel on the shoulder. He plunged across the edge of the gully, slithering and sliding on the loose stone, his legs trembling in an effort to stay upright. Miraculously, he did so, and skipping over the last two metres of gravel, bounded across the flat bottom in two steps, letting his momentum carry him up the lower bank on the other side. My mind dimly registered the Arabs shouting 'Stop, stop!', and then I was racing through the bush in full flight, weaving in and out of the trees, zig-zagging behind outcrops of rock, expecting a shot to crack out at any moment. I took a quick glance behind. The Arabs were not following, but I noticed that the younger boy was holding what could only have been the shiny black mass of a pistol. Another shock of ice-cold fear snaked down my spine, and I whipped the camel again, clinging on desperately as he plummeted through the bush, swerving behind some rocky outcrops, which gave me temporary shelter from view. I looked back again, and wondered how I had escaped. I could not believe that the Arabs did not trust themselves to the steep gully I had plunged into like a suicide-jockey. But perhaps they were more solicitous of their camels than I. I shook when I thought of how the camel's legs had almost given away.

I slowed down to a trot as the minutes passed. Then with another burst of adrenalin, I saw about a hundred metres away to my right, two shadowed heads bobbing up and down above the thornbush tops. The Arabs were circling around, keeping me in their sights. In a moment I was riding at a fast trot again, cutting away from those bobbing heads. I knew that I could not evade them for long. Eventually I should have to stop. Their camels were fresh, and they knew the country. Then, in the distance, I saw a collection of grass huts. To my right, the ominous, disembodied heads were still moving up and down. I changed course towards the settlement, galloping so that the scrub whirled past in a green blur, until minutes later I found myself coming down a slope towards a *zariba* of thornbush, where a young boy was herding some sheep. I halted my camel, trying to suppress my heavy breathing, and greeted the boy politely. Then I asked, 'What's your tribe?'

'Awlad Diqqayn, Zaghawa,' he told me.

Before the words had even registered, I found myself saying, 'Is this your village?'

'Yes,' he said. 'Welcome there!'

Without another word, I trotted towards the huts. They were built in typical Zaghawa fashion, though they were unkempt and derelict. Once inside the rough oval of the place, though, I felt a current of warm relief. At once a ragged old man came out saying 'Welcome!', shaking hands and leading me into the rough compound which surrounded his two huts. He instructed two plump girls and a young boy to unload my camel and set it out to graze. The old man spread out some mats for me in the shadow of the compound fence, and brought me water.

'Are you from the Gor'an?' he asked me. 'Where have you come from?'

'I'm English.'

'Is that a tribe from Chad?'

'No, I'm a teacher from Gineina. I . . .' The words froze on my lips, as through a hole in the fence I saw the two Arabs who had been following me. They were riding slowly and nonchalantly through the narrow street, outside, looking left and right. At once the old man noticed my expression.

'What's the matter?' he said.

'Those men,' I gasped. 'Who are they?'

'Umm Jallul,' he told me. 'They're herding camels near here.'

'I think they're bandits,' I said. 'They stopped me about half an hour ago. Now they've followed me here!'

The old Zaghawi chuckled to himself. 'They're not bandits,' he said.

'They have a camp near here. Were you travelling on the track? No, I thought not. That's why they stopped you. They thought you were a bandit, after their camels, heh, heh, heh!'

As the words of the Umm Jallul replayed themselves in my head, I saw at once that he was right. They had been afraid of me, and my reaction to their aggressive manner had made them even more suspicious. A simple misunderstanding, but one which could have been extremely dangerous. I could not, at first, join in the old man's mirth. Only later, when it registered that I had actually fled from Rizayqat Arabs and taken refuge with my old enemies, the Awlad Diqqayn Zaghawa, did I raise a smile at the irony of the situation.

The next morning, I gave the old man a present of sugar, and he led me about three miles across the *qoz*, back to 'Mr Moore's Road'.

'Don't lose the way again,' he said severely, 'or you may find worse than the Umm Jallul!' I thanked him, and bade him go in peace, watching the spare-framed athletic figure as he disappeared into the bush. Then I began to follow the 'road'. It was a narrow swath of brown and red, where the ground had been churned up by the feet of a million camels, horses, donkeys, cows, goats and sheep. I followed it eastwards as it wound into a lush green valley, thick with vegetation. Later I came across an area where the ground was blackened with fire, the trees cut and mutilated, many of the fallen trunks still smouldering. I guessed that the local Fur farmers had done this in an attempt to clear some fertile ground, but the sight saddened me. The ground might produce a good crop for a few years, but afterwards the sparse topsoil would be leached away by the rains, giving way to useless, sterile sand, another forward push for the relentless creep of the desert.

I ascended the steep incline of the mountain wall I had seen the previous day, a tortuous track between the lumps of hills, which led me down into another richly decorated gorge. I found some Arabs watering a flock of sheep from a deep well, and stopped to beg a drink. They were Awlad Rashid, and they told me to follow the wadi up into the mountains, where I would find a large encampment of their tribe.

In the hour before sunset I was still following the empty watercourse. It snaked down from the hills through groves of *heraz* and *hejlij* which pressed against its sheer, rocky sides. Its bed was a mosaic of blue stones and boulders, machined by the seasonal flow of water into all shapes and sizes. Suddenly, I was shaken by the sound of a piercing whistle which rang across the wadi, and rounding a twist in the bank I saw an Arab herdsboy with fifty or sixty camels. Obviously the whistle had been a warning to someone further up the water-course. I murmured a greeting to him as I passed.

As I rounded yet another convolution of the wadi, a magnificent sight lay before me. I could see along the whole dappled length of the creek as it climbed away from me, and all along its banks, on both sides, amongst the thorn thickets, scores of tents were being erected by hundreds of Arabs, men, women and children. In every patch of hard ground between the trees lay piles of saddlery, the frames of litters, folded rugs and blankets, leather and straw vessels. There were tents in various stages of construction, some already covered with canvas sheets, others no more than a wooden frame, the bare skeleton of a shelter. Women in their rainbow-coloured dresses swarmed excitedly around the camp, while men and boys herded the hundreds of camels which stomped around in the bushes. It was the largest camp I had ever seen, an entire Arab clan camping together.

As I made my way towards the first tents, a bullet-headed Arab with a clean-shaven face, a large pointed nose and piercing eyes called to me, 'Welcome, stranger! Come and drink!' I couched my camel amongst the piles of household effects, and squatted down with six or seven tribesmen drinking tea.

'You must stay with us,' said the bullet-headed man. He ordered the younger lads to strip my camel, and the men piled up the luggage beneath a tree, in my own private *dara*. I asked the Arabs which tribe they were and my host, the father of this particular section of the camp, introduced himself as Esa Ibrahim of the Awlad Rashid.

'We're the Zabob clan,' he told me. 'We're camel-men.'

'This is the entire clan?' I asked.

'Yes, this is all of us. We have come from near Kutum. The grass is worn out over there – and we're travelling south to better grazing. We stay here tonight, and maybe tomorrow – then we travel on.'

As the sunset wore on, the tents sprang up like mushrooms, blossoming amongst the trees. Twilight brought new shadows along the banks, but the shadows were cast back at the night by the glitter of fires which came to life all the way up the length of the wadi. The smell of wood-smoke drifted down to me as I watched the women moving about like graceful gazelles and the tiny children chasing the camels which must have seemed like mountains to them. Strings of camels brought water up the tracks and men stalked the creek bed on young calves. It was a scene of utter peace, soothing after the excitement of the previous day. Within twenty-four hours I had experienced both sides of the Arab coin: raw aggression, the volatile face of unrestrained energy; and total trust, the more authoritative power of complete stability. It was this stability and aggression which had sustained a society for millennia. These paradoxical qualities embodied in one spirit made, and still make, the Arabs a great people. In this ancient scene, the people had no expectations of me except that I should observe the rights and limitations of a guest. They were a self-sufficient people, and they had something more: contentment.

The sun of a new day was a golden globe, criss-crossed by the black fingers of the thorn trees, as I set off with Esa Ibrahim up the twisting track which led into the silver mysteries of the hills. At a tiny well we stopped to draw water, and Esa helped me lift the heavy waterskin on to my saddle. As we clasped hands, the Rashidi fixed me with his glittering eyes and said, '*Khawaja*, you've come far, but you have a long way to go. By the will of God, you'll get there.'

I mounted my camel and urged it forward, up the track, willing it into a slow, steady trot. I was setting off to another horizon, another noon, another sunset. I had come far, but the road ahead was longer. By the will of God, I should arrive.

15

A ROAD BEFORE ME

I have come, I know not whence, but I have come,
And I have seen a road before me, and I have taken it.

Eliya Abu Madi, *I do not know*

In Mellit I was invited to a banquet in the house of a rich merchant. It was a house-warming, and open to all comers, and we sat on plush carpets while servants brought in weighty trays of food of all kinds. After we had completed our 'shift' we removed ourselves to make room for others. Just as I was leaving, I heard a voice calling, 'Hey! *Khawaja!*'

I turned to see the broad face of a rotund gentleman, and for a moment recognition swam in my mind. Then I remembered him as one of the people who had witnessed my humiliating interview with the governor of Mellit. I had stood before them, eager and bedraggled, while four portly gentlemen in spotless *jellabiyyas* had laughed at my keen questions about the Forty Days Road.

The big man motioned me towards him, pulling me close, and said conspiratorially, 'You still want to kill yourself in the Libyan Desert?'

'I still want to go, yes, but . . .'

'Right! In El Fasher you will find a merchant called Osman Hasabullah. Some Arabs are taking his herd to Egypt in a few days' time, Rizayqat Arabs. Go to Fasher and contact him at once, if you still want to go.'

I walked away slightly dazed; I wondered if this large old man was trying to mock me. I said to the person next to me, 'Who's that big man over there?'

He squinted across the room, then said, 'Him! He's Mohammed Musa. The most important camel-merchant in Mellit. Why do you ask?'

'I think I'm going to El Fasher,' I said.

I felt now that I was ready to take on the challenge of the Libyan Desert proper. From the encounters I had had with the authorities in Mellit, I sensed that if the authorities in Fasher, the provincial capital, got to hear of my plans, they might prevent me from travelling, so I did not report to the police on my arrival there. Instead, I used a letter of introduction I had been given in Mellit to some members of the veterinary department, at whose mess in the Awlad Ariif quarter of the town I stayed. It was one of the veterinary surgeons, Awad Al Kariim, who put me in touch with the camel-merchant, Osman Hasabullah.

I first met him in Awad's office. He was a small, austere man, clean-shaven and with the brusque, no-nonsense manner of the uneducated rich. He wore a dazzling white *jellabiyya*, a costly silk headcloth and a woollen *tobe*, and he carried a walking-stick of shiny black *babanoss* with a carved handle. He greeted me in a rather peremptory way, telling me that his Rizayqat would be leaving after a few days, and inviting me to come to his house the next day to meet them.

When I arrived there the next day, there were six of the Rizayqat sitting with the merchant. They were dark-skinned with sharply defined features, as if their faces had been carved from some heavy wood. All wore calf-length Arab shirts of varying shades, and ragged *'immas* in twisted helixes across their close-shaved hair. They carried daggers, the telltale sheaths of which bulged under their sleeves, and most of them wore thin moustaches and curls of beard sprouting from their chins, in the style of nomadic Arabs. These men looked formidable and unfriendly, and I wondered how much they would accept me on such a difficult journey.

Osman Hasabullah introduced me to a short, thickset man with very bright, penetrating eyes. This was Ibrahim Hamed, the desert guide, known by his nickname 'Abu Sara', after his first-born child. His face was weathered and ageless, and he looked very powerful. As I seated myself amongst them, the merchant told me the names of the other Arabs, who glared at me fiercely as they were named. The last to be introduced stood out from the rest. They were short, lightly built and delicate, but he was heavy and broad-shouldered, with a wide, cheerful face and longish, curly hair. The others referred to him disparagingly as 'the Hamedi', since he belonged not to the Rizayqat, but to a nomadic tribe in Kordofan, the Dar Hamed. He was the youngest of the group, I thought, about my own age, and he seemed a little ill at ease among the glowering Rizayqat, whom I suspected regarded him as something of an outsider. This held an important lesson for me: if they did not accept this man, whose only distinction was that he belonged to a different, though related Arab tribe, how much more difficult would it be for them to accept me, who did not share their language, their religion or their cultural background.

Tea was served by the merchant's assistant, another Rizayqi called Juma. He was dressed in a fine shirt and a lace skullcap, but the expensive clothes did not disguise the deeply carved features of his tribe.

Abu Sara stared at me constantly as he drank his tea, and as he set the glass down he said, '*Khawaja*, the way across the desert is hard. It is summer, there will be thirst, severe thirst; there will be heat, there will be fatigue: do you understand that?'

'I understand,' I answered seriously. At least this was a positive attitude: it called for no fanciful explanations, merely the fact of acceptance.

'And you still want to go?'

'I want to go.'

Abu Sara explained that they would be taking a herd of a hundred and forty camels to the markets of Egypt, crossing the desert and touching the Nile near Dongola. From there they would follow the river to Egypt. However, he refused to take me further than Dongola, and it was some time before I discovered why. I agreed to meet some of the Rizayqat at the wells of Awlad Ariif the next day.

I arrived at the Awlad Ariif wells early the next morning, to find the Hamedi and three other Arabs watering about eighty camels of all sizes. One of them, Adem Mohammed, stood up to his calves in the muddy water which surrounded the troughs. He was a slim greyhound of a man, with silver in the stubble of his hair, which had been shaved close to the skull; he wore nothing but an old *sirwel* and a dagger in a sheath, and in his hand he held a long whip of hippopotamus hide with which he kept the camels in place at the troughs. Another, Saadiq Idriss, was crouching over a fireplace of three stones, making '*asida*.

Saadiq and the Hamedi called me over to eat, and as we settled around the pot, Adem came up with a fair-skinned lad called 'Ali. I sensed immediately that Adem was hostile, for he avoided looking at me and began to talk about me to the others as if I were not present.

'Is he a Muslim?' he asked.

'No, he's a Christian, of course, all *khawajas* are Christian!'

'Then he's an unbeliever!'

'Christians know God.'

'But he doesn't know Arabic. How can he travel with us?'

'He knows Arabic.'

'He doesn't know how hard the desert is in summer. He will not like what he finds. And look at that camel of his. It's weak and will probably die on the first day.'

I remained quiet throughout this invective, letting the others talk for me. I had no wish to begin an argument at this early stage with someone upon whom I might have to depend. I decided that discretion lay in silence, and hoped that one day I might be able to win the respect and acceptance of this proud and uncompromising man.

When the work of watering was completed, we mounted, and rode north into the *qoz*, driving the herd before us. It was the first time I had ridden with a mob of this size and I found the sight spectacular: a brown press of furred backs eddying over the plain with that familiar liquid motion which I had come to associate with these animals. The rest of the herd was grazing on a wide sward of thornbush some miles outside El Fasher. We passed through their lines, and couched our mounts by a cluttered camp where two more Rizayqat, oldish men, as lean as whippets, were brewing tea in the shade. Their names were Abu Musa and Abdallahi. I spent the rest of the day in their camp trying to become acquainted with the character and customs of these men, who were to be my companions on the way.

Here, outside the town, they seemed comfortable and at home in their natural environment. These Rizayqat were tough, resilient nomads, well used to the stringent discipline of the desert. They were rough diamonds, beside whom the other Arabs I had met seemed almost genteel. They were openly courteous, as all Arabs are, but I sensed beneath this an uncompromisingly suspicious attitude. I felt very much like an applicant for an exclusive club who had to prove himself to the established members. It was a club of which I could never become more than an associate member. To them I was not only a townsman, but also a non-Arab, a non-Muslim, and a *khawaja*. They were *al 'arab*, descendants of one of the purest races in the world, and their superiority was beyond question. I felt on the first day that all my actions were being closely studied: if I went away from the group, or merely tried to get something out of my saddlebag, I would hear one of them saying, 'What is he doing now?' or 'Where's he going?'

I had to reconcile myself to the fact that everything I did in future would be public property, for the desert allows no secrets, and the Arabs are men who know no falsehood amongst themselves. This harsh environment in which they lived exposed all pretension and reduced everything to its empirical essence. The privileges of wealth, skin colour and education were meaningless here: the desert equalized all, reducing each man to the elements of his nature.

I could understand why these men were so critical. The journey which we were about to undertake was no jaunt across the semi-desert, but a long period in one of the grimmest landscapes on earth. Each man would be dependent on the others for survival, and a weak link in the chain could lead to the extinction of all. My experience was without significance to these men who had been reared in the desert, who regarded all townsmen, even those related to them, with disdain.

For my own part, I knew that I was meeting these Arabs over an enormous cultural chasm: they had not chosen me as a companion, but I them. My world was a total mystery to them, though I had the advantage of knowing something of theirs. I was willing to make almost any sacrifice to gain their acceptance.

At sunset the Arabs began a flurry of activity, and Adem thrust a whip into my hand, and showed me how to run around the edge of the herd, drawing them close into the centre. There were to be no passengers on this trip: I was expected to fulfil my part of the work. When the hundred-and-forty-odd camels had been brought in, each one was carefully hobbled with a loop of rope called an 'uqal. The loop had a wooden peg at one end and was fixed around the knee of one of the camel's front legs to make it difficult for the animal to rise. Then the Arabs laid out their blankets in a rough semicircle in the midst of the herd.

It was a beautiful evening, calm and cool, and the scores of camel heads swayed around us like a forest of weird moving plants. The Hamedi began to sprinkle flour into a pot, making 'asida. Adem sat mending a broken 'uqal. All the time the Arabs kept up a solid stream of talk. Adem and Saadiq were comparing their respective journeys to Libya and Egypt, and often the others interjected. I felt, once again, how much of a luxury talk was to the Arabs. It was from this love of language that their powerful poetry and literature developed. The phrase 'Silence is golden' has no meaning to the Arabs of the desert. The men's raised voices were suspended in a background of teeth-grinding, grunting and chewing from the camels, and their smell drifted over to us as we sat there. Occasionally a large bull would flick sand over us with a sweep of his tail, and often one of them would hop to his three feet and begin antagonizing the seated animals. Then the Arabs would get up, whip in hand, and separate the culprits. As I sat writing my journal by torchlight, Adem came up and peered directly at my writing.

'Is that Arabic or foreign?' he asked.

'English,' I said.

'What are you writing about?'

'Oh, about camels, the country, anything I see.'

'Are you writing about me?'

'Some about you, yes.'

He scowled and withdrew, but from time to time I caught him casting resentful glances my way, convinced, I was sure, that I was some kind of spy.

That night I got little rest. My sleep was constantly disturbed by the roaring of camels and the shouting of the Rizayqat, 'Get down, dog! Bandit, get down! God curse you!'

In the morning, however, Abu Sara arrived and inspected my camel. 'It's too weak,' he said. 'It'll never make Dongola, by God! It has come a long way and needs rest. You must sell it at once and get another.'

'But when are we leaving?'

'Not for two days. Some of the camels are sick and have to be treated before we go. Ride to the market with Saadiq, and I'll see you there.'

Some time later, I found the guide in El Fasher animal market. Abu Sara took charge, and paraded the camel around as if he belonged to him, expounding to the potential buyers his qualities with polished oratory. Very soon he was sold, and a satisfied customer led him away. Then, Abu Sara and I began to search amongst the animals for sale, for what he called a 'clean' camel. We examined beasts of all colours, shapes and sizes, and finally Abu Sara turned to me and said, 'There are no clean animals here. They are either butchers' camels, or they are too weak.' I felt panic inside: now I was stuck without a camel, and the herd would soon be moving. 'There is a bigger market in Mellit tomorrow,' the pilot continued. 'Osman's assistant Juma is going there to buy camels. You go with him, and you can find a clean, strong beast.'

The market of herds in Mellit was no more than a *zariba*, or enclosure of stone, situated in the desert about two miles outside the town. There, far away from lorries and telephone wires, it was possible to imagine that nothing had changed for centuries. Camels were brought here from all over the west of the Sudan, and many different tribes, including the Zayadiyya, the Zaghawa, the Kababish, Berti and Meidob were represented.

On the morning that Juma and I arrived, there was a fierce *haboob* blowing from the north, and the air was gorged with a white mist of sand. Gradually the *zariba* filled with people. Camel-riders came like spectral apparitions, materializing suddenly out of the mist, their faces muffled with cloth, their bodies draped with swords and daggers. As groups of tribesmen formed with their camels, Juma walked around greeting old friends and inspecting the stock. I received some strange looks from people, though others seemed quite familiar with my story, and I gathered that the news had been passed on the Arab grapevine.

By the end of the morning, by supreme industry in the long-winded ritual of purchase, Juma had bought twelve camels for Osman Hasabullah, and I had bought a great battle-cruiser of an animal, pure white in colour, with an unusual mane of hair around its neck. It seemed rather slow, but Juma had persuaded me that it would 'go anywhere'. When the market closed, Juma and I went to drink tea, and he introduced me to an old Arab of the Zayadiyya, called Babullah.

'Babullah is taking Osman's camels back to El Fasher,' he said, giving me a wry smile. 'You'd better go with him and help to bring them back.' There was something in the way Juma said this that I did not like. I had no objection to helping Babullah, but I did object to being spoken to in such an imperious manner. Babullah seemed an old, old man. His hair was grey and he was as thin as a broom-handle. I found it surprising that he could actually ride a camel. He was occupied in tying up a saddle which Juma had given him, when the Rizayqi brought from his pocket two pounds and threw them in the sand at the old man's feet. 'Take that,' he said. 'That's your food. Now, get a move on, grandad, the herd's waiting for you!'

I was shocked by this behaviour, for Babullah was old enough to be Juma's father, and I knew that the Arabs generally respected old age. Babullah ignored this rudeness, however, and though I looked sharply at Juma, I knew I could not interfere. It seemed to me that he had been living for so long in the town, trying to become like the merchants, that the very worst of their attitudes had rubbed off on him. I stayed with Babullah as Juma stalked off, and when the old man had finished tying up the saddle, he said, 'You'll have to work with me. I told Juma that we needed another herdsman, but he's mean.' My half-suspicion had been correct – Juma had been trying to save money by using me as a second herdsman.

It was approaching sunset by the time we reached the outskirts of the town, having stopped on the way to get water and food. We descended into a deep wadi, the bed of which was lined with sand as fine

as gold dust, climbed out into thorn woods which became thicker as
the evening darkened. As we went, I got used to my new camel. He
was strong and steady, but slow, as I had thought, and I found it
difficult to keep up with Babullah, who was riding a three-year-old. He
kept shouting for me to catch up, but though I belaboured the camel
with a whip, he refused to change gear, and I began to feel frustrated
and angry. Had the bad-mannered Juma deliberately given me bad
advice, I wondered? If not he was as bad a judge of camels as he was of
men, for amongst the twelve he had bought for his boss, one had a bad
leg, and another was blind in one eye which caused it to wander off
constantly. There was also a *naqa*, a young female, which seemed to
have a route of her own mapped out.

I could see already that the situation was perilous: this old stager,
twelve wayward camels, and an assistant on a slow mount. Babullah
was having trouble with his own camel, which was young and im-
properly trained. Suddenly, it began to turn in dizzy circles while he
fought to control it. The other camels started to scatter in the dark
woods. 'Come on, *khawaja*!' shouted the old man angrily. I became
separated from the others in the darkness, and when I emerged from
the forest, I found that Babullah had halted the camels around a single
bush and was walking round and round them, shaking his head.

When he saw me, he cried. 'The *naqa*! Where is the *naqa*?' I slowly
counted the animals myself. There were eleven: somewhere in the forest
we had lost the errant female. I couched my camel by his, and he looked
at me accusingly, 'We've lost the *naqa*. Now what will we tell Osman
Hasabullah?'

Close up, I saw that his face was a mask of misery, and the situation
became clear to me in a flash. Babullah was a poor man, probably very
poor, and well into old age: he had no doubt worked with camels all his
life, and his reputation depended on his being able to transport them
safely from one place to another. Now he had lost one, the value of
which was more than he earned in two years. Everyone would laugh
and say he was 'past it': the bottom had fallen out of his world. He
looked exhausted and inconsolable.

I said, 'I'll go and look for her, she can't be far.' I set off back into
the thorn wood, but the shadows were thick and raven-black: I knew
that the only chance was to find her tracks, and I returned to the old
man.

'Perhaps she'll return to the wells,' Babullah said. 'We can go and
search for her at daybreak. We'd better stay here now.'

He unloaded his meagre possessions: a single blanket, ragged and torn, and an old saddlebag containing a few charred cooking pots and some food in twists of paper. He sank feebly on his blanket, and sat there motionless. I began to feel increasingly that the loss of the camel was partly my fault. I made a fire silently, collecting stubs of dry wood, and all the time the old man stared into space, not uttering a word, as if in a kind of daze.

We ate in a terrible silence, and almost immediately afterwards the old man hobbled the camels and went to sleep. I lay awake for some time, thinking about Osman Hasabullah, and how the news of the lost *naqa* would affect my chances of travelling with the Rizayqat. In my heart, though, I nursed a swelling grudge for Juma, who in my view was the real culprit, and who had brought what was almost a traedy into the dotage of this old man of the desert.

Before dawn Babullah was awake, saddling his three-year-old. 'I'm going back to the wells in Mellit,' he said. 'You stay here and look after the camels. Whatever happens, don't give the water to anyone!'

Less than an hour later, he was back without the lost camel. 'She's not there,' he said. 'But I found her tracks. I can't follow on this camel. It just won't behave!'

'Then take mine,' I offered. 'But it's slow!'

Babullah agreed, and I helped him to fill a small water-bottle from the skin. 'Don't move from here,' he instructed me. 'And don't forget about the water!'

In a few moments he had disappeared into the distance. I guessed that it would take all the skill acquired in a lifetime of experience to recapture the escaped camel.

Meanwhile, I looked around at my surroundings in the fresh light of morning. I was in an open stretch of desert beneath the volcanic plugs of two mountains, which rose like the fins of a giant marlin from the pale froth of the sand. There were some stunted thorn bushes near at hand, but none large enough to provide shade. I could not move the camels back into the wood, for fear of losing another. There was no alternative but to wait here in the blast-furnace of the day, until the Arab returned. As the sun came up, it began slowly to roast me. The hours passed, but Babullah did not appear. I wondered idly if he had decided to take my camel and escape to some camp in the desert, leaving me to face the consequences.

It became too hot to move, and I tried to bind my headcloth around me to provide a little protection from the strafing sun. I kept the waterskin covered, and occasionally sucked water from its mouth-piece, and this provided a welcome relief from the blistering heat. I was afraid to drink too much, however, since it seemed unfair on my companion. All day I saw nothing but a single camel-rider passing far off by the foot of the mountain, and a few children with some goats. I did not want company, for I was afraid of attracting the attention of thieves to these eleven all but unprotected camels. As I sat in the oven of midday, my mind wandered in strange corridors. I thought about the hostility of the Rizayqat, the unpleasantness of Juma, the potential wrath of Osman Hasabullah. Seldom had this world seemed so strange and incomprehensible. Often I asked myself why I was here, sitting out in the hot sun, watching a mob of camels somewhere in north-east Africa.

The sun was well past its zenith when the figure of Babullah appeared on the skyline. I saw immediately that the *naqa* was not with him. He approached very slowly on the large white, and as he came nearer I saw that his face bore an expression of absolute defeat. We did not speak as he couched the camel, and I noticed that as he stepped down his legs trembled slightly. He had been in the saddle all day, and was obviously shattered. There was nothing to be said, and we sat for a few timeless moments in silence, hearing nothing but a faint breath of wind playing across the surface of the sands.

'I saw her!' he said suddenly. 'By Almighty God, I saw her, but I couldn't catch her. That camel of yours is too slow.'

'What do we do now?'

'We must go on. The herd is waiting to move. We have lost a day already.'

Almost at once we packed up and moved off, herding the camels between us. It was a journey which I will never forget. The animals constantly wandered off and had to be chased back into line. The old man, after a whole day in the saddle without food, rode like a boy. We went on and on without a break. Sunset came and went, the hours of the night passed. Finally, not more than three hours before dawn, we made camp in a wadi and both fell into the sleep of the dead.

16

WHERE THE SUN BEATS

Away, for we are ready to a man,
Our camels sniff the evening and are glad.

James Elroy Flecker, *The Golden Road to Samarkand*

When we arrived at the camp of the Rizayqat the next morning, Juma, Osman Hasabullah and Abu Sara were there to meet us. They saw immediately that we had lost a camel, but to my surprise, they showed neither anger nor astonishment. They were much more concerned with our lateness. Abu Sara had collected together the rest of my equipment, and as I dismounted in order to load it on he told me that the herd was waiting to move.

'Come on, *khawaja*,' he bellowed. 'Ride! Ride!'

I had scarcely managed to get my breath before I found myself riding in the wake of the great herd, with the Rizayqat and the Hamedi positioned at intervals around its edges.

The mob moved like a single organism with a thousand elongated legs, swarming up a concave slope of sand as if drawn on by some terrible compulsion. My senses were choked with camels: the bitter-sweet smell of their bodies, the humped curvature of their backs, their inaudible flat-footed stride, and the high-pitched wail which they sent out as they went.

Abu Sara took up a post on the left-hand flank of the herd, occasionally shouting orders, 'One by one, brothers, spread out and keep them moving!' Mostly, though, he directed the movement by silent hand-signals. The others kept up a continuous barrage of sound, intended to urge the mob forwards; they cracked their whips and chased wanderers back into the belly of the herd with much swearing and many oaths by God. I could do nothing but ride bemusedly: I had not eaten for thirty-six hours and had ridden almost fifty miles after a day of being baked by the sun. My mouth was as dry as parchment, my head aching from the heat, I was too exhausted to appreciate fully the beauty of the scene I was witnessing.

Occasionally, Abu Sara would ride around the perimeter of the herd, to make sure everyone was in a good position. He rode an enormous bull camel, of superb lines, and carried a thick coil of *'uqals* which rattled as he rode. He pointed out to me an old bull which was dragging behind and I recognized it as one of the eleven we had brought from Mellit.

'That one won't last long!' he told me, as the bull wobbled errantly from side to side. Sure enough, within half an hour it had collapsed in the sand. We did not stop the herd, but Saadiq and Adem went back to truss the camel up. 'We'll go back for it this afternoon,' Abu Sara explained, 'when the herd is grazing.'

'Will it die?' I asked.

'God only knows!' he replied. 'Perhaps many will die on this road!'

After about two hours, when already I was beginning to think that I could travel no further without a drink, we came to a shallow depression where thornbush was growing. Abu Sara directed the camels into the trees and finally the Arabs couched their camels in the shade of a large *heraz* tree and began to make camp. I noticed that all of them, including the guide, were using the rough-framed pack-saddles. I had thought of myself as having very little equipment, but I was well supplied in comparison with these men who each had no more than a blanket, a canvas sheet and a ragged saddlebag made of sackcloth or leather. We had twelve full skins of water, which were loaded either side of the pack-saddles.

There were six Arabs and myself in the group: Abu Sara, Adem, Abdallahi, Saadiq, Abu Musa and the Hamedi. Still I found them distant and uncommunicative – only the Hamedi seemed friendly, and I suspected that this was because he too was an outsider. The Arabs continually kept themselves busy, twisting new *'uqals* from pieces of bark, repairing saddles, sharpening daggers. Abu Musa, a tall man with a bullet-shaped head and a thick black beard, began to cook parts of a sheep which he had brought with him. Abu Sara sat down on the sheets we had laid out, and I took the opportunity to ask him about our route.

'We go north, though the country of the Zayadiyya,' he told me, 'then into the *dar* of the Kababish. That's where we have to be careful, by God, for they don't like us, and where is the government in the desert, if not them?'

I asked him how many times he had made this journey before.

'Believe me, *khawaja*, I've been a desert man since I was a youth. That's how I learned to be a "pilot", I've seen over sixty rains, so I must have been this way fifty times at least!'

I was aghast at the revelation of his age. If he had said forty, I should have believed him, for he exuded strength and alertness. I tried to imagine myself at the age of sixty, riding a camel across one of the earth's most severe deserts, and failed. Yet Abu Sara was not the oldest of the group; Abdallahi claimed to be over seventy, and to remember the days of Sultan Ali Dinar.

Throughout the journey, in fact, I was constantly surprised by the toughness of these Arabs. Only the Hamedi was under thirty, yet though the Rizayqat lacked his large muscles and his youth, they seemed far more resilient than he. It occurred to me that the physical shape of the Rizayqat was the result of natural selection in an environment where only the strong survived.

When the sheep was cooked, Abu Musa laid out the meat in a dish. It was only ribs and head, which were raw in some places and charred in others, but nevertheless I relished the meal, especially as Abu Sara told me it would be the last meat for some time. While eating, the Arabs crouched around the pot in such a way as to prevent the soles of their feet from facing the food, which was considered very impolite. Before dipping their hands into the communal dish, each man would say *bismillahi!* literally 'in the name of God', an epithet which preceded everything the Arabs did, whether mounting camels, cooking or washing their hands. During the early stages of the journey we washed our hands with a little water before eating, but licked them clean afterwards. As we moved further into the desert, however, we used only sand to clean ourselves.

After the meal, we drank a cup of hot, sweet tea. Arab tea was usually very strong and very black because the water which they carried was always tainted. The making of the tea was a long ritualistic affair, requiring great precision. The tea-maker, a man of some standing in the group, constantly tested his product, sipping it from a spoon or pouring a few drops from a glass. Tea is regarded by the Arabs as a great luxury, and after a few days in the Libyan Desert, I began to understand why. Like them, I began to crave its stimulating effect.

After tea had been drunk, Saadiq and Adem rode off to see how the collapsed camel had fared. They returned several hours later and told Abu Sara that it had died.

The guide shook his head, and said, 'That Juma, he's a bandit. Why does he buy such camels?'

I decided against expressing my whole-hearted agreement since I remembered that Juma was from Abu Sara's tribe, but I was pleased that someone else had discovered the truth.

Abu Sara went to fetch his camel, and suddenly the camp erupted into activity, the Arabs rushing about and shouting. I wondered what was happening, and the Hamedi said, 'We're going!' I was mystified at the sudden animation, and put it down to the fact that this was the first day of a new journey. In fact, I found that the Arabs constantly behaved in this way, shifting from neutral to top gear without any interim build-up.

We moved the herd out, following a series of rocky outcrops into undulating land. It was only then that I understood that after all the months of planning and speculation, I was actually on my way into the Libyan Desert. The land was scattered with volcanic rock, the many shades of which glinted amongst the roots of the thorn trees which punctuated the landscape. We carried on as the afternoon sun drooped towards the western horizon, casting a silver silicon sheen around the massed insect-like feet of the camels. Shortly after sunset, we dropped down into a wadi with a bed of hard-packed sand, and halted the herd. As we began to make camp, I asked Abu Sara why we had moved such a short distance. He told me that we would be travelling relatively slowly for the first few days, in order to make the best use of the grazing in this area. Further on there would be no grazing, and we would be travelling until late every night.

When we made camp at night, the camels were not left to feed freely, because of the danger of their wandering away or being taken by thieves. First, the riding-camels were unsaddled and the equipment dumped on the ground. We had with us a pack-camel, carrying four heavy sacks of flour, which was to be our food as far as Dongola, and this also had to be unloaded. While two of us carried out this task, the others would go about the painstaking job of hobbling each of the hundred and forty camels. Not until this work was completed did anyone drink water.

The heavy waterskins were never left on the ground overnight, but were hung on the sides of the pack-saddles which made admirable frames. The water would be poured out into a wide bowl and each of us would drink in turn, squatting down on our haunches: to drink while standing was considered rude. At first, I sipped the liquid in small mouthfuls, thinking that it would be assimilated less quickly this way, but I noticed that the Arabs quaffed it in great draughts, and soon I was copying them. Certainly I never felt bad effects. Often on our journey to Dongola we were thirsty, but as time went on I found thirst far easier to withstand than the scorching heat of the desert. No one ever drank water alone, or without offering it first to another. At the evening halt, indeed, there were constant protests by the one to whom the bowl had been handed that one of his fellows should drink first, and often the reciprocal protests became quite animated, despite the fact that we were all very thirsty.

After we had drunk, each man would lay out his meagre bedding with his saddle at his head. The Arabs slept on their canvas sheets with a single blanket for cover. They always slept very close together, despite the vast area at their disposal.

That first night in the wadi, the air seemed electric with the chatter of the Rizayqat as they sat on their blankets stripped down to their *sirwel* and busied themselves. Abu Musa lit a roaring fire. The Hamedi and Saadiq went off to collect firewood, while Adem and Abdallahi set to work stitching sackcloth over the rough straw pads of their saddles. Abu Sara began pasting spare waterskins with *gotran*, which prevented the empty skins from becoming hard.

I sat a little apart from the Arabs. I didn't yet feel part of this group. One of the problems was that I found their dialect a little difficult to understand. Although my Arabic had become proficient, the Rizayqat had many terms and expressions which were unique to them. When talking to them individually, I was able to hold my own, but when they spoke together I had difficulty in understanding them.

Abu Musa cooked *'asida*, and when it was ready, Abu Sara called me over to join them at the pot. The *'asida* was served in a large dish, with two saucepans of gravy. Everyone took massive chunks and ate them fast, and with great relish. I ate with the same gusto as the others. If someone stopped eating before the food was finished, the Arabs would shout 'Eat! Eat!' in great earnest. Usually, however, the other would mutter *alhamdulillah*, 'praise be to God', repeatedly, licking his fingers until the eaters were convinced that he was really satisfied.

When we had eaten, and drunk more tea, the Arabs began on their evening prayers. On this first night they made many *raka'*, in an attempt to make up for those they had not done during the day. This was a strictly irregular practice in Islam, though it probably seemed logical to the Rizayqat, none of whom had read the Koran. I noticed that once we had penetrated deeper into the desert, and became more exhausted, some of my companions performed their prayers far less frequently.

Before going to sleep, I smoked a cigarette, the one luxury I had allowed myself. The Arabs generally did not smoke, though Hamedi and Saadiq occasionally asked me for a cigarette. Some of them used *tombak*, a kind of snuff which was inserted between the gum and the lower lip. The effect was pleasantly anaesthetic, but the long-term effect on the nervous system probably devastating.

In the morning I awoke to the sound of the Rizayqat reciting their prayers, and a little later, I rose to join them at the fire. The first task to be completed was the loosing of the camels so that they could graze. When this was done we huddled together around the hearth and splashed a little water over our faces. Occasionally we ate cold *'asida*, left over from the previous night, with oil, but generally we had only two meals a day. After the tea-drinking, Abu Sara would fetch his camel and begin to saddle. This was the silent signal for the rest of us to 'scramble', and it always followed this strict sequence, with the guide saddling first. I once inadvertently saddled before Abu Sara, and incurred his severe wrath. He had Saadiq explain to me that the organization in the desert was 'like the army'. I did not repeat the action.

The mob which we escorted were to be sold in Egypt for meat. They were mostly males, some of them gelded, with the well-developed humps which showed that they had been reared for this purpose. The riding-camels we used were all bulls, since the western tribes of the Sudan never rode females, and all had undersized humps from the constant bearing of a saddle. However, a riding animal put out to graze could develop a full-size hump within a year.

The wooden pack-saddle which the Arabs used was a large frame like a double clamp, joined at either side and resting on coils of straw. It was held in place by a cord of bark fibre looped around the camel's neck and under its tail. My own saddle was much easier to manage, since it depended only on tightening the girth, and because of this I was often ready before the others.

I never saw the Rizayqat treat their riding-camels badly: this was because, in the desert, their lives depended on them. The death of a man's camel meant a reduction in his chances of survival, and if he were alone, death was almost certain.

When we were ready to go, we would mount and begin to gather the herd by galloping around its skirts and forcing the camels into the centre. Once they were shoulder-tight, they would be forced into a bottleneck made by two riders, and Abu Sara would count each one as it walked through. This painstaking process had to be gone through twice a day, in the morning and after the midday halt. When the counting was finished, the guide would take up his position on the left-hand side, and we would move out, forcing the herd onwards. Although we never travelled faster than a walk, the camels actually made fast progress, covering an average of thirty miles a day. The Rizayqat drove them with their traditional herding songs, some of which had words, and others merely consisting of a series of sounds, such as *'wei wei oooh wei!'* The Hamedi hardly ever stopped singing. This would have been fine, if it had not always been the same song that he sang: a mysterious little number which he called the 'Dar Hamed Maidens', and which was accompanied by an inordinate amount of whistling and grunting.

I was sometimes irritated by these men, their arrogant attitude, their hostility to everything which was strange to them, their imperative way of speaking and their quickness to excitement. But I knew that I was among men whose lives were not at all affected by all the things which my upbringing had taught me to hold precious. In fact, they owned almost nothing belonging to the twentieth century, and as we travelled deeper into the Libyan Desert, I felt that extraordinary sense of timelessness which I had experienced so often with the Arab nomads. When I looked at my companions, or listened to their talk, I saw nothing which set them in a particular time: it could have been any age within the span of a thousand years or more. Reading and writing had no place in their lives. Their alphabets lay in other spheres: the tracks left by camels in the sand, the colour, texture and value of the grazing, the worth of a camel or goat. Their picture of the world was quite different from my own. They did not measure distance in miles or kilometres, did not know that the earth was a sphere, or that it moved around the sun, that the stars were anything but lights to guide their way or that the moon was more than a means of judging the flux of the seasons. I found this refreshing. Metaphysical questions did not concern them: there was One God and all things stemmed from him. Their store of practical knowledge was supremely adequate for the lives they led, and I envied their simple, uncluttered concept of existence.

Generally, we would travel until the sun became hot, around noon, then make camp under a tree for the afternoon. If there was no adequate shade, the Arabs would erect blankets and sheets as a temporary shelter. During these siestas, the camels would eat whatever was available, but even these hardy desert creatures would stop eating in the middle of the afternoon and seek out any shade they could find. We would take turns to leave the shelter of the camp in order to watch the herd, making sure that none of the animals strayed too far, and keeping an eye out for thieves. I often had to steel myself for the foray into the blistering inferno of the afternoon: the heat seemed to crush one with its massive pressure. Even in the shade of our makeshift tent it was too hot to move, but out in the open desert it was almost unbearable. I appreciated my Arab headcloth and its voluminous layers. On my first day, sitting on my haunches, being slowly simmered by the sun, I was reminded of T. S. Eliot's *The Waste Land*:

> *. . . where the sun beats,*
> *And the dead tree gives no shelter, the cricket no relief,*
> *And the dry stone no sound of water.*

After three days we arrived in El Koma, a village near the wells of Abu Ku' where I had met the Zayadiyya, in the heart of the country of the Awlad Jerbo clan. The Rizayqat were expecting to water the herd there and we camped near the wells amongst some scrub. It was evening when we arrived, and I was stunned by the splendour of the scene: the sun going down wreathed in plumes of magnolia, the moon coming up like an inflated yellow balloon in the east. The acrid smell of the camels touched my nostrils as they shuffled about, champing the sparse grasses, and I heard the startled cry of an enormous vulture, and the snap of its wings as it launched itself heavily into the sunset.

Abu Sara and Abu Musa rode off to the wells, and I helped the others to hobble the herd. Abu Sara and Abu Musa reappeared later with long faces. They were accompanied by a stranger and as we gathered to greet the newcomer, Abu Sara growled, 'The wells are dry. There's no water for us here. We'll have to go on to Umm Hejlij.' Then he introduced our guest to us as Shaykh 'Ali Mohammed of the Zayadiyya, and told us that he would be our *rafiq*, as far as Umm Hejlij. I was intrigued by what had been left unsaid. Abu Sara's manner was slightly resentful, and I wondered if 'The wells are dry' was a euphemism for 'These sons of dogs will give us no water!' I wondered too if 'Ali Mohammed had been sent to keep an eye on Zayadiyya grazing.

The next morning, as we moved out, I rode alongside the Zayadi. I

asked him guardedly if there was likely to be any trouble from camel-
thieves in Zayadiyya country.

He laughed, and replied, 'There are bandits everywhere, why should
there be none here? But by the will of God, there will be no trouble.'
He gestured expansively towards the landscape. 'Look at this country.
There is grass; there is thornbush; there is water. Our people are few
but our herds are large.'

It seemed to me that 'Ali Mohammed was something of an uninvited
guest; nevertheless, the Rizayqat treated him with respect and courtesy.
Often on this journey other Arabs attached themselves to us with
hardly a by-your-leave, yet they were usually welcomed without reserve. Arab traditions of hospitality are born of necessity. In this arid
land survival often depends on cooperation between individuals; it is a
case of do-as-you-would-be-done-by. To the Arabs no invitation is
necessary: *karm*, hospitality, is simply the custom, to be expected and
received with equanimity. Woe betide all who fall short in the exercise
of this tradition.

A little later on, after the meal, old Abdallahi sidled up to me and
asked for some medicine for his headache. I guessed that he wanted
more of the morphine substitute which I was carrying, and which I
had inadvisedly given him previously. The Arabs constantly asked for
medicine of any kind, and seemed to suffer a great deal from headaches
and stomach trouble. At least half of the time, however, I suspected
them of taking pills without reason as if they were some kind of magic
potion. This was confirmed towards the end of the journey, when I
explained that I had nothing left but chloroquin, for the treatment of
malaria. They insisted on taking it, though they obviously did not have
malaria, and the following day asked for more.

This time I explained to Abdallahi as well as I could that I was
keeping the drugs he wanted in case something serious happened and
sent him off, glowering resentfully, with some Aspro. I returned my
attention to the conversation, to find that Adem was baiting Saadiq,
who claimed that he had once been a pilot, taking cows from Darfur to
Omdurman.

'How did you know the way?' Adem asked.

'I followed the stars.'

'You followed the stars by day! By the life of the Prophet! You're a
better man than all of us!'

Everyone, except Saadiq, guffawed with laughter, and I warmed to
Adem's sense of humour. He was by far the most talkative of the

group, and his mouth was always full of jibes and jests. His wit was often directed at Saadiq, who had a well-known tendency to romance about his experiences. Although I was no less a target for his acid tongue, I came to like and respect this clever and cheerful man who always seemed to be in good spirits, though the others might be depressed.

The Hamedi remained the most openly friendly of the Arabs, though he lacked Adem's sense of humour. By the end of the first week he seemed very tired, and he confided that this was his first trip across the desert. Unfairly, though, he seemed to get the lion's share of the work, and at first I suspected that this was because he was from a different tribe. But I knew that it was customary amongst the Arabs for the youngest member of a family to perform the most menial tasks, and realized that their treatment of the Hamedi was a reflection of this rather than a deliberate slight.

Abu Musa was a quiet, good-natured man who remained steady and unperturbed in most circumstances, though I found his way of speaking particularly hard to understand. I came to dislike the old Abdallahi for his constant wheedling. The others respected him for his age, and even Abu Sara tended to listen more open-mindedly to his demands than to those of the others.

On the second morning out of El Koma, we awoke to find that two of the camels were missing. They had broken their hobbles and disappeared in the night, no doubt in search of water, for it was now five days since they had drunk. Abu Sara and Abu Musa saddled up and rode off to follow their tracks, while we took the herd slowly on, moving in open order so that the camels could make use of any grazing which they passed. At noon the pilot and his friend returned empty-handed.

'We followed the tracks for a long way, by Almighty God!' declared Abu Musa. 'But they must have been moving fast, not stopping to eat. They'd gone too far for us to catch them.'

'The blame is on that Hamedi!' said Abdallahi acrimoniously. 'Son of a donkey! He should have been watching them!'

'By God, O people, I can't stay awake all night!' shouted the Hamedi defensively.

'That's enough!' cried Abu Sara. 'They're gone, and that's the end of it. Never mind. God is generous. Now we must think about water for the herd.'

Indeed, as we moved out that afternoon, I noticed an eerie, rumbling moan from the camels, faint at first but growing steadily louder into a curiously harmonious, haunting descant. Saadiq told me that this was their 'song of thirst'.

That evening we camped in open desert near Umm Hejlij. Abu Sara, 'Ali Mohammed, Saadiq and I rode to the wells where we found a family of Zayadiyya. The men were bearded and fair-skinned, and the girls beautiful, with braided hair. We sat in a semicircle in the sand and they brought us fresh water in a bowl.

'How is the water?' Abu Sara asked.

'The water is little,' answered one of the Zayadiyya.

'We have a hundred and forty camels to water.'

'By the will of God, there will be more tomorrow, but now there is scarcely enough for our own animals.'

'It would be better to return in the morning,' agreed 'Ali Mohammed.

Abu Sara grunted, then chuckled bitterly, 'By the life of the Prophet, I'm glad these camels aren't mine!' He agreed reluctantly to come back the next morning, and we rode back to the herd disconsolately, 'Ali Mohammed staying with his kinsmen at the well.

All night the camels rumbled and moaned, and before sunrise Abu Sara was off to the well. He returned an hour later as we sat around the fire.

'Those sons of a dirty whore!' he exclaimed. 'Would they give us water? By God that 'Ali Mohammed gave me no help, father of two tongues that he is. I won't forget him! Look, brothers, they sent me off with two skinsful! Two!'

'Curse their fathers!' said Saadiq. 'But what do we do now? If the camels don't drink soon, they'll die, by God!'

'No, not yet, not yet!' cried Abu Sara. 'I've seen them go for ten days without water in summer. But we must leave immediately for Umm Qozein.'

I had wondered often since my first days with a camel how long these beasts could actually survive without water. Everyone I had asked had given me a different answer, and I had long since understood that the question was as futile as asking 'How far can a man walk?' The answer depended on many factors, including the size and age of the camel, the season and temperature, how fast the animal was moving and where it had been bred. A camel raised on the fringes of the Libyan Desert, for instance, would be far hardier than one brought up in the damper pastures of South Darfur. A camel feeding regularly on green vegetation in the cool season may not need to drink for forty-five days, whereas camels travelling fast in summer and eating little, as ours were, felt thirst every four or five days. The six days our camels had lasted was already considerable.

We pushed the herd on all morning, but they moved slowly and resentfully, and at midday we found a copse of bush where they could feed. Some Zayadiyya appeared from nowhere with a sheep, and Abu Sara bought it. At once all the Arabs offered their hands to Heaven, asking God to bless the animal, and Abu Musa recited the first verse of the Koran. Then he slit its throat with a single stroke, still murmuring prayers, and the carcass was hung from a nearby tree. Saadiq and Abu Musa proceeded to butcher the animal, with my assistance, first peeling back its skin, then removing the intestines and stomach.

Meanwhile Adem lit a fire, and when the flames of the matchwood had died down, the ribs and brains of the sheep were placed on the glowing embers and eaten almost raw. The remainder of the meat was made into a stew, served in two great pots; the Arabs used all edible parts of the animal, mixing them with strong pepper and spices. The Zayadiyya joined us for the meal, thinking nothing of the fact that they had sold us the sheep, and one of them asked for, and received, the fleece. Afterwards they stalked off without thanking us or wishing us well. It is the custom of the nomads to leave without fuss. Greetings are lavish in the extreme, whereas farewells are usually peremptory. Since hospitality is something expected rather than considered a special favour, thanks are not thought necessary, or even understood, in this context.

That afternoon we moved through petrified forest where the sand lay blood red between the cleft hooves of the bushes. I was able to see the skill of Abu Sara in a new perspective. I marvelled at the way he managed to keep the herd together through the tangled obstacle course of the scrub. It seemed almost as if he had an instinctive feeling for the job, a kind of extrasensory empathy between himself and the camels, as well as the skill resulting from years of experience. He told me later that the herd had a structure and organization of its own. He pointed out the 'leader', a huge buff-coloured bull, which walked always at the apex of the herd. If this individual could be directed correctly then the others would follow, for the herd instinct was very strong. This was easily seen if we halted our riding-camels for a moment while the herd carried on. They would fret and roar, acting uncontrollably until they were back in the ranks of the mob.

My large white camel was too slow for herding, but Abu Sara allowed me instead to ride a spare riding-camel from the herd, and I was able to learn some of the skills of the camel-man. Urging one's own animal forwards at a fast pace, without allowing it to break into a run, was difficult and required constant concentration. Travelling behind the herd, we determined its speed, cracking our whips and singing. Two riders always stayed at the rear flanks, keeping the animals pressed tightly, but constantly one would stray off course and would be followed by a detachment of others. Then one of the Arabs would shout 'Chase that camel!', and the nearest rider would break off and pursue the splinter group. It was this situation which required the most skill, for the pursuer had to handle his camel so as to force the runaways back towards the body of the herd, without allowing the group to fragment further. It was easy to make the runaways move in the opposite direction to the one required. This caused endless trouble, for it meant that at least two riders had to leave the main herd to retrieve the absconders. Gradually I learned how to angle the break-away group back to the mass, and to work in concert with the other riders, anticipating and correcting the camels' movements.

The night covered us like a blanket, without moonlight, and we lay on a gravel plain west of Umm Sunta. After eating, we retired in the usual way. I slept soundly, exhausted after the hard ride of the day, but a short time later I was shaken awake by Saadiq, who said, 'Get your camel, quick, we're going to Batatikh!'

'What's up!' I asked.

'A Kabbashi came from the wells at Umm Qozein, and said there's no water, we've got to move quickly now. The camels must drink!'

The others were already up and saddling their camels amidst great excitement and exclamation, and moments later the herd was moving through the unreal, gilded sheen of the moon, newly risen. For hour after hour we rode in that eerie other-world of the desert shelf. The camels rumbled with thirst, now louder than before, like a growl of distant thunder, and the Arabs moved back and forth round the edges of the herd. All around us lay the boundless nothingness of the desert night. Our world was an island in that vast sea, an island of six Arabs, an Englishman and a hundred and forty-seven camels which were slowly dying of thirst. The night stretched forwards and backwards, impenetrable and infinite. I was unable to monitor the time, as none of us had a watch, and I was aware only of the rocking motion of my camel, the silvery coalescence of the herd moving before me, and the wraithlike figures of the others, in soft focus, beyond its perimeter. The aches in my back and legs felt like hot irons, and I was constantly fighting sleep, sometimes drifting into that dream world between the unconscious and the conscious where illusions become reality and reality illusions. I felt shattered, but I was determined not to let it show, nor to succumb, for I knew that the ethos of these desert men did not encompass nor allow for the admission of weakness. I suspected, however, that they were suffering too, for often one of them would dismount and run along behind the herd, obviously afraid of falling asleep in the saddle.

The going became harder and harder, and I had to will my body to carry on. We could not even stop to drink, for our water was scarce, and my throat was as rough as plaster. I was battling against the mounting tonnage of exhaustion which pressed down upon me. I had lost all sense of time, and began to fill the vacant, monochrome hours singing folksongs, in opposition to the Hamedi, who kept up an unflagging version of his favourite song, 'The Dar Hamed Maidens', on an almost operatic scale.

The moon described a half-parabola above, and I watched it, waiting for its descent, when a faint, hardly perceptible glow appeared on the horizon. At first, partly because I had no idea how long we had been riding, I imagined that it was yet another optical illusion to add to the many I had seen in the dream world of the night. But slowly, unmistakably, the light increased. It was the dawn, like the answer to a prayer. Never had the coming of day seemed to welcome or so magical.

Suddenly, Adem broke away from the herd, and rode directly over to me. 'Morning of goodness, brother!' he said, smiling.

'Morning of light!' I replied.

'And upon you be peace,' he said.

One of the hardest experiences of my life was over. I felt, with a rush of emotion, that this man, this uncompromising Arab who had never before said a friendly word, nor made any allowance for me, had with this standard formula of greeting saluted me more than a thousand assurances of friendship could have done. I felt within his words the first budding of a brotherhood born of a shared hardship. From that moment onwards I began to feel no longer an outsider, but part of that tight little world which we had created amongst the seven of us.

I knew then that the route I had taken across the desert was not and never had been important. I was no explorer, and other Europeans had been here before me. Others would come after, but most of them would come by truck or Land Rover, cut off from this hidden dimension which I had found. The desert was only sun, rock and sand, but its treasure lay in the hearts of these men who lived within it, these desert Arabs, the last survivors, not of a race, but of a culture in its original form, whose like had all but disappeared from the rest of the earth, and whom it had been my privilege to know. This, I realized, would be the prize which would stay with me always.

As sunrise burned red and gold in the throat of the skyline, we stopped to make tea. Abu Sara said to me, 'By God, it was a hard night, wasn't it?'

I suspected, wrongly, that I was somehow being tested, and replied with false nonchalance, 'It wasn't too bad.'

The old desert guide just smirked, and said, 'It was hard and it's going to be harder: we're not at Batatikh yet. It's a long way from here. We'll stop to drink tea, then we go!'

It was another six gruelling hours before we drew the herd in by the wells at Batatikh. The Hamedi had fallen a little behind and I guessed that he was as drained of strength as I. Abu Sara and Abu Musa were towers of control, and even old Abdallahi seemed in remarkably good condition. Obviously proficiency and resilience in desert travel was proportionally related to age and experience. I estimated that we had been riding for twenty-seven hours out of the last thirty.

There was no grazing for the herd and they huddled together in the raw power of the sun, bleating pitiably with thirst. It was now eight days since they had watered, and even Abu Sara considered the situation critical. He went off to the wells, and returned within half an hour. He dismounted and unsaddled silently, and we sensed immediately that he had once more been turned away. He sat down heavily and said, 'No water, the wells are dry!'

No one spoke. It seemed that the tremendous effort we had put into the previous day's ride had been wasted. We ate 'asida and the remains of the sheep morosely, and afterwards held a council.

'The herd must drink in the next two days,' said Abu Sara. 'It's eight days since we left El Fasher, and they haven't watered. We cannot afford to find another well dry.'

'What about Umm Badr?' suggested Abu Musa. 'There must be water there!'

'But it's so far away,' cut in Adem. 'The camels will die before we get there.'

'There is no other way,' said the guide. 'If we move as fast as possible, we may just make it, by the will of God.'

'By the will of God!' they echoed.

Umm Badr was a settlement in the territory of the Kawahla and Kababish tribes, where there was a perennial water pool in a depression in the rock. It was certain to have water, for these tribes watered their vast herds there in summer. The problem was one of distance. Was it possible for our herd, already weak, to reach Umm Badr before they began to collapse?

During the night we had crossed the border between the *dar* of the Zayadiyya and that of the Kababish. Amongst the valleys and dry watercourses which we passed that afternoon, I saw tents of woven wool, with knots of camels couched around them. Fine herds of buffs and whites grazed amongst the thornbush, and occasionally we saw riders in the distance, travelling at a tripping speed, the hooves of their camels hardly seeming to touch the ground.

The Rizayqat seemed more wary and alert in this territory. I rode for a while with Abdallahi and he pointed out the white tents of a Kababish encampment in the distance.

'This is Kababish country,' he said. 'There is no government here. If you so much as touched one of their goats, schchch –' He drew a finger across his throat. 'Weapons rule here.'

I was surprised that the Rizayqat, who had a reputation as fierce fighters, should be in awe of the Kababish. When I saw how well the Kababish were armed, however, I realized that their wariness was well-founded, since they were carrying nothing but daggers.

That night we camped on a narrow plateau east of Umm Sunta, and for the first time, Abu Sara explained that one of us must be awake all the time in order to watch for bandits. As usual it was the Hamedi who bore the brunt of the work, and for some time I sat up with him, watching the stars and listening to the grunting and moaning of the herd. It must have been about midnight when we saw two riders approaching on light camels. They stopped a short distance from the camp and shouted a greeting.

At once, Abu Sara woke up. 'Welcome, welcome!' he shouted. 'Come near, come near!'

The two guests brought their camels into the camp and couched them, then joined us around the rekindled fire. I noticed as they sat in the firelight that they were quite distinct in appearance from the Rizayqat. While my companions were very dark, with close-cropped skulls, the newcomers were a shade lighter, with soft black hair which fell in unkempt rats' tails around their ears. They introduced themselves as Kababish of the Umm Badr clan, and assured Abu Sara that he would find water there, if we could reach the place before our camels foundered.

'What is your people?' asked one of the Kababish, when he had finished giving us information about the route ahead.

'Zayadiyya,' replied Abu Sara, without batting an eyelid. I was astonished that he should have lied to them. I kept quiet, however, and took no part in the conversation, letting it flow to its natural conclusion, while I sat well back in the shadows.

When I awoke the next morning, the Kababish had gone. I asked Abu Sara why he had lied to them.

'I told you before,' replied the guide. 'The Kababish have no love for the Rizayqat. There is hostility between them. Only a few years ago my cousin was killed by Kababish near Jebal Esa on the way to Libya. They took his camels, and left his body in the desert. They are dangerous men and they are the law here. They have weapons, we don't. We can't defend ourselves. The Kababish are friendly with the Zayadiyya, but their accent is close enough to ours for the Kababish not to know the difference.'

'Why didn't you bring weapons?' I asked.

'It's difficult enough to get past the police on the Egyptian border, even without weapons,' he explained. 'We'd never get through if we were armed.'

That day we moved slowly so as to spare the herd, but the way was difficult, up and down depressions littered with loose shale and dominated by great brown dolmens of rock which broke the surface of the ground, some shaped like upturned pudding-bowls and others like the vertebrae of some giant, half-buried fossil. We passed over dried-up watercourses with soft, sandy beds, scattered with cowrie shells. We moved towards a line of mountains, the colour of which changed from grey to scarlet as we approached. The sky was onyx-blue, blemished only by a tall wisp of bluer smoke from an Arab camp fire which appeared in the distance. We left the bush land far behind and moved on to a tilting slope of sand, fringed with the crags of jutting hills. With startling force a *haboob* began, lashing our faces like a leather-thonged whip. I bound my headcloth tightly around my face so that only the eyes showed. Suddenly, over the wind, I heard the Hamedi shout from behind me, 'One of the camels wants to die!'

I wheeled around to see a young animal lying on the ground and shivering in pain. Quickly, Abu Sara halted the herd, and I watched as he and Adem poured out the last of our water into a dish. Instead of letting the camel drink, they poured a little of the water over its nostrils. Still it shivered silently, as the *haboob* blasted by. Abu Sara suddenly drew his dagger, and began to make small, deft slits around the camel's nostrils. He cut until the blood ran down its jaw, mixing with the fine sand borne on the wind. Then Adem poured more water over its head. Miraculously, it stopped shaking. Adem allowed it to drink the remains of the water, then he, the guide and the Hamedi began to kick and tug at the beast, until finally it staggered to its feet, its legs trembling unsteadily like those of a new-born calf.

'Come on! Mount up!' bellowed the guide. 'We've got to get to Umm Badr today, or they will all go like this.'

Now there was a new atmosphere of desperation as we pushed forward into the evening. All of us knew that if we failed to reach Umm Badr that night, we would be lost. The desert lay before us, pale as paper, seemingly without landmarks. But I knew that if there was anyone who could find water in this wilderness, it would be Abu Sara. Sunset came as we descended a great dune, leaving a trail of colours in the sky, prussian blue, magenta and scarlet. In the darkness which came down like a blind, Adem and Saadiq began a faltering camel-chant, '*weh weh oooh weh*', and I tried to join in, but our mouths were so rasped with dust and dryness that the effort soon failed and we rode grimly on. Even Abu Sara rode without speaking, and I caught myself thinking, over and over again, 'It can't be far now!' But the hours passed blindly on, as featureless and empty as they had been on the way from Umm Sunta.

Then, just as I was starting to think that perhaps Abu Sara was lost, after all, he called to Adem. 'Go over that ridge and see if there's water.'

Adem broke from the ranks of the herd, urging his mount into a trot, a shadowy figure, undulating silently over the hard sand, until he was swallowed up whole by the predatory darkness. We continued for a silent lifetime. Then Adem reappeared suddenly out of the blackness like a figure from a pop-up picture-book. As soon as he drew near, Abu Sara shouted, 'Is there water?'

'By God the Great, brothers, there's a sea!'

'Praise be to God!'

Everyone blessed the Almighty and the Prophet repeatedly. One more night, we all realized, and half the herd would not have been able to carry on.

Within minutes we were over the ridge, and I saw the dim reflection of the starlight in the pool. The camels plunged in, smashing the mirror image, slurping up the water noisily, gagging and heaving in their efforts to push their way through the crowd.

Saadiq filled a bowl and handed it to Abu Sara. 'In the name of God, the Compassionate, the Merciful,' he whispered and took a long draught. Then each of us drank in turn: the liquid had the consistency of weak glue and approximately the same taste but none of us complained.

'God is Generous!' said Abu Musa.

'Amen!' echoed the others.

We sank back into the soft sand, catching a few moments' respite while the camels drank. My mind drifted off. All I knew was that I was here, and that somehow by this experience I had transcended the life I might have lived. For I knew instinctively that this experience was going to be a seminal one in my life, that a serious and fundamental change had taken place within me, and that I should never, as long as I lived, be quite the same again.

17

A SMALL NEST OF
LIVING CREATURES

Life here evaporates like a vapour.

Antoine de St Exupéry, *Wind, Sand and Stars*

The pool seemed a miracle when I awoke the next morning. It glistened like glass as the first ruby fingers of the dawn kindled its fire. I ran down to the water's edge and plunged in; it was so cold that it stung. Afterwards I sat in the sand for some time, admiring the beauty of the place. It was a desert-man's heaven: a cool, shaded oasis, surrounded by crusty terraces of sand. The water was as smooth as marble, skirted by grey cliffs on one side and ivory beaches on the other. There were groves of *nim* trees on the open side, and above the cliffs a hundred black eagles played around each other in spiralling flight paths. It was a vision of paradise that one could keep in one's heart always in the oven of the Libyan Desert.

A bevy of Arab women came down to the water driving a score of donkeys carrying empty goatskins. They were Kababish women with coffee-coloured faces and shoulder-length hair, as black as jet. They began splashing about in the water, floating the skins and filling them, and the sound of their cheerful, feminine laughter drifted up to me like music after the tensions of the journey.

Already in the distance I could make out the minuscule shapes of camels being watered, and as time passed more and more were brought out of the desert for the nomad's perennial task of watering. The camels were accompanied by ragged, biblical-looking figures: old men with Santa Claus beards of ash grey and younger ones with long straggly mops of hair who walked barefoot in the hot sand. Very soon, there were camels as far as the eye could see. I had never imagined that there were as many camels in the world as I saw at Umm Badr that morning.

When I returned to the camp, I found the Rizayqat in conversation with two Kababish tribesmen. They were lean wolves of men with thick black beards, who seemed outwardly friendly. Yet I sensed tension as I shook hands with them and answered the usual catechism about my background.

'Which way are you going to the river?' one of them asked.

'By the black mountain, Jebel El Ain,' Abu Sara said.

'We could travel with you,' said the Kabbashi. 'We're from the Ruwahla, and our country lies in that direction.'

'Well, we're leaving at dawn tomorrow,' Abu Sara said. 'You can meet us here.'

The Ruwahla agreed, and walked off towards the pool. As soon as they were out of sight, the guide turned to us and said, 'Get the camels ready, we're going as soon as possible.'

'But what about them?' I asked.

'I'm not travelling with them, by God!' the pilot said. 'I don't trust them at all. They're bandits. Didn't you see the way they looked at our camels? And the way they asked us about our tribe? They didn't believe we were Zayadiyya. Curse their fathers, these Kababish miss nothing!'

The guide seemed really nervous, and I knew that to have deceived the Ruwahla like this he must be convinced of the danger. Luckily they did not return, and we prepared the camels as quickly as we could for departure.

We left the rainwater pool a few hours later, moving behind the camels whose bellies were now bloated with water. As we climbed one of the ivory-coloured dunes which swept down to the lake, I realized that we were leaving the last 'civilization' of any kind between here and the Nile. What lay ahead of us was five hundred miles of almost waterless desert, inhabited only by a few scattered families of Arabs.

Now something had changed in our relationship. I felt proud and happy to be riding with the Rizayqat. For their part, their treatment of me had become no more indulgent, but I sensed a new current of acceptance under the rugged surface of their manner. I knew that I could never be totally accepted by the Rizayqat: the linguistic and cultural barriers were too great, but I was pleased with the melting of the initial aura of suspicion.

The first afternoon out of Umm Badr was like riding in a furnace, the sun out like a scythe slashing at its flesh-and-blood chaff. The Rizayqat called an exceptionally hot day such as this *abu farrar*, 'father of axes', since they said it was able to strike a man down with a single blow. I estimated that the temperature was about 45° Centigrade, which made this one of the hottest places on earth. We climbed up and down dunes and into dry watercourses, passing huts and tents of the Kababish stuck on the bald contours of hills without any protection from the sun. I found it incredible that anyone could live in these conditions. We were travelling towards a wedge of grey mountains which seemed mystic and eerie beyond the pale sands, and the desert itself displayed a palette of colours: orange, scarlet and brown, ornamented by rock of ivory and silver. We rode slowly until sunset came like a blessing, and camped in a watercourse.

That night as usual we took turns to watch the herd. Abu Sara seemed particularly restless on this occasion, and I knew he was still thinking of the Ruwahla. I realized that it was quite a strain on him and the others to lie about their origins in this way, especially for the sake of someone else's camels, for they were proud of their tribe. I wondered how Abu Sara felt about Osman Hasabullah, and asked if the merchant ever rode with the herds.

'Him!' scoffed the pilot. 'By the life of my father, he's a *zurqi*! He wouldn't know the camel's head from its tail! Perhaps he might do it on a donkey!'

This was rather unfair, for Osman's tribe, the Berti, had camels, though they were not of Arab ancestry. I saw that the Arab idea of superiority also applied to the merchants.

'That man's nothing but a robber!' the guide went on. 'They're all bandits that lot! How much does he pay me for this journey? Three hundred pounds, that's all! And one hundred for the others. Look at the work we do! Is it easy? And he sitting in his big house sipping coffee! We should let the Ruwahla take everything, by God!'

The Arabs' wages were certainly meagre. For what amounted to a three-month round journey in atrocious conditions the herdsmen received the equivalent of fifty pounds sterling, and the guide with all his responsibility only a hundred and fifty. When I thought of those I had heard disparaging the Sudanese for their laziness I had to smile to myself. These Arabs worked like ants from dawn far into the night, an endless cycle of toil in merciless temperatures which alone were enough to cripple lesser men. It seemed to me that rarely had I seen so little reward won with so much hardship.

However, Abu Sara and Saadiq both owned a camel in the herd, by which they hoped to gain a little extra on their mean wages. Saadiq pointed out his camel to me; it looked weak and I hoped it would reach the market. I noticed that he was worried about its condition.

After supper that night I sat and talked to the Hamedi. The journey had taken its toll on him and he looked thin and tired, hardly able to stay awake. I asked him if he liked travelling in this way.

'There's great fatigue here,' he said. 'Heat and thirst. This isn't like the land of the Dar Hamed, by God. In our land there's plenty of grass and trees and water, the camels thrive. Here there's nothing but sand and dead trees.'

I asked what he would do after the journey and he told me, 'I'll go back to my camp in our *dar*. I'll spend my money in Egypt on camel-whips and pans and canvas, then I'll sell them to the nomads.'

I wanted to ask how he felt about the Rizayqat, but it would have been impossible in the close confines of the camp, where every word was a public announcement. This was a good thing, for the constant sharing of information gave the group a muscular unity and prevented fragmentation, which would have been disastrous under these conditions. The Arabs talked from the moment they woke up until they went to sleep, and at night, after we had eaten, the time would be filled in by endless rounds of storytelling. Often the stories were repeated over and over, though no one objected much.

Adem was the best storyteller, though Abu Sara had the most interesting tales, especially of his adventures as a young man, and about inter-tribal battles and incidents. It was from him that I learned that the governor of Mellit had not been entirely correct when he had told me that the Forty Days Road was no longer in use. He claimed that he had come down from Egypt that way as a young man, though he called it the White Mountain Route.

'Of course, no one goes that way except the bad ones,' he said, his eyes glittering in the firelight. 'They go that way to avoid the police and the customs. No honest man would use it.'

'Then you're a bandit, by God!' said Adem.

'Listen, brothers, I was a youth then. We were bringing weapons down from Egypt. They were rifles, English I think. I remember they were beautiful weapons, by God, packed in boxes. But that way was hard, believe me. Where was the water? Where was the food for our camels? There was none. After seven days we arrived at the oasis of Selima, and thought we were safe. We had to get water there, but it was bad, and there were some Kababish. They came into our camp, talking and drinking tea. Then they said, "Show us your rifles!" "How do you know we have rifles?" we said. "No one comes by this way unless they have rifles," they said. "It would be better to give us some of these rifles, then no one will know which way you are going." You understand, brothers? They wanted payment for silence.'

'And what happened?'

'How could we refuse? How could we fight the Kababish in their own land? We gave them a box and left the next morning. By God, but these Kababish miss nothing!'

Why then, I asked Abu Sara, if the Kababish were so rapacious, did they not just take our camels? The old guide laughed and said, 'Maybe they will, by God. God only knows what they will do! But Jebel El Ain is the dangerous area. Once we are in the land of the Nuba no one will touch us, by the will of God!'

Another story which Abu Sara told was about how the war between the Mahriyya section of the Rizayqat and another Arab tribe, the Bani Halba, had begun in the late seventies.

'It was like this,' he said. 'One day three camels belonging to a young man of the Mahriyya wandered into some sorghum belonging to the Bani Halba. The Bani Halba captured them, and took them to their camp. Then the owner came along on his riding-camel, with his rifle, to get them back. "By Almighty God," he said, "those camels are mine, give me them." "By God," they said, "those camels belong to us, for we found them in our fields!" "Then I will buy them from you!" said the Mahri. "What is your price?" "Never," they said. "They will stay here!" "Then I'll fetch my family, and we will see, you sons of dogs!" The Mahri rode away on his camel, but as he did so, one of the Bani Halba women, who had been angered by his last remark, said to her sons, "If you are men you will take his rifle, and I will use it to stir the 'asida!" Then one youth from the Bani Halba ran after the Mahri and stopped him. "Give me your rifle!" he said. "You've had my camels," said the Mahri. "Now if you want my rifle you must pay for it!" And he shot the youth dead. Then two of the boy's brothers came running, and he shot them too. That was how the war started. After that there was much killing.'

'How did it all end?' I asked.

'They held a great meeting, the government, the elders and the tribesmen. Fourteen of the Bani Halba had died, by God! And six of the Mahriyya. It was decided that the Mahriyya should pay twenty thousand pounds to the Bani Halba. But even to this day, the Bani Halba hate us!'

Old Abdallahi rarely told stories, but on several occasions he spoke about his younger days during the time of the Anglo-Egyptian Condominium. He spoke of Guy Moore in the thirties and forties: 'Sultan Moore was a generous man! By God I've seen him throw money to the people, so that they scrabbled for it like chickens! But he was a man who did not play. There were no bandits around when he was Sultan. It was the whip or the rope for anyone who was dishonest!'

It had taken me some time to realize how famous Moore was in Darfur. Many people, even those who were too young to remember him, were familiar with his name, and some of the Arab tribes had oral poetry about him. They often referred to him as 'Sultan' almost as if he had been independent ruler of North Darfur rather than just a district administrator. Evidently he had been a most unusual character, and I wished I could have met him. Abdallahi asked me if I knew him, and I told him that I didn't, though I thought he had died recently.

I asked the Arabs if they had heard of Wilfred Thesiger, who had been Moore's assistant in Kutum. At first no one seemed to know what I was talking about, then suddenly Abdallahi said, 'You mean Sejjar! Of course I remember him! He was a big, tall man. Very young and strong, and always killing lions. One day a lion came charging at him out of the bush. His men wanted to kill the lion with spears, but he said, no, let it come. Just as he fired, his foot trembled, but he hit it right between the eyes. Afterwards he took off his shoes and threw them away. "Why did you do that?" someone asked him. "Because they're no good," he said. "They let my foot tremble!"'

The Arabs connected me with Moore and Thesiger simply because these were the only other Englishmen they knew of, and imagined that we were from the same 'tribe'. During other journeys in Darfur, when meeting people who had difficulty in understanding that I was an Englishman, I referred to myself as being the *Awlad Moore* ('Children of Moore') tribe. I rarely found anyone over forty who did not grasp this immediately.

The second day after leaving Umm Badr, we camped for the night on a plain of hard, flat sand. Shortly after we had made camp, two camel-riders arrived. As they came out of the shadows to greet us, we saw immediately that they were the Ruwahla we had met in Umm Badr. After shaking hands with each of us, they came to join us at the fire, their angular, hawkish faces turned to Abu Sara.

'You left without us!' one of them said.

'Yes,' replied Abu Sara, unflinchingly. 'We decided that it would be better to move on as quickly as possible. We didn't know where to find you.'

'Never mind. God is generous.'

'Yes.'

'Which clan of the Zayadiyya did you say you belonged to?'

'I didn't say, but we're the Awlad Jerbo.'

'Do the Awlad Jerbo take their camels to Egypt in summer?'

'These camels aren't ours. They belong to Osman Hasabullah in El Fasher.'

'Which way did you say you would take to Egypt?'

'By Jebel El Ain.'

'That way is dangerous. There are many bandits. It is better to go another way.'

The air was suddenly charged with pressure. I scanned the faces of the Rizayqat. They were impassive, yet something about their composure suggested a taut string, ready to snap.

Then Abu Sara said with slow authority, 'There is no other way. There may be bandits in the desert, but does Arab rob Arab as dog eats dog? God will reckon their sins.'

'But some of these men are wild, and don't know God.'

'But God will go with us.'

I looked at the Kababish. Their predatory eyes were now wide open and staring at our guide.

'Some of your camels have Ruwahla brands. Perhaps they are stolen.'

'I have papers for each one of them.'

'They might have been stolen before you bought them. By the law of the Arabs the original owner may take them back.'

Suddenly Abu Sara's eyes opened wide. The slow, easy-going manner dropped from him as if it had been a mask, and he fixed the Ruwahli who had spoken with a glare like a knife-thrust. 'Are any of these camels yours?'

The other man seemed hesitant for the first time, 'Well . . . no, I don't think so.'

'And you?' said Abu Sara to the other Kabbashi.

'No, they are not mine.'

'Good.' It seemed at once that Abu Sara had grown in stature, his true being showing through in its hardest, most uncompromising aspect: he looked, as he was, a man who had grown strong from a lifetime spent in the world's most severe school. 'Then it is better not to say that they are stolen. For anyone who tries to take camels by force must answer for it.'

'God is generous,' said one of the Kababish.

'Amen,' agreed Abu Sara.

Without another word the tribesmen rose and mounted their camels. A few moments later they were nebulous, ghostly figures in the moonlight. Then they merged with the thicker strains of the shadows and were gone.

'We might have trouble with them,' Abu Sara said, finally.

'They're treacherous those Ruwahla, by Almighty God!' said Saadiq.

'They may come back at any time, brothers, and they may bring others. This is their country, don't forget. We must watch the herd all the time,' said Abu Musa.

'Yes,' continued Abu Sara. 'We'd better move on as quickly as we can to the wells at Rameiti. Then we'll be in Handab country. I have friends there who will help us if there is trouble.'

'They won't come back now,' said Adem. 'You scared them off.'

'By the will of God you're right. But only God knows.'

Later, as we lay down to sleep, there were flashes of electricity in the depth of the sky, veins of metallic yellow which split and branched as they ripped the night's velvet. Far away I heard the soft boom of thunder, and I thought of Eliot's 'Dry sterile thunder without rain' from *The Waste Land*. And in that thunder, it seemed, lay a profound warning from nature about the gathering storm which lay coiled and waiting across our future.

There were purple streaks in the sky as I awoke and went to join the others at the fire. In minutes the streaks had grown blue and brilliant, and I watched the familiar dark-swathed figures moving around the circular mass of the herd, hearing the clink of the 'uqals as the camels were freed. The day was humid and uncomfortable, and my palms sweated as we moved off that morning. The clammy atmosphere depressed me, so that even the beauty of the landscape, the vacant miles of sand, the crusted mountains in the distance failed to stir me. As the temperature dropped in the evening, however, my spirits soared, and we moved on mile after mile in the inky darkness which was so thick that we could hardly make out the camels before us. The darkness drew the camels together with an instinct as old as time, and the Arabs sang and shouted relentlessly as if to remind each other of their own existence. On and on we travelled, going always a little to the east of the pole star, which Abu Sara kept at his left shoulder. To the west I could see the golden asterisk of Venus which the Arabs called *zahra*, by whose slow descent Abu Sara judged the time.

Later we made camp, and as I drifted off to sleep after the meal, I was woken suddenly by a yell from Saadiq.

'What is it?' I gasped, as the others started up.

'Two riders!' he said, pointing. 'There!'

For many minutes we sat straining our tired eyes in the darkness, but we saw nothing but the eternal stars littering the silk screen of the night, and heard nothing but the rhythmic mastication of the herd.

'You imagined it, by God!' declared Adem, always ready to ridicule Saadiq.

'Never!' replied the other. 'I saw them. They passed over there.'

No one commented further. All of us had in mind the menacing figures of the Ruwahla whom we had met the previous night. Abu Sara detailed a strict watch on the camels, but so exhausted were we from the day's ride that none of us was able to stay awake for long.

The next day we moved across trackless nothingness which stretched to every horizon. Occasionally jagged necks of hills raised themselves from the hard, flat sand, and I was sure that Abu Sara was navigating on these, having memorized the exact shape, colour and texture of each. I tried to do this myself, but after a short while I found that my mind was only able to retain a blurred, imperfect image. Before the sun's heat came out like a spear from its housing, a *haboob* set in with devastating force. We covered our faces and battled on towards the horizon, the Rizayqat bent forwards over the horns of their saddles, accentuating the strange jutting profile which walking camels present. The landmarks were lost in the chalky mist of the storm and I felt entombed in this infinite place, lost with a group of mortals, surging on some incomprehensible compulsion to the bounds of the earth and its wilderness.

It was a relief when Abu Sara called a halt, but as we crouched in the lee of the camels we were immediately covered by sand. The water, already foul and greasy, was laced with sand as soon as it was poured, and we could do nothing but cover our faces and wait till the storm passed. As the force of the wind began to drop, a figure appeared out of the nothingness: it was a bent old man, like a haunting leprechaun.

'Welcome!' shouted Abu Sara, and the figure advanced towards us. After we had greeted him and given him some of our gritty water, he said, 'You're near the well of Ruweiba. What is your people?'

'Arab, Zayadiyya.'

'There are some Ruwahla at the well. They said that some *zurqa* were bringing a herd up this way. They must have spoken of another herd.'

'Either that or they're lying. We've seen no one else.'

When the wind had dropped enough, we lit a fire, and the old man stayed to eat some of our *'asida*, before heading off back to the wells, which were in a nearby wadi. Abu Sara decided that we would press on to Rameiti, but when the time came to count the herd, we discovered that one animal was missing. This time it was Abu Sara who blamed the Hamedi for supposed idleness, and cursed him loudly.

Adem said, 'He'll make for the well.'

It was decided that Saadiq should go off and search for the animal, but before he mounted Abu Sara said, 'Watch out for those Ruwahla, brother.'

We waited for his return. Half an hour passed, then an hour. Abu Sara fidgeted nervously. Then Saadiq appeared on the skyline and we saw immediately that the camel was with him. He arrived in the camp mumbling disgruntledly to himself, 'Curse their fathers, those Kababish!'

'What is it?' Abu Sara asked.

'The camel was at the well and it had drunk. The devils made me pay fifty piastres for the amount of water. Fifty!'

We laughed uproariously when we thought of what might have happened. Saadiq, however, refused to see the funny side, 'They cheated me!' he said. 'No camel can drink fifty piastres' worth of water! Money is money!'

'Did you see the Ruwahla?' Adem asked.

'Yes, they were there but they didn't speak. *Zurqa!* I'd like to *zurqa* them, by the life of the Prophet!'

For the next three days we moved deeper and deeper into the wasteland, beyond tracks, beyond the stark huts of the Kababish. All around us was nothing, except an endless beach of flat, featureless sand, a monotony unbroken even by a rock, a blade of grass or a dead tree. The environment both humbled and exalted. It seemed that the stature of the Rizayqat increased steadily in proportion to the severity of the surrounding landscape, and I never ceased to be amazed by their hardiness. At the same time the vast emptiness of the desert reduced our tiny, struggling world to absolute insignificance: a small nest of living creatures with no more permanence than a gust of wind playing across the face of the ocean. A *haboob* blew almost constantly, and each day was a quarterless battle against an alliance of unbeatable foes: thirst, heat and exhaustion. During the lulls in the battle, I discovered that my surroundings were having a strange effect. My mind became unusually clear and lucid, and I found myself following logical trains of thought for several hours without losing the thread. I was able to think more profoundly about myself than I had been for years, to examine my motivations, aims and objects in a new and surprisingly fresh light. This was totally unexpected, and I guessed that it was a result of the low sensory input which one experiences in the desert. In our normal environment, our thoughts are constantly bombarded by information gathered from our surroundings which are in a state of perpetual change. In the desert, though, the surroundings are static and featureless, liberating the mind and allowing strings of ideas to run and develop in logical chains. I had read about the effects of sensory deprivation, and even experienced them during a Special Air Service 'resistance to interrogation' exercise. In this, though, the situation had been induced artificially and in a deliberately unpleasant way, so that the principal effect had been disorientation. In the desert I experienced it as something valuable and satisfying. I wondered if the Arabs were experiencing it too, or if perhaps their minds were constantly on this level. It might help to explain why they were customarily so keen and observant.

By day we rested in our tent of canvas and wool, and after sunset we laid our bedding in the sand and awoke to find ourselves half-buried in drifts which had piled up in the night. We had loaded the pack-camel with firewood, since none was to be found in this quarter, and we used it very sparingly. Our greatest problem was water: although we had enough to drink, what we had was filthy and fetid with a nauseating smell, and even strong Arab tea could not disguise its rankness.

One evening, after the meal, I got out my Michelin map in order, purely for the sake of interest, to make a rough estimate of our position. This was a new diversion for the Arabs, who jeered and laughed when I tried to explain it to them, and Adem asked me if I thought the map better than the guide. For a long time afterwards I considered the skill of Abu Sara. It seemed quite remarkable that this man could navigate so accurately without instruments, except those he was born with. For him the desert was a familiar place, and what seemed so difficult for me was second nature to him. His proficiency was a simple necessity for survival: from an early age he had learned that it was a matter of life and death. The pilot was the pivot of the herd both physically and mentally; he knew the water sources, the grazing areas, the places to find shade and firewood. Already I had doubted whether the survival of man in such conditions was possible without the camel; now I wondered how long any of us would have survived without the expertise of Abu Sara.

I once asked him his opinion of the desert, having explained my own impressions of its beauty and grandeur. He looked at me uncomprehendingly, then said, 'The desert! The desert is a bitch!'

After three days of back-breaking toil against head wind, a vague black line of what appeared to be jagged rocks, shimmering like a mirage, appeared on the horizon. As we approached, the nebulous shapes materialized into the form of trees. This was the wide, empty watercourse of Wadi al Milik. During the autumn it transferred water from the damp lands of the sub-Sahara into the Nile near Ed Debba, but its trees, *kitir, sayal, hejlij* and *heraz*, were now dry and lifeless, and the wadi bed nothing but sand and rock-hard, cracked mud. We camped for the afternoon amongst the bare trunks, grateful to have found some respite from the ceaseless *haboob*.

For moments after we had unsaddled we lay there, our minds drifting, enjoying the rare luxury of shelter. All of us were exhausted, and even Abu Sara was less bubbling with energy than usual. Suddenly, Saadiq let out a subdued cry which cracked the pleasant cosiness of the afternoon rest and sent us scrabbling to our feet to see what was happening.

'It's them!' Saadiq yelled. 'They've followed us here.'

This time there was no mistaking it. Not more than a few hundred yards away, two riders approached at a jaunty, walking pace. I could already make out their pale faces and the distinctive yellow tint of their shirts.

'It is them, by God the Great!' said Abu Sara. 'And we can do nothing but sit!'

Although the shrubbery in the wadi was quite thick, no Arab could have failed to notice the herd spread out under the trees. We watched as the riders came nearer. On the faces of the Rizayqat, beneath the fatigue, I saw that sudden terrifying alertness, a bowstring taut and ready to fire. If the Rizayqat had been armed, those two Ruwahla would have been dead men. The riders came within a hundred yards of the trees, then turned north-east at an oblique angle, following the line of the wadi. We watched silently until they went out of sight.

'They must have seen us,' agreed Abu Sara, 'but it's a strange thing – if they want something why don't they make a move?'

For some time we turned the matter over in our minds, all of us disturbed by this latest development which had come so unexpectedly. It was just possible that the Ruwahla were following us by pure chance. Somehow, though, I doubted this, and I remembered Ian Fleming's quip about chance encounters: 'Once is happenstance, twice is circumstance, and the third time is enemy action.' It seemed to us all that this third meeting heralded enemy action.

As soon as the sun had passed its zenith, we moved away from the grey-green vein of the wadi. The camels were now travelling slowly, for the pangs of thirst had once more tightened their grip upon them. I will never forget the sunset of that evening. The sky was a loose, billowing cloth, the sun drenched in golden liquid; all around us on the endless proscenium arch of the desert a free film show was in motion. The clouds carried sparklers of colour, crimson, salmon pink and burnt sienna, lying across beds of turquoise and prussian blue. Momentarily our world was washed in a glaze of gold, and everything passed into the dimension of the surreal: the impossibly elongated spider-legged shadows of the camels, the sickly pale sheet of the desert floor, the Arabs slumped towards the arched necks of their camels. Abu Musa rode sage and timeless with his great whip held over his shoulder, with Adem and Saadiq in perfect cameo against the skyline, Abdallahi and the Hamedi, angelic with light on the other side, and Abu Sara occupying his usual position, showing nothing but the determined set of his shoulders, rocking slightly with the unfaltering motion of his mount. Then without further warning, the sun was gone, leaving only the dying tracers of fire in the sky to tell of its going.

The next two days were the hardest I had experienced so far, and I felt myself becoming physically weaker as we rode deep into the timeless desert nights. Finally we arrived at the well of Rameiti, a single water-hole in a clump of acacia and *ushur* bush. As the herd broke around the bush we were greeted by a group of Handab Kababish. They were small, knotty-muscled men, much darker than the Ruwahla, and at once I sensed that their friendliness was not only due to the fact that they knew Abu Sara, but was also the genuine delight in meeting outsiders felt by inhabitants of the inner desert. For the first time in this alien country, it seemed that we had found some allies.

Almost at once we went about watering the herd. The Arabs began to mould a great dish of wet mud and sand from which the camels could drink and some youths of the Handab began drawing water from the well, which was quite shallow. The liquid was stagnant and almost the colour of milk, yet it tasted as sweet as wine after the foul stuff we had been carrying. The dish was only large enough for the camels to be watered in pairs, and at intervals the well would run dry, which meant that the task was a protracted one.

Much of the day I spent sitting in the shade of an *ushur* bush, talking to the Handab. The darkness of their skin showed that there was some Nubian blood in these men, though their stocky, light frames were well adapted to the desert environment. Abu Sara seemed relaxed and at ease with them, and I guessed that they knew his true origin. At noon, Saadiq cooked two huge pansful of *'asida* and the Handab obviously relished the food, since they existed for most of the year on camels' milk. As we drank tea after the meal, Abu Sara asked them if they had seen any Ruwahla.

'There were two of them here last night,' replied one of the Handab. 'They said they were going to Dongola, but I didn't like the look of them, by God the Great! Listen, brothers, they said some *zurqa* were bringing stolen camels up from the south. But where were the *zurqa*? There was no one except you!'

'Look, I think these men are bandits,' replied Abu Sara. 'They've followed us from Umm Badr, by God! Where did they go?'

'They're nearby, camping in the wadi.'

The watering took the rest of the day and most of the night, but though dead beat from the work, we left early in the morning with a group of Handab. The Handab rode tiny, immature camels which seemed to suit their own dimensions perfectly. We followed the line of a small wadi, but did not travel far, for all of us were tired, and we made camp under some *lalob* trees. After eating, the Arabs went to sleep almost at once, and I wrapped myself up in a blanket and dozed.

I awoke to find that two more Arabs had arrived in the camp. They were sitting by the remains of the fire, with the Handab, and two lean camels were couched in the sun, outside the ring of shade afforded by the trees. With a sudden shock I recognized the two Ruwahla who had been following us. They sat amongst four of the tiny Handab, smouldering and dangerous, their eyes sparkling darkly, their bearded chins thrust forwards in defiance. Abu Sara and the Rizayqat roused themselves, moving with a deliberate slowness which held that familiar coiled menace. I moved closer to hear what was being said.

'Why have you come, brothers?' asked one of the Handab.

'We think some of these camels are stolen. Some of them have Ruwahla brands.'

'The guide is a trustworthy man. I have known him for many years. These men are not bandits! They have papers for all their camels.'

'What is this talk of papers? A stolen camel is a stolen camel, paper or no paper!'

'You are the Father of Two Tongues,' the Handabi said suddenly. 'You came here telling us that these men were *zurqa*, but I know they are Arabs.'

'They say they are Zayadiyya, but their tongue is not like that of the Zayadiyya. They lie!'

The discussion went on for some minutes. The Rizayqat said little, as insult and counter-insult were fired. It seemed that the Ruwahla were trying to persuade the Handab to support them in their claim to our camels. Slowly, though, the Handab with their calm, heavy voices began to wear the others down. The voices of the Ruwahla were raised in objection: 'You are not Kababish to support such men!'

'These Arabs are honest. You are not. You come here telling lies and expect us to help you. Go, and do not come back to this land!'

The Ruwahla stood up, and I thought for a moment that one of them was about to draw his dagger: his hand rested on it momentarily. Then with a deft movement, one of the Handab reached below his blanket and brought out a short automatic rifle. It was a Kalashnikov with a folding paratroopers' butt. He did not point it at the Ruwahla, nor make any threatening gesture. Rather, he held it as if he had brought it out for cleaning. But the meaning was clear. I recalled Abdallahi saying, 'Weapons rule here!'

The Ruwahla scowled darkly, as if they were about to let fly a string of curses. They looked at the Handab, at Abu Sara and the Rizayqat, and met the reflection of their own harsh, narrow-eyed stare which is the hallmark of the desert Arab. For moments, it seemed, no one spoke. Hollow time washed amongst us, this ossified group of humans, frozen for ever in an aggressive attitude, and no more than a microscopic blemish on the surface of the great Libyan Desert which stretched away infinitely on every side. Then the Ruwahla turned and mounted their camels in perfect unison, cocking their legs over the saddle horns and launching immediately into a trot, back across the yellow sands. We stood silently, wondering if these ghosts which had haunted us were finally exorcized.

'They are bad men!' said one of the Handab.

'I thought you were going to kill them!' said Abu Sara.

'Kill them?' the little Arab looked surprised, and there was an un-expected 'clunk, click' as he drew back the cocking handle of his weapon. No bullet was ejected into the sand: the rifle had been empty. 'I got it out for cleaning, that's all. But I don't think they'll follow you again!'

We thanked the Handab, and paid them for their water. With minds easier and less exhausted we set out that day on the last stretch of our journey to the river.

18

RETURN TO THE RIVER

The next morning we awoke beneath a sheer scar of smooth black rock which formed a continuous wall as far as the eye could see. This was Jebel El Ain, a mysterious flat-topped shelf which runs unbroken across a hundred miles of desert. If the fear of Ruwahla raiders was behind us, then this last section of the journey to the river was a continuous battle to hold back the tide of fatigue which threatened to engulf us.

The floor beneath the mountain was hard-packed sand, perfectly flat and featureless, without the faintest hint of vegetation. Each day resembled the previous one, so that the journey became a dissembled blur in my mind. I found it difficult to keep track of dates or times, and was always aware of the continual heaviness in my body, and the blinding fire of the sun which seemed to penetrate deep into my being.

Now it was hunger and weakness which wore down the herd. Every day we saw nothing but sand and the solid, intractable black face of the plateau. We were totally immersed in our own tiny universe of men and camels, seeing no one and nothing beyond our own microcosm of society. Now I saw why unity amongst us was essential, why Abu Sara's unquestioned authority was the order of things. It was survival, pure and simple, for here there was nowhere to run, nowhere to hide from disagreement. It seemed at times as though I was living in a bizarre dream world, a fantastic Salvador Dali landscape, arid beyond imagination, wandering through a desolation of sand, without end or beginning.

All day the camels festered in the sun, for now there was no shadow, no blade of grass or leaf or tree to help ease the grip of thirst. They stumbled on, following the irresistible dictates of herd instinct, to certain death. A great change had been wrought in their condition; they were weak and thin, and flaps of useless flesh hung in obscene folds from their ribs. My own white had become feeble and Saadiq's bull seemed to be on its last legs. To our riding-camels we now gave a little water, poured into a depression in a canvas sheet, and mixed with a little rock salt.

I had grown familiar with many of the camels in the herd: the small red with the limp, the large buff with the white eyes, the playful female, the black with the over-developed hump. I felt almost sad that after such an heroic journey these animals should end up on some butcher's slab in Egypt. I asked Abu Sara how many beasts were sent to Egypt each year, and he answered that although he was not sure, he guessed that at least ten thousand went from the west of the Sudan alone.

'It is not possible to know,' he continued, 'for they are taken across the border in secret.'

'Smuggled?' I asked.

'Yes. Every merchant or tribesman is supposed to pay tax on each camel exported to Egypt. But of course no one pays, and we enter the country by secret ways. If the police stop us, then we give them money. They will let us through, but they won't let you in. They will know you are *khawaja* by your face.' When I pressed him, he insisted, 'It is a big problem as things are with the police. You think I have a passport? No. And if they found you they would say that you are a spy and we helped you. That is why I won't take you!'

I could see that his word was final, and although I had been told this at the beginning of the journey, I was still disappointed. I knew, however, that from Dongola the herd would be following the Nile into Mahas country, the 'Belly of Stones', an area which I had already explored extensively, and I felt a little consolation in this.

I wondered how the Rizayqat felt now the conditions were becoming harder. It was obvious that each of them was affected in some way for they had become more sharp-tempered and irritable. Every night, for instance, after the herd had been hobbled, there would be the same endless argument over the number of *'uqals*, some of which were always lost during the day. This was doubly annoying, for it was an unspoken rule that no one could drink until the hobbling had been settled. Luckily such disputes were soon forgotten.

Some of the camels began to go lame, red sores developing on the velveteen soles of their feet. This was usually amongst those of the herd which had been reared in the grasslands of the south, and which were unused to the scorching desert sand. When this happened, the Rizayqat cut out patches of leather from a thick sheet they carried, and sewed them on to the wounded feet like shoes.

One day, during a particularly severe *abu farrar*, augmented by a blustering wind which blew a breath of steel across our vision, we struggled to erect our little tent. To my surprise, Adem said, 'This is like a war, O people! And this desert is the enemy!'

It was the first time I had heard any of the Arabs express such an opinion of the desert, and I realized that though the desert was far more familiar to them than it was to me, they no more regarded it as a friend or ally than I did, but as a quarterless foe against which all one's strength was required merely to survive. Often though, the desert moved me intensely with the utter enormity of its scale, and lost in the grasp of its deep spell, I would forget the herd and allow them to stray, only to raise cries of 'Chase that camel!' and curses from the others. They had no concept of natural beauty in this sense; when I tried to explain to Abdallahi, he looked puzzled, and after a time said, 'Well, at least it's clean.' This, I realized, was a concession to my eccentricity.

The journey started to turn into an endurance exercise. By day I dreamed unwillingly of coolness, smooth falls of water over rock, gurgling white-foamed mountain streams, ice-cold lemonade. We rode until midnight every evening and now, when I dismounted, I noticed that my legs wobbled for the first few minutes, and I was horrified to see how emaciated they had become. Abdallahi once poked me in his irritating way and told me, 'You've become weak!'

I scoffed at him, yet inside I knew he was right, and I felt embarrassed beside this thin old man who was old enough to be my grandfather, yet who could survive so well in this hostile world when I, a young European, raised on protein and orange juice, was struggling so hard. The Hamedi, however, seemed in a worse state than I. Each night he would fall asleep as soon as the hobbling was completed and have to be shaken awake when it was time to eat.

We left the plateau of Jebel El Ain far behind and entered a region where sand was piled up in immaculate pieces of natural sculpture. Abu Sara told me that he could recognize individual dunes from previous journeys.

One morning, after leaving the mountain, I noticed a stream of blood and matter pouring from the rear end of one of the females.

'She wants to give birth!' Adem told me.

I was amazed at this apparent miracle, for I had not even been aware that she was pregnant, so thin had she become. As we moved, the stream became more effusive, and suddenly, in a shower of liquid, a small sac was deposited in the sand. Inside was a perfect baby camel, stillborn. The mother did not even stop to inspect the dead offspring, but carried on in the omnipotent compulsion of the herd. The Rizayqat were quiet and I sensed that they, like me, felt a poignant sadness at the merciless privations of this wilderness. No Arab, I was sure, could fail to be moved by the potential birth and subsequent death of a camel, since they regarded these animals as a gift from God. The Prophet Mohammed himself was a desert guide, and must have spent hours watching these fascinating creatures. It seemed to me that the history of the camel and that of Arabs and Islam were inextricably bound.

Later that same day during the afternoon halt, I was roused by a shout from the Hamedi, 'Saadiq's camel has collapsed!'

I joined the others around the prostrate beast which was shivering piteously in the last throes of exhaustion and hunger. Some water was brought, and Abu Sara began to slit its nostrils with his dagger. The other Arabs thumped and kicked at the animal, pulling its tail and trying to make it stand, but the camel showed no sign of reviving. 'It's finished!' said Saadiq sadly, shaking its head. We left it shivering in the sand, to die alone, far from the ranges of its homeland, to become yet another pile of bones, another signpost on this relentless road to the Nile. Saadiq was heartbroken. He had gambled all his money in a game of chance with a savage enemy and lost.

'The desert is hard!' he said. 'It's a place for men, by God!'

'God is generous!'

'Amen!'

The next day we entered a plain of laval rock where the sand had been leached away from the surface, leaving nothing but massive metallic clinkers of stone. The sore-footed camels found this terrain difficult, for their velvet-padded feet were adapted to the flat sands, and this new obstacle only added to their misery and fatigue. It was so hot that the heat drove one almost to madness, but as we laboured on into the afternoon, Adem said unexpectedly, 'There! Smell the woodsmoke! It's a camp!'

Sure enough, passing over the brow of a hill, we saw a clump of scrub, within which was a well. Outside the perimeter of the bushes, in the desert itself, were four wooden cabins, belonging to a family of the Umm Metto Kababish.

We drove the camels into the trees and began to unsaddle, when a ragged group of Arabs came out to greet us. Like the Handab they were small and wiry, with skin like uncured leather and straggly black beards. Most of them wore nothing but tattered *sirwel*, and some were bare-footed. Their faces were more strikingly Semitic than any I had yet seen and they spoke with a slow, deliberate diction which seemed to reflect their character.

The houses of the Umm Metto were constructed of layers of brushwood and stood in the sun among a cluster of dunes. Around them I noticed some women and children. The women were beautiful, with shoulder-length black hair, worn loose and unbraided. They were naked except for loincloths and their skin shone as if it had been oiled.

The Umm Metto were desert Arabs who lived all the year round in this wilderness, seeing no one but the Arabs who brought herds and caravans on the route to the Nile. They owned camels and some goats, but their lives seemed hard in the extreme. Apart from their livestock, they owned nothing but cooking pots and saddlery. I saw, though, that most of them had automatic rifles which they kept close at hand. They wore the desert like a mantle, as if it was their natural environment. They were the *bedu* whose vision I had been following since I set out from Dongola so long ago, and whose reality had taken me down many strange paths. It was ironical that I should find them within a stone's throw of the place I had left months before.

The Kababish had once been a poor tribe of sheep-herders, but had grown strongly by control of the watering-places on the desert routes to Libya and Egypt. They had increased their strength by raising livestock from tribes such as the Hamar, and now had the largest number of camels in the west. It was difficult to equate the knowledge of their tribe's power with the apparent poverty of these Umm Metto, especially when, within a few minutes of meeting them, two men had asked me for *libess* or underclothes. It was Saadiq who solved the mystery for me, 'They're not really poor men,' he said. 'They just look poor. They live in the desert, and never go into towns to buy cloth, so their clothes wear out and they look like beggars. When you ride a camel, your *libess* is the first thing to wear out. That's why they always ask for *libess*.'

In the desert, material possessions are disadvantageous to survival, and therefore the Umm Metto live a frugal life and avoid ownership of much other than their herds. To these Arabs camels represent wealth: not their market price, but wealth itself, a precious commodity like gold and gems. Since their status system within the tribe is also based on camels, they hate to sell them, although it is occasionally necessary in order to obtain essentials such as tea, sugar, flour and spices.

A little later we moved a few miles further on to a well which had more abundant water, and began watering the herd again. I sat and watched the Umm Metto boys straining on the leather ropes, their brown bodies glistening as they frantically filled the hollowed-out tree trunks from which the camels could drink. This was not a labour of love, or a free service for travellers: the Kababish charged fifteen piastres per head for the water and since they used little money, this represented to them a substantial income.

After sunset, when the work was finished, the Rizayqat lit a fire and began to cook massive helpings of 'asida. The Umm Metto began to arrive, coming suddenly out of the darkness, and seated themselves by the fires, until there were about ten of the small dapper men whose bearded faces were reflected in the flickering firelight. They reminded me of gnomes, with their curly hair and beards, their long noses, their small stature and their leather slippers, the way they sat in the sand with their legs drawn up and their slow, drawling way of speaking, which contrasted so markedly with the mercurial patter of the Rizayqat.

After the meal, which the Umm Metto enjoyed, for they rarely ate 'asida, the two groups sat in the moonlight ruminating over the tariff of the well. It seemed simple enough to multiply a hundred-and-forty-odd by fifteen, but the discussion was complicated by the fact that we needed to buy some tea from them, and so it went on for more than an hour. Everyone was allowed to express an opinion, and Abu Sara even asked me if I could work it out by my 'afranji reckoning'. I gave him the correct answer, but it made little difference to the debate. The Umm Metto merely nodded sagely, let the number click over in their minds, and finally arrived at the same conclusion by their own processes.

When they learned that I was a teacher, one of the Umm Metto said, 'Why don't you stay here in the desert, and teach my children?' I imagined myself living for ever in the Libyan Desert with these free and happy people. It was an offer I had to consider for a long time before refusing.

After the sum had been duly paid, it was prayer-time, and both tribes lined up, in order to pray together. The *imam* was an elderly man of the Umm Metto with a straggly horse-tail of a beard. As I watched their devotions, I thought of how the concept of a single God had originated amongst people just like these. It was significant, I thought, that the three great monotheistic religions had begun in desert regions: a reflection, I was sure, of the power of the desert to affect the spiritual nature of man. In the Arabian Peninsula, even before the era of Islam, the scattered tribes had some concept of a supreme God. The Prophet gave shape to this idea, promoting the notion of submission, 'Islam', the idea that all humanity is subject to the will of God.

The next morning we moved off on the final stretch of the journey to the river. We left the brushwood shelters of the Umm Metto far behind, entering a region where the sand lay like a smooth pastel carpet, piled up here and there into great crescent dunes. In patches it glistened silver from the mineral salts it contained and occasionally we crossed stretches of hard black magma strewn with polished rocks and boulders.

'How is the desert?' Abu Sara asked with a knowing smile.

'Perfect!' I answered.

'It's like this as far as Egypt, you know,' he said. 'Neither grass nor tree, just desert!'

At night, the sky filled with electricity again, great flashes of orange and steel blue, without a hint of thunder or rain. On the morning of the next day, however, a savage wind hit us with staggering force. There was a crushing boom of thunder which shocked us all and brilliant forks of lightning filled the air, splitting the banks of cloud and driving down to the desert floor. The intensity of the storm was frightening, and suddenly the rain came splashing across the sand like a hail of bullets. The horizon turned bleach grey, and we knew at once that we were in for the granddaddy of all *haboobs*, travelling in its very eye. The camels turned tail to the wind with an instinctive movement, as its brute force whipped sand and rain across our faces. There was nothing we could do except dismount and cower in the lee of the camels. The Hamedi and I tried to keep the herd together, but the wind was so strong that it was difficult to stay vertical.

As suddenly as it had appeared, it was gone. The Arabs came out of their shelters, like animals from their holes, and we lit a fire, using as much wood as we dared to dry out our clothes and to warm our insides with tea.

'That's like your country, Makil!' said someone, for I had told them that in my land it rained continuously.

'Yes,' I said. 'But not as fierce as that!'

'You would not believe it, by God!' said Abu Sara, 'Only two days in the year it rains here, brothers, and this is one of them!' Certainly, if before the journey I had been warned to expect rain, I should not have believed it.

During this part of the journey, water was no longer a problem, but we were short of food and ate little. Like me, the Arabs became weaker and more bad-tempered as their exhaustion grew. They described this desperate kind of movement as 'going cold', which I found ironical since it was the opposite of the reality. *Abu farrar* was the rule rather than the exception, and the sun chased us with predatory deliberateness, as savage as I had known.

On the afternoon of the second day out of the Umm Metto camp, however, a small incident occurred which raised our spirits. The Hamedi let out a yell, and I saw something small and black on the sand. It was a dove, and quickly the Hamedi dropped from the saddle and tried to catch it. He was far too slow, and the bird flew off, and circled high above us. The find was significant, however, and the Arabs began to mutter, 'The sea! By God, it's near!'

It was not until the next morning that we made out the dim smoky line of the palm trees which marked the river, like a mirage in the far distance. Then the vision was lost again, shielded from our eyes by a range of dunes. But there was a tremendous change in our morale now, as we rode forwards like demons, pursuing that image of shady palm groves and cool, fresh water.

Several hours passed, and the trees came into our sight again, glistening with a deep shade of green which I had almost forgotten. Then we were almost upon them, crossing a desert track from Dongola to Khartoum which was marked with black and white poles. I suddenly remembered having travelled down that same track in the back of a Toyota truck with Katie, long ago, living in a different, more naïve world. I could hardly recognize myself in that fleeting memory, but it produced a lump in my throat as I remembered my first days in the north, how Katie and I had become friends, how the dream had been born. This double perspective, seeing the desert as if from both sides at once, treading on a piece of ground I had once trodden, crossing the same track, produced within me a sense of anticlimax. But it was dispelled when a few moments later I saw the Nile glinting like mercury beyond the palms and the *sunt* trees. I saw neat Nubian houses nestled in the palm groves, and suddenly we were greeted by a man on a donkey, who led us down to the river.

Its beauty was overwhelming, a vision of life itself, as it flowed cool, deep and silent between its green banks. The camels stampeded across the shingle down to the water's edge, and we couched our animals to let them drink. The Rizayqat were behaving with their usual composure, waiting until the herd had been organized before drinking. I myself stood for a second watching the smooth inviting flow of the water, then plunged in fully clothed and splashed about in the blissful chill of the current. A few minutes later, though, Abu Sara put an end to it by shouting 'Hey, Makil, you're frightening the camels!' and I understood that my antics were preventing them from their much needed drink. As I hoisted myself out of the stream, Adem said, 'Makil, you're home!'

'*Alhamdulillah!*' I said.

Later we sat on the shale bank, and some Arab farmers who Abu Sara knew came to join us. After a little discussion, Abu Sara persuaded them to buy my camel for two hundred pounds. It was a considerable loss, but I thought myself lucky when I remembered Saadiq's camel, by now a dry heap of hide and bones, somewhere out there. At last, the end of the road was in sight. In one more day, I told myself, I should be in Dongola. Often on the journey I had been irritated by the Arabs; now the thought of leaving them brought a hollow feeling to my stomach.

That night we camped near Dongola, and before I slept, I asked Abu Sara how soon he would be going this way again. The guide shook his head and said, 'By God this is the last time for me. I'm getting old. Osman Hasabullah can keep his camels. I'll go back to my goats and my wife and I won't travel further than the market ever again!'

I knew that this was empty talk. Abu Sara was a desert man: he would never leave the desert until they buried him in it.

The first thing I saw the next morning was an oddly shaped blue object which seemed to flutter like a flag above a distant dune. Then I realized that it was the windsock of the airport outside Dongola, that place from which I had first been captivated by the Libyan Desert several years before. I changed into European clothes and packed up my things for the last time. I gave Abu Sara and the others some money out of the two hundred pounds which was all I had in the world, and shook hands with each of them. Then Adem and I rode off towards the airstrip, the last sad ride out of the dimension of the desert and into the world of Sudan *afranji*. As we rode a truck suddenly appeared before us and Adem tried to flag it down. It grated past in a shower of dust and Adem said, 'See, brother! It won't stop for an Arab on a camel!'

His words brought into sharp focus the border between the two dimensions, the border I was about to cross. In the desert, the Arabs were their own masters, sleeping and moving as they pleased: within its harsh anarchy, they were free. In this other world, man's machines controlled and limited them, trucks confined them to tracks and roadways where roadside coffee-shops marked the route. I felt like a man fallen by accident from another planet.

Adem and I rode right up to the airstrip, where I saw a knot of Toyota pick-up trucks. As I dismounted, one of the drivers came over to us. He was a young man of the Danaqla tribe whose family I knew slightly.

When he saw me, his eyes opened wide in amazement, 'Mister Michael, what are you doing with that camel?' he said, giggling.

I was about to answer when Adem cut in, 'That man has just ridden from Darfur on that camel. Why do you laugh?' The Dongolawi stepped backwards in disbelief, and I looked up to Adem and grasped his hand.

'Thanks, brother,' I said.

'Go in peace,' he replied.

I watched as he led the two camels back into his world, the world that for a short time I had shared.

Sitting in the back of the Toyota, the Dongolese plied me with questions. 'Been riding a camel, then?' someone said, and laughed. But I was not listening. Instead I was looking out at the desert, the lonely desert which I had crossed. Like a woman, it looked its most beautiful at the time of parting. I was seeing too the ghosts of the Rizayqat and the Hamedi, which I knew would always haunt me. I was seeing Abu Musa, sitting back comfortably in the saddle as if it were an armchair, grumbling and mumbling to himself; Adem, as slim as a desert fox, perched shoeless on the edge of his *hawiyya*; Saadiq, like an image from the Arabian Nights with his tightly bound turban and sharp goatee beard; Abdallahi, the old man who rode like a youth, strangely elegant in his tattered clothing; the Hamedi, broad, simple, good-natured, singing endlessly into the night; and Abu Sara, the man upon whose skill and courage all our lives had depended. I knew that this was how I would be seeing them for the rest of my life. As I strained my eyes across the shining sand, it seemed to me for a moment that I could hear the shrill cry of '*weh weh oooh weh!*', drifting across to me from that other world.

Then the engine started, and we were off to Dongola, along that same road by which I had entered the town on that first day. It was the same road, but I knew that I was not the same man. All that I had experienced in the desert had left a mark upon me. The brand of the nomad, as indelible as if it had been made by a burning iron, could not be erased. Those moments were the beginning, not the end of everything, for it was then that I knew that nothing could prevent my return.

LIST OF TRIBES

The following is a rough classification of tribes mentioned in the text and is not intended as a comprehensive classification of tribes of the Sudan.

Nubian	Danaqla	
	Mahas	
Arabo-Nubian	Shayqiyya	
Ja'aliyyin Arabs	Ja'aliyyin	
	Jawa'ama	
	Jellaba Hawara	
	Bederiyya	
	Kawahla	
Juhayna Arabs	Hamar	Jiledad
	Zayadiyya	Awlad Jerbo
		Awlad Jabir
	Rizayqat	Mahamid
		Mahriyya
		Umm Jallul
		Erayqat
	Kababish	Umm Badr
		Ruwahla
		Handab
		Umm Metto
		Atawiyya
		Awayda
		Ribayqat
		Bani Umm Ran
	Awlad Rashid	
	Bani Hissein	
	Dar Hamid	
	Bani Halba	
	Messeriyya	
	Baza'a	

Nilo-Saharan cultivating tribes	Fur	
	Mesalit	
	Tama	
	Erenga	
	Jabal	
	Gimmar	
	Tungur	
Central Saharan nomads and semi-nomads	Zaghawa	Ango
		Kobbe
		Awlad Diqqayn
	Bedayatt	
	Gor'an	
	Tubu	
	Berti	
Others	Kiniin Tuareg	
	Dinka	
	Beja	Bishariyyin
	Meidob	Ababda

GLOSSARY

abbala	camel nomads
abu 'ashara	Lee-Enfield .303 rifle
abu farrar	lit. father of axes – a very hot day
afranji, pl. *afranj*	foreigner, western person
ahsaas	natural insight; sense
akhdar	green
alhamdulillah	lit. praise be to God
araagi	long Arab shirt worn by nomads
'asida	sorghum porridge
azraq	blue, black
babanoss	tree with dark wood similar to mahogany
baqqara	cattle nomads
barashoot	smugglers
bayt kibiir	lit. big house – main hut of a compound
bedu	noble, camel-rearing tribes of Arabia
bishari	breed of fast camel from the Butana
bismillahi	lit. in the name of God
conflet	type of shirt worn by Chadian tribes
damin	a guarantor or agent controlling animal sales
damra, pl. *damr*	semi-permanent camps of nomads, for the old and sick
dar	house; area; country
dara	hearth or guests' area in nomads' camp
dobbayt	sung verse of the Arab nomads
donki, pl. *dawanki*	artesian well
ghautiyya	hut of mud or straw
gotran	kind of tar made from melon seeds
haboob	desert wind, usually from the north
habsha	water mixed with sugar and flour, or buttermilk
hawiyya	pack-saddle for a camel
hejlij	*Balanites aegyptiaca*
heraz	*Acacia albida*
heskaniit	*Cenchrus biflorus*
hiq	young camel, three or four years old
howdaj	nomad women's litter

imam	prayer-leader in Islam
'imma	long strip of cloth wound round the head
ingleez	English, British
jebha	guerrillas
jellabiyya	long Arab shirt, named after *jellaba*, merchants
jongola	camel saddle designed for carrying tents
jowloon	gallon
Kalash	Kalashnikov AK47 rifle
karm	hospitality and generosity, part of the Arab code
khabiir	lit. expert – usually a desert pilot or guide
khalwa dyuuf	special quarters for guests
khawaja	lit. gentleman; sir – also white man, European
kirkadea	*Hibiscus sabdariffa*
kitir	*Acacia laeta*
lalob	*Balanites aegyptiaca*
libess	underclothes
mashat	braided hairstyle used by Arab women
merissa	sorghum beer
mowta	southern movement of the nomads
mukhayyit	*Boscia senegalensis*
nabak	*Ziziphus abyssinica*
naib	leader, adult camel
naqa	female camel
nim	*Azadirachta indica*
qayd	hobble for the front legs of a camel
qeshsh	dry grass, hay
qoz	rolling sand-dunes
raba'	'adolescent' camel, six or seven years old
rafiq	companion
raka'	prostrations made during Islamic prayers
rakuba	flat-roofed sheter
sadiis	fully grown adult camel, over seven years old
salaam 'alaykum	standard Islamic greeting, lit. peace be upon you
sayal	*Acacia tortillis*
sharaat	nervous camel
shorta	police
silsil	chain, device for controlling a camel
sirwel	baggy Arab trousers
sunt	*Acacia arabica*
suq	market
tobe	(1) woollen garment worn by men; (2) colourful robe worn by women
tombak	a type of chewing tobacco
umda	senior shaykh

upchachumba	pure spirit alcohol made from sorghum or millet
'uqal	hobble for a camel's knee
ushur	*Calotropis procera*
ustaz	sir; professor; normal title of a teacher
'utfa	nomad women's litter
zabata	defect of camel's shoulder
zahra	the planet Venus
zariba	enclosure, usually of thornbush
zurqa	Arab name for black people

MORE ABOUT PENGUINS, PELICANS, PEREGRINES AND PUFFINS

For further information about books available from Penguins please write to Dept EP, Penguin Books Ltd, Harmondsworth, Middlesex UB7 0DA.

In the U.S.A.: For a complete list of books available from Penguins in the United States write to Dept DG, Penguin Books, 299 Murray Hill Parkway, East Rutherford, New Jersey 07073.

In Canada: For a complete list of books available from Penguins in Canada write to Penguin Books Canada Ltd, 2801 John Street, Markham, Ontario L3R 1B4.

In Australia: For a complete list of books available from Penguins in Australia write to the Marketing Department, Penguin Books Australia Ltd, P.O. Box 257, Ringwood, Victoria 3134.

In New Zealand: For a complete list of books available from Penguins in New Zealand write to the Marketing Department, Penguin Books (N.Z.) Ltd, Private Bag, Takapuna, Auckland 9.

In India: For a complete list of books available from Penguins in India write to Penguin Overseas Ltd, 706 Eros Apartments, 56 Nehru Place, New Delhi 11019.